Oracle Web Applications

PL/SQL Developer's Introduction

Oracle Web Applications

PL/SQL Developer's Introduction

Andrew Odewahn

O'REILLY®

Beijing · Cambridge · Farnham · Köln · Paris · Sebastopol · Taipei · Tokyo

Oracle Web Applications: PL/SQL Developer's Introduction
by Andrew Odewahn

Copyright © 1999 O'Reilly & Associates, Inc. All rights reserved.
Printed in the United States of America.

Published by O'Reilly & Associates, Inc., 101 Morris Street, Sebastopol, CA 95472.

Editors: Deborah Russell and Gigi Estabrook

Production Editor: Madeleine Newell

Printing History:

September 1999:	First Edition.

ISBN: 1-56592-687-0   [3/00]
[C]

Table of Contents

Preface

Although the philosopher who gave us the phrase "May you be cursed to live in interesting times" probably didn't have Oracle application development in mind, there's no doubt that the saying is as applicable to us today as it was to the ancients.

Since the World Wide Web exploded on the corporate landscape, it's been an exciting time for information technology professionals of all stripes: our skills are in demand, there are lots of exciting new things to learn, and people at dinner parties are actually interested in what we do and no longer recoil in horror at the mere mention of the word "computer."

For most of us, though, the advent of the Web has been a mixed blessing. While there are many ways it can make life better, the steep learning curve has made it hard to take advantage of this potential. Even worse, we're expected to deal with all these issues while keeping existing systems running smoothly. What most of us need is an evolutionary, not a revolutionary, approach to the Web: one that allows us to use our existing skills to solve immediate problems, yet gives us the breathing room to adapt to new concepts and tools.

Oracle Corporation's latest database, Oracle8*i* (the *i* stands for Internet), provides just such a framework. Oracle8*i* allows you to use all your hard-won Oracle skills—data analysis and design, performance tuning, and SQL—to manage web content, develop web applications, and integrate those applications with your existing production systems. In an Oracle8*i* application, Internet skills are almost as important as SQL, normalization, data design, and the host of other database skills. This book will help you start learning these Internet skills and give you a foundation for entry into the new world of Internet computing.

Goal of This Book

The goal of *Oracle Web Applications* is to help Oracle SQL and PL/SQL developers who have little or no web programming experience to learn to develop useful web applications, using technologies most IS developers can grasp fairly quickly: WebDB, Oracle Application Server (OAS), PL/SQL, HTML, and XML.

In addition, the book introduces several other Oracle8*i* technologies—Advanced Queuing (AQ), the Internet File System (*i*FS), interMedia, InternetLite, and Java™—and shows how they form a cohesive development framework that addresses the pressing issues of web content management, application development, and application integration. While there have been many changes in Oracle8*i*, it's still just a database, and there's no need to panic: data is data, whether it comes from the accounts payable system or from the Internet.

This book acknowledges that you're a busy person. Since most of us simply don't have time to read and digest an 800-page book on each individual technology, I've tried to present fundamental elements of the topics you'll use most often in your daily development efforts. This book will get you started and solidly on your way, but it's not, obviously, the ultimate reference. Rather, it is a "Cliff Notes" of Oracle web development—enough to help you pass the test, but not enough to help you appreciate the finer points. Once you've read the book, however, you'll be ready to delve into the various areas (WebDB, PL/SQL, Java, etc.) more deeply. Your first step on that journey should be to consult the appendix for information on further resources.

Structure of This Book

This book is divided into nine chapters and one appendix, as follows:

Chapter 1, *Introduction,* provides some motivations for using the Oracle database as a web platform, introduces Oracle8*i* and its major products, then lays out a strategy to help you get ready for Oracle8*i*.

Chapter 2, *Foundations,* provides some background information necessary for the discussion of web technologies. It describes TCP/IP, HTTP, and web browsers, explains the content delivery model used by Oracle's web tools, and presents the basics of database/web integration and security issues.

Chapter 3, *WebDB,* describes Oracle's WebDB product, which you can use to develop database-driven web applications and sites.

Chapter 4, *Oracle Application Server (OAS),* describes Oracle's OAS product, which uses plug-in "cartridges" to allow you to develop database-driven web sites in a variety of languages, including Java, Perl, and PL/SQL.

Chapter 5, *HTML*, describes the basics of HTML (HyperText Markup Language), the standard language used to create web pages.

Chapter 6, *PL/SQL*, describes Oracle's PL/SQL, a procedural language built on SQL that supports a wide variety of language constructs, including packages.

Chapter 7, *The PL/SQL Toolkit*, describes the set of PL/SQL packages supplied by Oracle specifically for use in developing PL/SQL web applications.

Chapter 8, *Developing Applications*, describes two real-world web applications that demonstrate how you can use the tools described in this book to do actual web development.

Chapter 9, *XML*, describes the basics of XML, an emerging standard for creating structured documents.

Finally, the appendix, *Resources for the Oracle Web Developer*, provides a list of online and offline resources for further information on Oracle and the Web.

Conventions Used in This Book

The following conventions are used in this book:

Italic
> Used for script, file, and directory names

`Constant width`
> Used for code examples, HTML tags and attributes, and XML tags and elements

`Constant width italic`
> In code examples, indicates an element (e.g., a parameter) that you supply

UPPERCASE
> Generally indicates Oracle keywords, including package names

lowercase
> In code examples, generally indicates user-defined items such as variables and procedure names

|
> In code examples, a vertical bar indicates that you must choose only one from the list (e.g., `IN | OUT | IN OUT`)

 The owl icon indicates a tip, suggestion, or general note. For example, we'll tell you if you need to use a particular Oracle version or if an operation requires certain privileges.

The turkey icon indicates a warning or caution. For example, we'll tell you if Oracle does not behave as you'd expect or if a particular operation has a negative impact on performance.

Comments and Questions

We have tested and verified the information in this book to the best of our ability, but you may find that features have changed (or even that we have made mistakes!). Please let us know about any errors you find, as well as your suggestions for future editions, by writing to:

O'Reilly & Associates, Inc.
101 Morris Street
Sebastopol, CA 95472
800-998-9938 (in the U.S. or Canada)
707-829-0515 (international or local)
707-829-0104 (fax)

You can also send us messages electronically. To be put on the mailing list or request a catalog, send email to:

info@oreilly.com

To ask technical questions or comment on the book, send email to:

booktech@oreilly.com

For corrections and amplifications to this book, as well as for copies of the examples found in the book, check out O'Reilly & Associates' online catalog at:

http://www.oreilly.com/catalog/oracleweb

For more information about this book and others, see the O'Reilly web site:

http://www.oreilly.com

Acknowledgments

In reviewing the "Acknowledgments" section of other O'Reilly Oracle books, I was really not surprised to almost invariably find Debby Russell at the top of the list. In addition to being a great editor who has a careful (if not downright hawk-like) eye for both style and substance, she's also a warm and funny human being. During the final editing phase of this book, my wife and I were in the midst of a 2000+ mile hike on the Appalachian Trail. Debby was wonderfully patient and understanding during our hike, and kept her sense of humor even during my frantic calls from places like the Nolichucky Campground. Many thanks also to Michael

Blanding for greatly improving both the style and organization of the book, Lorrie LeJeune for creating a special order boll weevil, Gigi Estabrook for providing editorial support during the production process, Madeleine Newell for her careful edits and comments, and Jim Cupan for providing much needed NT support. Finally, thanks to all the many other people at O'Reilly who transformed this book from a rough draft into the book you're holding now.

I'm deeply indebted to everyone who has provided invaluable technical feedback. Thanks to those who read this book in its earliest stages: Chris Albee for commenting on the very roughest drafts, Sandy Bickford for being my technical mentor, Steven Feuerstein for his sage PL/SQL advice and for introducing me to Debby at ECO'98, and Steve Muench and Victor Oppenheimer for their feedback on XML. I'm also especially grateful to everyone who reviewed the book and provided excellent suggestions for improvement: Rick Greenwald for his help navigating the sometimes treacherous Oracle waters, Dave Kreines for the feedback on the foundations of Oracle technology, Steven Leung for his advice on WebDB, and Bill Pribyl for his careful analysis of almost everything in the book. (Bill even caught typos in the code comments—now that's dedication!) Thanks to everyone at Oracle who answered questions and provided many excellent materials: Martin Graf for his help with Oracle Lite, Tom Grant for *i*FS, Steven Leung for WebDB, Joe Mauro for interMedia, Mahdu Reddy for AQ, and Thomas Kurian and Ashok Swaminathan for explaining how it all fits together. Thanks also to Steve Hilker at RevealNet for letting me use PL/Formatter to format the book's code examples. Despite the hard work of all these people, any errors, omissions, and oversights in the book are solely my own.

Many others have provided help without even knowing it: thanks to the people at Someday Café in Davis Square for the strong coffee, the folks at Burdick's Chocolates in Cambridge for the delicious chocolate mice, and the chefs at Blue Fin for the fresh sushi. Also, my deep appreciation to everyone who has been so amazingly nice to us while we've been on our hike, especially Dennis and Mary Hutchins at the Laurel Creek Lodge in Hampton, Tennessee. Thanks to the people in my life who have provided encouragement and support: my parents Joyce Odewahn and Charles Odewahn, my brother Steve and sisters Anne and Cathy, my in-laws Ben and Maxine McManus (who gladly chauffeured us throughout the most obscure corners of Appalachia), and especially my sister-in-law Stacy McManus, who in addition to just being great is also mailing us our food while we're on the trail!

Finally, last but not least, I thank Amy McManus, my wife, friend, confidant, and traveling companion on the trail of life. Without her emotional, spiritual, and financial support none of this would have been possible. In the words of singer and poet Jerry Jeff Walker, "without you there'd be no light in the window, nobody to laugh with late at night . . . there'd be no reason to write . . . ."

Introduction

Since it burst on the scene in the early 1990s, the World Wide Web has transformed from a way (to quote Homer Simpson) to "let us know some nerd's opinion on Star Trek" to a whole new way of doing business. Hardly an area in the information technology industry has been unaffected. Developers who only yesterday were using COBOL to write accounts payable systems are now being asked to create a broad range of new Internet-based applications, including electronic commerce (e-commerce) web sites, internal data warehouses, and enterprise resource planning (ERP) systems.

Unfortunately, the filesystem architecture of most web systems is beginning to show its age. The new breed of web application, which is quickly becoming critical to companies' survival, demands a platform that provides production-quality tools for content management, application development, and application integration.

The new release of the Oracle database, Oracle8i, attempts to meet these and other objectives by building web technology on top of a relational database system, rather than on a filesystem. This type of development enables companies to apply well-understood, reliable, production-quality database methodologies to web content management. Oracle8i also supports a wide variety of application development platforms and tools that are tightly integrated to the core database. Finally, Oracle8i supports technologies that help you tie your web-based systems to legacy applications.

In this chapter, I'll examine these issues in more detail. I'll start with a look at the new web applications and why current web technology isn't an ideal platform for building them. Next, I'll look at how Oracle8i and its related products attempt to address the failings of previous web technologies. Finally, I'll lay out a roadmap you can use to get started with Oracle8i web development, so you can take full advantage of the Web.

The Internet Grows Up

Flush with both the successes of the World Wide Web and its potential to generate new revenues, companies are scrambling madly to exploit Internet technologies. Internet technology is now commonly required for at least four different types of projects: internal application projects, like data warehousing; mobile application projects, like sales-force automation; electronic commerce, like Internet storefronts; and enterprise resource planning (ERP) systems for automating business operations.

Internal applications are critical resources for a variety of users within a company. For example, developers must build web interfaces for data warehouses that often contain several terabytes of data. In addition to responding quickly, these systems must often meld several different kinds of data—table data, images, and even videos—into an attractive page.

Once these systems are in place and successful, developers are asked to create new systems called *mobile applications* that can extract subsets of the data warehouse for use on portable devices like laptops, PalmPilots, or other Personal Data Assistants (PDAs). These systems, often used by salesman or technical support personnel, allow users to work even when not connected to a network. The data these users enter is synchronized with production systems when the users reconnect to the main network.

Internet storefronts and other *e-commerce applications* let customers buy things over the Web. Increasingly, these applications are expected to integrate with existing order entry systems, provide continuous availability, and protect both the customer and the business from attacks by malicious hackers.

The most ambitious companies use Internet technologies to reduce costs through business-to-business enterprise resource planning systems, which let systems in one company communicate directly with systems in another company over the Internet. For example, an ERP system might let the purchasing system in company A place an order directly with the order entry system in company B. The goal is to automate everything from paying invoices to ordering paperclips. These hybrid sites must integrate many different application systems, from accounts receivable, to accounts payable, to order entry, into a single, cohesive unit that performs a complex series of transactions quickly, accurately, and securely.

Despite the diversity of these application systems, they share several characteristics:

- Each system may deal with a variety of data: traditional relational data, multimedia data such as video or audio clips, structured files like spreadsheets, unstructured documents like emails or text, and web documents like HTML and, increasingly, XML.

- The information in each system must be available to many types of clients: a workstation connected through a LAN or WAN, a web browser connected through the Internet or an intranet, a PalmPilot connected through a modem, or even an email client connected through a POP server.

- Each system must understand and be compatible with multiple communications protocols, from Internet standards like HTTP, FTP, and CORBA, to proprietary protocols like Microsoft's SMB.

- Most application systems are built by developers who are overworked and overstressed from keeping production systems running, maintaining legacy systems, and fighting the daily fires caused by hardware, software, and user problems.

It's tempting to keep trying to extend current web technologies to meet the additional demands of the new generation of Internet web sites and applications. Unfortunately, this effort is probably doomed to failure. While today's web servers comply with the requisite protocols, they are simply not designed to manage complex information, because they are, at heart, little more than networked extensions of traditional filesystems.

Current Web Techniques Are Inadequate

Sure, anyone with Microsoft FrontPage can put a human resources policy manual on the Web, but creating production web sites with existing web technology is simply too much work. Three broad problem areas in current web technology make it hard to build these new applications:

Content management
Although web servers are good at presenting content, they are bad at managing it. This is partially due to their filesystem-based architecture, which often does not include the ability to build searchable, maintainable, and auditable information systems.

Application development
A production setting requires tools that can scale both up and down, fit the needs of a specific user base, and are part of a complete developmental framework. Few, if any, current development techniques meet these criteria.

Application integration and electronic data exchange
It's too hard to integrate different systems. To make e-commerce and ERP a reality, a platform must provide a simple method to link different applications, whether they all reside in one site or are spread across multiple sites. Current web servers are only just beginning to address this issue.

Let's look at these problems in detail.

Content Management

Web servers are great for making information available to a wide audience. Unfortunately, they do very little to help web site developers manage all this information. An ideal platform would help us develop sites that make it easy for users to find what they are looking for, are easy to keep up to date, and allow easy tracking of site content changes.

Finding what you need

There's universal agreement that good web sites make it easy to find what you need. Unfortunately, the filesystem architecture of most web servers makes it difficult to put searches into specific, meaningful contexts.

Filesystems are used to manage files on the operating system level. To make it easier for users to find their files, the system automatically keeps various attributes, such as the file's name, size, creation date, and owner. When we create a spreadsheet, for instance, the system saves it and its attributes within the file structure. Later, if we forget the particular name of the file, we can search for it based on its attributes. For example, in DOS we can enter `dir *.xls /s` to find all Excel spreadsheets within the various subdirectories, then look at the name or date to find the file we want.

This works great when you are sitting at a command line looking for a file that you created. The model breaks down, however, when you attempt to extend it to the Web. When people are searching for files on the Web, they don't care about the file's name or size (unless they're using a 14.4 modem!). Since they care about the file's contents, not its properties, the attributes maintained by the filesystem are largely irrelevant.

Some sites use search engines to overcome this shortfall. When a user enters a search term, the engine churns through an index of all the documents and returns a list of links to the files containing the search terms. Some of the most popular sites on the Web, like Yahoo! or AltaVista, attempt to do this for all files on the Internet.

You only have to look for the term "sexual reproduction" on a web search engine to see how laughable this effort really is. While keyword searches can be helpful, they almost always fail to put the search into a meaningful context. For example, suppose I want a list of all works by Harper Lee. I should be able to enter something like "Give me a list of all works where Harper Lee is the author." With a keyword search, however, in addition to her only book, *To Kill a Mockingbird*, I'm likely to get dozens or hundreds of additional documents ranging from a brochure about Harper's Ferry, West Virginia, to a retrospective of Bruce Lee movies.

The simple fact of the matter is that effective searches on the Web require a broader, more flexible set of attributes than filesystems maintain. In addition to simply describing a file, a web server should automatically keep meaningful *meta-data** about the file's contents that puts a search into a specific context. This meta-data should extend to all files, regardless of format. What if a document isn't ASCII at all or doesn't even represent a spoken language? For executable binaries, for example, it would be nice to be able to directly assign searchable attributes like "purpose" or "platform."

Keeping sites up to date

A second problem with the current web server technologies' lack of integrated content management features is that it is too hard to keep a complex site up to date. Hyperlinks on the Web act as a mapping function between a logical name, like "Andrew's Homepage," to a literal file that resides on a specific machine, like *C:\andrew\web_stuff\default.htm*. These links, created through URLs, let us navigate from one page to another. The problem with this dual mapping system is that we have to make every update in two places, in the filesystem and in the URL. If someone deletes or moves a file, but forgets to change the corresponding URL on every page on which it appears, we are guaranteed to have broken links. It's probably impossible to manage this process manually on a large site.

This two-step process also creates extra work for the webmaster. Publishing a new document, for example, requires the webmaster to manipulate various files by hand: she must use FTP to copy the new document to the web server and must then edit an existing document (such as the home page) to add a link to the new file. While this process is fine for dozens, maybe even hundreds, of individual documents, it is unrealistic to expect to keep a site completely up to date when there are thousands, or even millions, of individual documents. Consequently, sites contain inaccurate information, broken links, and pages perennially under construction.

Tracking changes

Finally, current web servers don't have a way to automatically track all changes to a document. While some operating systems, like VMS, have automatic versioning systems web developers can exploit, most do not. Since the ability to audit changes is a fundamental requirement for any production information system, an ideal web system would handle it automatically.

Suppose a webmaster or an end user updates a file, and it turns out later that he or she made a mistake. How do we track down exactly what was changed and fix

---

* Metadata is data about other data. For example, a file's size is metadata because it is data about the file, not part of the file itself.

it? Most filesystems don't automatically maintain logs that let us reconstruct a complex sequence of changes. Instead, we must either rely on the webmaster's memory or reconstruct the sequence of events from backups. Filesystems are simply not designed to handle complex audit tracking.

Application Development

The Internet has also blurred the traditional line between applications and data to the point where it's unclear how to classify many sites. While a static HTML document is "content" and a Java applet is a "program," how do we classify hybrid systems that are a little bit of each? For example, a data warehouse might have a web interface that seems like a normal web site, but behind the scenes each page is generated dynamically by running a database query. Is this really a web site as we normally think of it, or is it closer to an application acting on underlying data? Although there is no clear agreement, the term *content-driven web site*, implying equal parts of data and application, is one of the best names for these sorts of sites.

In web parlance, the applications and programs that create content-driven web sites are called *dynamic resources*. Dynamic resources are unlike documents created with an HTML editor such as Microsoft FrontPage, although both types of documents are accessed over the Web using a URL, and both return an HTML document. A dynamic resource is a program that creates a page upon a user's request, not a static file that exists beforehand. While such a program traditionally generates HTML, it can create any type of content; for example, you could write a system to create a graph in GIF or JPEG format, using sales data stored in a database table.

As technology has progressed, it has become possible to create more and more complex dynamic resources. Once limited to simple operating system scripts, developers can now choose from a host of viable languages for creating content-driven sites: Perl, Visual Basic, C, C++, Java—even COBOL or FORTRAN! In addition, web servers now support more sophisticated invocation methods. The list of technologies is growing longer every day: CGI, application servers, cartridges, Java servlets, Object Request Brokers (ORBs), and on and on.

The explosive growth of these different technologies and techniques has made it difficult, if not impossible, to select a single platform that can meet all of your current and future needs. Ironically, the overwhelming number of development options is one of the most unsatisfactory things about web development. How do you know which one to pick? Will that technology exist in five years? Is it a viable commercial product or someone's Ph.D. thesis?

The profusion of options has led to two related problems. First, no single platform can meet the needs of every type of application and user group. Second, developers have to use a variety of platforms, depending on the type of application they are building, which stretches their ability to become proficient with any particular technology.

No single platform is scalable enough

Current development platforms rarely scale in both directions. For example, suppose you develop a really slick web application for your department using Active Server Pages on Windows NT. Word gets out around the company about how great it is and hundreds of people want to start using it. Suddenly, your application, which was designed for use by 10 or 20 people, has to accommodate hundreds. What can you do to scale it up? Conversely, suppose you need to build a small, specialized system that is to reside on its own server. You know it will never have more than a few users. Will you really use a Sun Ultraserver to build it? No, you'll go with something smaller and more affordable. As developers, it's hard for us to remember that technology decisions should scale in price as well as performance.

Developers must know too many platforms

Ideally, developers should be proficient on just one development platform that can scale across different hardware platforms, from Intel to Alpha to Sparc, and operating system platforms, from NT to Unix to VMS. Unfortunately, this is not the case with current web server application development. Developers wander from one platform to the next, worrying, like Goldilocks, that "This one's too small" or "This one's too big," when they need one that's just right.

You must factor in the skill levels required by each option. One of the worst situations is that each platform requires its own specific skill set, so you wind up with a development team that is split along platforms. For example, you may have one group of programmers that uses Perl, one that uses Java, one that uses Oracle Forms, and one that uses PL/SQL. Since it's impossible to master all the techniques available on each platform, you wind up with systems that only a small group can support.

Application Integration and Electronic Data Interchange (EDI)

As if content management and application development aren't enough of a challenge, the new breed of application must seamlessly interact with internal applications and electronically exchange data with external systems. Data entered by remote users must synchronize with the production systems. Orders placed on your web site must flow into an order entry system, which must then send the customers email notifying them that their orders have been received. Purchase orders must flow from your system into the order entry systems of your business partners.

These types of tasks are well beyond the scope of almost all the web servers currently available. While it's possible to build this functionality, it is usually a kludgey process performed with uploads or downloads or, God forbid, rekeying the information by hand.

Web server vendors are attempting to address this problem by defining universal standards for interoperability and object-to-object communication; some of the most promising solutions, such as CORBA and COM, are already available. However, the battle over what will be the general standard is already brewing and promises to make the browser wars look like a game of touch football at a retirement home.

Oracle's Solution—Oracle8i

To steal a phrase from James Carville, consultant to Bill Clinton's 1992 presidential campaign, "It's the data, stupid." Large companies have realized for years that file-systems are unsuited for sophisticated data management, and have instead relied on *relational database management systems* (RDBMSs).

These databases have quietly provided scalable, secure, and manageable access to the most critical corporate information for over a decade. Companies understand how to plan for auditing, disaster recovery, capacity, maintenance, and application development. There are well-understood tools and proven techniques, and developers know how to build database systems. Given that content will be king for the new generation of web sites and applications, doesn't it make sense to graft web server capabilities onto a database, rather than a filesystem?

Oracle has had over 20 years of experience designing information systems that manage the most important corporate data. As the largest database vendor in the world, they have (arguably) the world's most sophisticated and powerful database. Over the past several years, Oracle has moved diligently to apply professional data management concepts like scalability, security, auditability, disaster planning, and so on to an unruly world of Internet content management. With Oracle8i, the "Internet database," these plans have come to fruition.

Oracle8i is a soup-to-nuts platform for web site and web application development that addresses the pressing issues of content management, application development, and application integration by extending traditional database concepts to web content. Oracle8i replaces the traditional filesystem used by most web servers with a database management system, and it supports—either directly or through various add-on products—a mind-boggling variety of technologies. Table 1-1 summarizes the most important of these; asterisked items must be separately licensed from Oracle.

Table 1-1. Major Web Technologies Supported in Oracle8i

Technology	Description
Internet File System (*i*FS)	An Oracle extension[a] that allows Oracle8*i* to store files inside the database. It combines this capability with a wide variety of networking protocols to let various clients use *i*FS as a native data store. These clients can include email products like Qualcomm Eudora, productivity products like Microsoft Excel or Word, and HTTP clients like Netscape Navigator. In addition, *i*FS supports sophisticated version control features, such as check-in and check-out for documents shared by multiple users.
HTML	An ASCII-based markup language used to create web pages. HTML is a non-proprietary specification.
XML	An emerging standard for creating documents that contain structured information. XML, syntactically similar to HTML, allows you to define your own markup tags. XML is expected to be a key technology in electronic commerce systems because it simplifies data interchange among various systems.
PL/SQL	A structured programming language similar to Ada that combines procedural constructs with standard SQL. PL/SQL also supports reusable components called packages; you can write your own packages and use those built into Oracle8*i*. Like Java, PL/SQL is executed directly in the database. Unlike Java, it's supported in Oracle8 and Oracle7.
WebDB*	An Oracle development environment for building and monitoring content-driven web sites and data-driven applications. WebDB allows users to use a web browser to access and store information in the Oracle8*i* database. It's also compatible with Oracle8 and Oracle7.
Oracle Application Server (OAS)*	An extensible web server that uses plug-in programs called cartridges. OAS allows you to develop database-integrated web systems in a variety of languages, including Java, Perl, and PL/SQL. It's also compatible with Oracle8 and Oracle7.
Java	An object-oriented language similar to C++. Oracle8*i* includes a built-in Java™ Virtual Machine (JVM) to allow Java programs to execute directly inside the database. Java is probably the single most important new technology in Oracle8*i*.
InternetLite*	The collective name of a set of Oracle products for developing mobile Internet applications. These products are: Oracle Lite, a small footprint version of Oracle8*i*; EnterpriseSync Lite (ESL), a set of replication technologies that includes AQ Lite, a disconnected version of AQ; and the InternetLite (IL) server and API, a set of software products for replicating both data and applications to mobile applications.
Oracle interMedia*	The collective name of a set of Oracle cartridges for storing multimedia content inside Oracle8*i*. The cartridges include interMedia Text for storing text information, Visual Information Retrieval (VIR) for storing image and audio files, and Oracle Spatial for storing geographic data.

Table 1-1. Major Web Technologies Supported in Oracle8i (continued)

Technology	Description
Advanced Queuing (AQ)	A queue-based messaging system that allows programs to communicate asynchronously. While Oracle8*i* is built on the AQ system available in Oracle8 and Oracle7, it supports a "publish/subscribe" model not available in the earlier versions.

[a] Available in Oracle8*i* Release 8.1.5.

As you can see, Oracle8*i* supports an extensive number of products and technologies for developing web sites and Internet systems. We'll look at each product in a little more depth in the next several sections.

The Internet File System

The *Internet File System* (*i*FS) allows Oracle8*i* to masquerade as different types of data servers, including a file server, an FTP server, and an email server. This makes data accessible to almost any type of client, whether it's a Windows 95 workstation, a web browser, or an email client. *i*FS supports several networking protocols to accomplish this sleight of hand:

SMB
> Allows Windows 95, NT, and 98 clients to treat files stored in Oracle8*i* as if they resided on a normal Windows file server

FTP and HTTP
> Allow FTP clients and web browsers to treat data stored in Oracle8*i* as if it resided on an FTP or web site

SMTP, IMAP4, and POP3
> Allow email clients like Eudora and Microsoft Outlook to treat data stored in an Oracle8*i* database as if it resided on an email server

For example, a user on a Windows workstation can define a network drive like *E:*, *F:*, or *O:* that points to an Oracle8*i* database instead of to a file server. The user sees no discernible difference between an Oracle8*i* volume and a file server, and she can open, update, or save Word and Excel files in the usual way.

Although *i*FS is not available at the time of writing, Oracle has laid out the following basic model for its use in conjunction with XML:

1. You create a TYP file (an XML document) to describe the structure of each type of document that can be stored in the *i*FS repository. Each element in the TYP file is mapped to a corresponding column in a database table.

2. Users can use almost any client to access the *i*FS repository, including FTP and HTTP clients, email clients, and Windows (SMB) clients. The client treats the *i*FS repository as it would a native data server. For example, an email client can

see Oracle8*i* as an email server, and a Windows client can see the same information as a network volume.

3. *i*FS executes a server-based event, a chunk of code analogous to a database trigger, whenever a user inserts, deletes, updates, or views a document in the *i*FS repository. You can develop your own event servers, using Java and CORBA, to override basic *i*FS functionality. For example, you might want to send an email when a certain type of document, such as a purchase order, is saved to the repository. *i*FS also has a built-in XML parser to process XML documents.

Using *i*FS, you could define a purchase order document and associate it with various events. A customer could place an order electronically by emailing a purchase order document to the Oracle8*i* *i*FS repository. This could trigger a "Send Thank You" event that would send an email thanking the customer for the order and a "Process Order" event that would move the document into an order entry system.

HTML

HyperText Markup Language (HTML), the language used to create web pages, is a specification for marking up text documents using a fixed set of tags that control how the document is displayed in a web browser. For example, text enclosed between the <b> and </b> tags is displayed in bold, and text enclosed within <i> and </i> is displayed in italics. Tags can also have attributes, parameters that act like instructions. For example, the <a> tag, which is used to create a hyperlink within a document, has an attribute named `href` that specifies the location (the uniform resource locator, or URL) of the page the user visits when he clicks on the link.

HTML is also used to create simple data entry forms you can use to store information inside an Oracle database. Here, for example, is the HTML code needed to produce a guest book screen that asks for a web user's name, email address, and comments:

```
<html>
    <title>Sign the guest book</title>
    <body>
        <form action="guestbook.insert_entry" method="post">
            <b>Name:</b>      <input name=i_name>  <p>
            <b>E-mail: </b> <input name=i_email> <p>
            <b>comments:</b>
                <textarea name="i_comments" rows=5 cols=40>
                </textarea>
            <p>
            <input type=submit>
        </form>
    </body>
</html>
```

Figure 1-1 shows how the form is displayed in a web browser. You can learn more about HTML in Chapter 5, *HTML.*

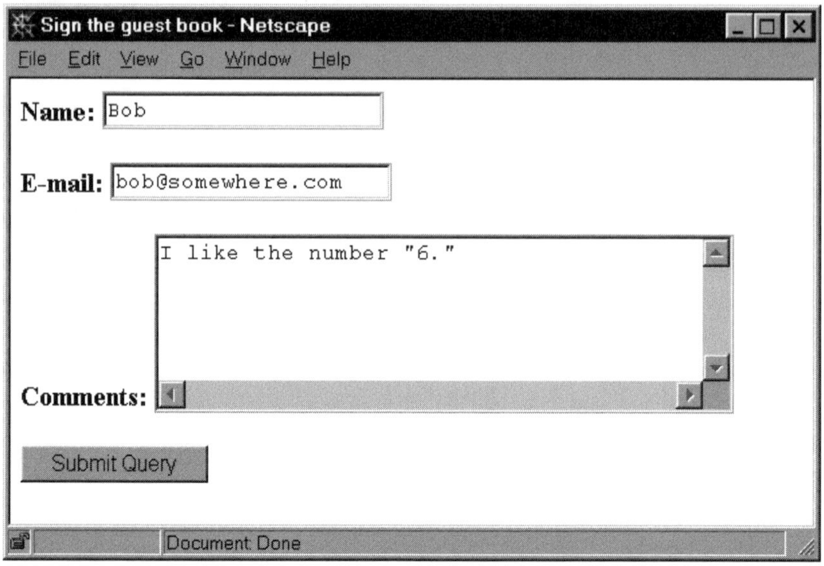

Figure 1-1. An HTML form

XML

Extensible Markup Language (XML) is an emerging standard for creating structured documents using an HTML-like syntax. Although much of the current enthusiasm for XML is focused on its ability to create complex user interfaces for web systems, XML has much broader applications in the following areas:

- Creating complex, browser-based user interfaces. At the time of this writing, though, few browsers support XML (Microsoft's Internet Explorer version 5.0 supports most of the new XML specification).

- Defining a universal data format for use in productivity tools like spreadsheets and word processors.

- Applying complex, hierarchical relationships to unstructured data.

- Providing a platform-independent specification for exchanging information among a variety of electronic systems, including different database systems.

Surprisingly, XML is also fairly easy to learn and use. The following example shows how you could use XML to create an electronic invoice:

```
<?xml version="1.0"?>
<!DOCTYPE INVOICE SYSTEM "invoice.dtd">
<INVOICE>
    <INVOICE_NUMBER>876514234</INVOICE_NUMBER>
    <DATE>05/21/1999</DATE>
    <CUSTOMER>Megaplex Industries</CUSTOMER>
    <INVOICE_ITEMS>
      <ITEM>
         <ITEM_NAME ITEM_NUM="PN-5342">Widget 1</ITEM_NAME>
         <QUANTITY>5</QUANTITY>
         <PRICE>19.99</PRICE>
      </ITEM>
      <ITEM>
         <ITEM_NAME ITEM_NUM="PN-6354">Widget 2</ITEM_NAME>
         <QUANTITY>2</QUANTITY>
         <PRICE>9.99</PRICE>
      </ITEM>
    </INVOICE_ITEMS>
    <TOTAL>119.93</TOTAL>
</INVOICE>
```

XML allows you to define your own tags and attributes, then set up rules that these tags must follow. An XML parser program reads each document to make sure that it follows these rules and, if it does, moves it into a hierarchical data structure called a document tree. You can then manipulate the structured information using Java or PL/SQL. You can learn more about XML in Chapter 9, *XML*.

PL/SQL

PL/SQL is Oracle's procedural language extension to the SQL language. PL/SQL is a structured language that has been extended in Oracle8 and Oracle8*i* to handle object types and support other object-like features. PL/SQL is especially well suited to modular programming since it allows you to build stored procedures, functions, and packages to perform database operations. PL/SQL provides a rich set of datatypes and supports conditional processing, loops, cursors (for row-at-a-time processing), and collections (PL/SQL's version of arrays, formerly called PL/SQL tables).

Packages are an especially powerful PL/SQL construct. A *package* is a container for other PL/SQL elements, such as variables, constants, procedures, functions, and datatype definitions. Packages let you build standard code libraries with well-defined APIs. In the web environment, for example, you might create standard libraries to handle security, formatting, and other reusable functionality.

You can learn more about PL/SQL in Chapter 6, *PL/SQL*.

WebDB

WebDB is an excellent tool for developing database-driven web applications and sites. WebDB lets you perform everything from database administration to application development using only a web browser. Your applications and content area are stored inside the database. WebDB's capabilities are divided into these broad categories:

Database administration
> WebDB lets you use a web browser, rather than a "fat" client like Oracle Enterprise Manager (OEM), to perform routine database administration tasks. These tasks might include viewing the definitions of database objects, administering WebDB and database security, and monitoring database and application performance.

Application development
> WebDB provides *wizards* that simplify the development of database objects (e.g., tables and views) and user interface components (e.g., forms and reports).

Content-driven web management
> WebDB lets you use a browser to build and edit complex sites, add content (e.g., PDF, presentations, papers), and integrate other WebDB applications. You, and better yet, your end users, can add web content directly from a browser and can manage it like any other information.

You can learn more about WebDB in Chapter 3, *WebDB*.

Oracle Application Server

Oracle Application Server (OAS) is another good tool for building web applications. Whereas WebDB may be the most appropriate tool for quickly building and deploying Internet applications, OAS is probably best for electronic commerce and enterprise resource planning applications. OAS performs all the functions of a traditional web server, but in addition, it provides tight integration to an Oracle database.

OAS is built on a system of plug-in *cartridges* used to execute certain kinds of resources. Several language cartridges come with OAS: PL/SQL, used to execute PL/SQL stored procedures; Java, used to execute server-side Java programs; and Perl, used to execute Perl scripts. Other cartridges are also available; for example, the ODBC cartridge executes ODBC (Open Database Connectivity) statements and returns the results directly to your browser.

You can learn more about OAS in Chapter 4, *Oracle Application Server (OAS)*.

Java

Java, a popular object-oriented language, is becoming a good choice for developing and deploying Oracle-based web applications. Oracle8*i* is completely integrated with Java, and supports a wide range of data access and development models. These include:

JDBC™

> The standard specification for interaction between Java and relational databases, as defined by Sun Microsystems. JDBC is the Java version of ODBC. Programmers can take advantage of Oracle's extensions to JDBC, such as convenient access to Oracle-specific datatypes like ROWID.

SQLJ

> A precompiler technology (similar to Pro*C or Pro*COBOL) that allows the programmer to embed static SQL statements directly into Java code. The SQLJ translator and runtime libraries are available both inside and outside the Oracle8*i* server. SQLJ also provides access to Oracle-specific datatypes.

Java stored procedures (JSPs)

> Stored programs that let you invoke static Java methods from Oracle's SQL or PL/SQL languages. The mechanism for publishing Java methods in this fashion is proprietary to Oracle.

CORBA server objects

> Objects that are developed according to Object Management Group (OMG) specifications and that can be distributed. They can communicate with other objects regardless of location. Using CORBA, you can integrate both Java and non-Java applications. CORBA server objects in Oracle8*i* can both call and be called by CORBA objects outside the server. CORBA is supported by a variety of languages and environments.

Enterprise Java Beans™ (EJBs)

> An approach especially helpful in large distributed systems. EJBs are coarse-grained, reusable components that comply with Sun's EJB specification; they rely on the Oracle8*i* EJB "execution container" for services such as component location, activation, security, and transaction support. EJBs can be used with non-Java applications.

Java servlets

> Java programs that generate HTML for presentation in a web browser. The Oracle8*i* server provides HTTP service and a servlet execution environment by incorporating a special version of Sun's Java™ Web Server™.* Servlets can

---

* This capability is in beta form in Oracle8*i*'s initial release.

read and write database data using any convenient database access model (JDBC, SQLJ, etc.) and generate any form of HTML.

Consult the appendix for a list of references concerning Java development.

InternetLite

InternetLite is a toolkit for building mobile applications that allow users to work while disconnected from a network. A mobile application has two basic parts: a *master site* and a *snapshot site.* The master site is usually a complete, production Oracle database. When a user needs to disconnect from the network and use the database on the road, he copies a subset of the production data from the master site to his own local database, the snapshot site. The user makes various changes to the snapshot site, each of which is recorded in a log, until he is ready to reconnect to the master site. At this point, the snapshot site and master site must be *synchronized* so that changes on the snapshot site are applied to the master site, and vice versa. The logs are reset once the master site and snapshot site are in synch.

As you can imagine, handcoding the mechanics for each of these steps can be a tedious, difficult process. The various InternetLite products act as a sort of operating system for distributed computing that provides these services automatically; it handles data and application replication issues, allowing you to concentrate on designing your application without worrying about lower-level details. There are four individual products in the InternetLite product suite: Oracle Lite, EnterpriseSync Lite, AQ Lite, and the InternetLite server and API.

Since it's helpful to look at each product in the context of a specific example, let's suppose you want to create a mobile expense sheet application. The system should allow users to record their expenses while they're on the road and, when they return to the office, automatically upload these expense items into the production database.

Oracle Lite

Oracle Lite functions as a miniature version of the full Oracle8*i* database, which runs in just under one megabyte of memory and supports the major database application objects, such as tables, indexes, and sequences. The Oracle Lite database is used to maintain the snapshot site in a mobile application.

Oracle Lite supports two modes for application development: client/server and Internet. Client/server mode allows developers to use the Oracle Call Interface (OCI) to write C programs, Open Client Adapter (OCA) to write Developer/2000 applications, and ODBC to write applications using Visual Basic, Access, PowerBuilder, etc. Internet mode supports two access methods: JDBC or the Java Access Classes (JAC), an API for creating data-aware Java servlets.

To return to our expense report example: Oracle Lite is the application data store that contains the expense items. Our first step in developing the application is to define the various tables, such as the different types of expenses (lodging, mileage, food) and the actual expense items (person submitting the item, date, expense type, dollar amount). We can use Oracle Forms, Java, and an ODBC client such as Microsoft Access to write the application and then use EnterpriseSync Lite to develop a replication strategy to move data between the master and snapshot sites.

EnterpriseSync Lite

EnterpriseSync Lite (ESL) is the second product in the InternetLite suite. As its name implies, ESL is used to handle the synchronization phase of a mobile application. ESL provides a replication API, called REPAPI, that defines how the table data is moved between the master and snapshot sites.

ESL is based on Oracle's database table *snapshot* technology. A snapshot is basically a copy of a table that's based on a SQL query. For example, to create a snapshot of the expense item table, I could use the command:

```
CREATE SNAPSHOT expense_item_snap AS
    SELECT * FROM EXPENSE_ITEMS;
```

Periodically, the snapshot must be refreshed to reload the information from its base query. There are two refresh options: complete and fast. A *complete refresh* will reload the entire table. A *fast refresh* will reload only the rows that have been changed or added since the last refresh.

 As a rule of thumb, the fast refresh is faster only when fewer than 10% of the rows in the underlying master table have been changed. Otherwise, the complete refresh is faster.

ESL automates the process of creating the snapshot site by allowing you to define how and when the application loads and refreshes the snapshot data. Hooking your program into the REPAPI provides a behind the scenes way to move data from the snapshot site into the master site and vice versa. ESL supports two replication modes: synchronous and asynchronous. In *synchronous mode,* the user must be connected directly to the database over a standard SQL*Net (Net8) connection; data is transmitted using the standard Oracle protocol. In *asynchronous mode,* the user uses a file transfer process, such as email or FTP, to send an export file of her snapshot log and receive an import file of snapshot refresh data. The advantage of this approach is that users can synchronize their systems off-site using standard products like Qualcomm Eudora or Microsoft Outlook.

AQ Lite

EnterpriseSync Lite also includes AQ Lite, a scaled-down version of Advanced Queuing (AQ, covered later in this chapter), that's used to create distributed messaging services. Messages are queued to the snapshot site's local data store and sent to the production queues when the user synchronizes.

InternetLite server and API

The InternetLite server allows you to synchronize both data and applications on mobile clients, eliminating the problem of installing the correct version of an application on mobile clients. The advantages of this approach should be clear to anyone who has ever tried to provide phone support to an irate user (usually calling from the client's site!) who has a corrupted database or a Dynamic Link Library (DLL) conflict.

The catch is that the applications must follow the Internet development model; the client/server model isn't supported. The development process works something like this:

1. The developer defines the master and snapshot sites using Oracle Lite as a local data store.

2. She then writes the application using Java servlets. Typically, these applications use an HTML user interface to access the underlying database tables.

3. Next, she sets up a replication profile for each mobile client that defines the snapshot tables and application components that are replicated.

4. When the user connects to the IL server, it receives the data in the master site as well as all the Java servlets required for the application. IL replicates everything the user needs to run the application in disconnected mode, including the Oracle Lite database engine and the necessary Java classes.

The InternetLite server, which performs these operations, is a plug-in cartridge for OAS version 4.0. Figure 1-2 shows the architecture of an IL-based system.

Consult the appendix for a list of resources that will help you learn more about the InternetLite product suite and building distributed systems in general.

Oracle interMedia

Oracle8*i* has three plug-in cartridges that can manage multimedia data: the interMedia Text cartridge, the Video Information Retrieval (VIR) cartridge, and the Oracle Spatial cartridge. These three products are collectively called Oracle interMedia, and allow Oracle to manage text, multimedia, and spatial data.

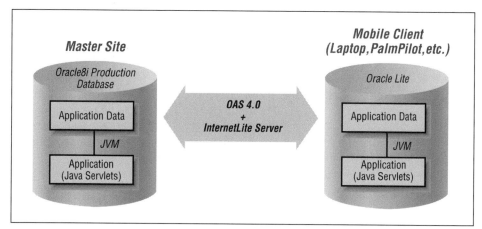

Figure 1-2. Architecture of an InternetLite-based mobile application

Text data

The Oracle interMedia Text cartridge is used to manage documents (either inside or outside the database) by automatically indexing them with smart attributes. You can then use SQL to perform a variety of complex searches, such as searching for an exact phrase or performing a fuzzy search to find the closest matches for the search criteria. Text can index nontext documents, such as Word, Excel, Power-Point, WordPerfect, Adobe PDF, HTML, and XML, using a filter that converts the document from its native format into one the database can understand. Currently, there are more than 100 such filters.

Multimedia data

interMedia can manage traditional multimedia files, such as video or audio clips, as well as static image files. Video Information Retrieval (VIR) can store video clips in a variety of formats, including AVI, QuickTime, and MPEG. It can store audio clips in AUF, AIFF, AIFF-C, and WAV formats. These clips are accessible through any streaming server, such as RealNetworks or Oracle Audio/Video Server. interMedia can also store image files in a variety of popular formats, including TIFF, GIF, and JPEG. Audio, video, and image data are all compatible with popular authoring tools like Symantec Visual Page or FrontPage, via the interMedia clipboard.

Spatial data

interMedia's Spatial cartridge provides support for a range of geocoding systems that specify a latitude and longitude with a specific piece of information, such as a zip code or an address. This information can be used to calculate distances between locations or to represent information in geographic information systems (GIS). For example, using this information, you could create a query system for a bank that returned the ATM locations closest to a specific address.

Advanced Queuing

Advanced Queuing (AQ), first introduced in Oracle8, is a message-based queuing system you can use to bind a variety of different systems together. A universally accessible API used to send complex messages from one system to another, AQ is built on procedures and functions stored directly in the database. This architecture allows applications in any language or platform, from COBOL to PL/SQL to Java, to communicate through a system of queues maintained in the database.

For example, an OAS storefront could use AQ to send an order from its order entry system. This system, perhaps written in C, could use the AQ API to retrieve and process the request. This universal application-to-application communication eliminates the need for clunky import and export routines.

As an example of AQ in action, suppose you want to write a simple web site that lets registered customers buy or sell stocks over the Internet. The customer can use a variety of clients, such as a Java applet, an HTML browser, or an Oracle Forms application, to place an order to buy or sell stock. Another program, perhaps written in Pro*COBOL, periodically processes and fulfills the orders placed so far. The next sections illustrate how to design an AQ-based solution. Figure 1-3 illustrates its basic architecture.

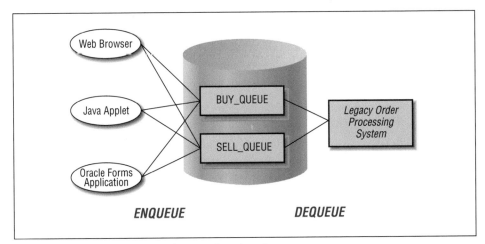

Figure 1-3. Basic architecture of an AQ-based stock system

Define the message payload

The first step is to define the structure of the message contained in the queue, which is done with the SQL command, CREATE TYPE. Here, for example, is how we might define a simple payload for the stock example:

```
CREATE TYPE aq.customer_order AS OBJECT (
    customer_id NUMBER,
```

```
    stock_symbol VARCHAR2(20),
    num_shares NUMBER );
```

Create and start the queue tables

The next step is to use the AQ administrative API to create the queues inside the Oracle database. Each queue is associated with a payload definition and (by default) follows the first-in-first-out protocol. In our example, we want to create two message queues: one for "buy" messages and one for "sell" orders. After you create the queues, you can start and stop them to control when they can receive messages. The following code snippet illustrates these steps for our example:

```
-- Create BUY and SELL Queues
EXECUTE DBMS_AQADM.CREATE_QUEUE_TABLE (
    queue_table => 'aq.BUY_QUEUE',
    queue_payload_type => 'aq.customer_order');

EXECUTE DBMS_AQADM.CREATE_QUEUE_TABLE (
    queue_table => 'aq.SELL_QUEUE',
    queue_payload_type => 'aq.customer_order');

-- Start the Queues
EXECUTE DBMS_AQADM.START_QUEUE (
    queue_name => 'BUY_QUEUE');

EXECUTE DBMS_AQADM.START_QUEUE (
    queue_name => 'SELL_QUEUE');
```

Enqueue and dequeue messages to/from a queue

Once you've created and defined the queues, you can begin *enqueuing* (inserting) and *dequeuing* (retrieving) messages. To create a message, you create an object based on the queue payload, set the values you want to insert, and call AQ's ENQUEUE procedure. For example, a browser-based client could enqueue an order at any time by calling the following PL/SQL procedure:

```
PROCEDURE buy_stock (
    i_customer_id   IN VARCHAR2 DEFAULT NULL,
    i_stock_symbol IN VARCHAR2 DEFAULT NULL,
    i_num_shares    IN VARCHAR2 DEFAULT NULL
    )
IS

    the_order aq.customer_order;
    queueopts dbms_aq.enqueue_options_t;
    msgprops dbms_aq.enqueue_properties_t;
    msg_id RAW(16);

BEGIN
    the_order :=
        message_type (
            i_customer_id,
```

```
            i_stock_symbol,
            i_num_shares
        );
    DBMS_AQ.ENQUEUE (
        queue_name => 'BUY_QUEUE',
        payload => the_order,
        enqueue_options => queueopts,
        message_properties => msgprops,
        msg_id => msg_handle
    );
END;
```

Dequeuing reverses the process by extracting the item from the queue. To dequeue a message, you create a payload variable and then use the AQ's DEQUEUE procedure to extract the first item off the queue. In our example, we could fairly easily retrofit our legacy system (for example, a Pro*COBOL program) to loop through each item on the BUY and SELL queue.

You can learn more about AQ in *Oracle Built-in Packages*, by Steven Feuerstein, Charles Dye, and John Beresniewicz (O'Reilly & Associates).

Functional Summary of Oracle8i Web Products

Table 1-2 illustrates the role each Oracle8i web product plays in fulfilling the requirements for the new generation of systems laid out at the beginning of this chapter.

Table 1-2. Uses for Oracle8i Web Technology

	AQ	HTML	iFS	interMedia	IL	Java	OAS	PL/SQL	WebDB	XML
Content management			✓	✓					✓	
Application development	✓	✓	✓	✓	✓	✓	✓	✓	✓	✓
Application integration	✓		✓			✓				✓
Electronic data exchange										✓

In addition to supporting a range of tools for content management, application development, and application integration, Oracle8i (as well as Oracle7 and Oracle8) scales across three related dimensions: performance, platform, and price. Oracle8i's multithreaded architecture ensures high performance through clustering, connection pooling, and multiplexing; it also has a resource management system to precisely control the CPU time given to a user or a group of users. Oracle8i runs on an enormous number of hardware and software platforms, which can range from a palmtop (via Oracle Lite), to a workgroup server, to a mainframe; porting an application from one platform to another is often as simple as exporting and importing the schema. Finally, since Oracle8*i* is supported on so many different systems, you can decide how much you're willing to spend on an application without locking yourself into a platform that can't, if necessary, scale up.

Finally, Oracle8*i* addresses the pressing problem of development fragmentation by allowing developers to master a single platform that can meet most foreseeable future demands. Of course, there's just one little problem.

A Roadmap to Oracle8i

There's way too much new stuff to learn! You could spend the rest of your life—including the additional 100 years you'll get because of Y2K—learning the technologies listed in Table 1-2 and still not master them all. Oracle Corporation is far ahead of most of us; we're lucky if we can keep our existing production systems running, much less learn dozens of new tools and methodologies.

Given the increasing importance of the Internet, though, we need development skills that we can use right now, not in the distant future. Additionally, some sites, for one reason or another, haven't even moved from Oracle version 7.3 (or even 7.0) to Oracle8, much less Oracle8*i*. What are they supposed to do?

In this section I'll suggest an approach to building web applications for Oracle8*i* that you can learn in just a week or two, even if you currently know nothing about the Web and even if you're still using Oracle7. Everything I'll cover will migrate smoothly to Oracle8*i*. In this way, you'll have time to start learning the other technologies even as you develop new systems. The approach I suggest here uses a subset of the technologies listed in Table 1-2: OAS, WebDB, HTML, PL/SQL, and XML. I'll also tell you why I think Java should be your second step.

Connect the Database to the Web Using OAS or WebDB

The first thing you'll need to do is connect the Oracle database to the Web. The simplest way to do this is to use either OAS or WebDB. Both products work with Oracle 7.3 or above. I'll cover each in its own chapter, focusing on what you, as an application developer, need to know to use and understand the technology.

Develop Web Applications with HTML and PL/SQL

Once you've seen how to connect the database and the Web, you can start learning how to write web applications by combining HTML, the language used to create web pages, with PL/SQL, the SQL-like language used to develop Oracle stored procedures. The next three sections explore the reasons for choosing these tools.

Why HTML?

HTML is based on a simple principle: a limited syntax composed of tags and attributes can define almost any document, from a quarterly report to an online catalog. Each tag affects the text between the start tag and the end tag. Tag attributes act like parameters that refine the tag's behavior. There are several reasons why HTML is an appealing user interface:

HTML is easy to learn

> HTML uses a simple, forgiving syntax to create documents. These documents can range from a text-only listing of all employees in a particular table to a complete data entry form that inserts or updates a record in a table. This simplicity is in stark contrast to the host of proprietary languages that try to be all things to all people.

HTML is platform-neutral

> A browser running on a PC, a Macintosh, or a Unix system will display a document in roughly the same way. Because virtually all browsers support HTML, you can concentrate on developing the contents of a page without worrying about how it will be distributed. If you build an online employee directory, anyone with a browser can access it through an HTML interface, regardless of the type of machine they have.

HTML is simple to deploy

> With a browser and a TCP/IP connection, a user can access any application on your network by simply typing in the appropriate URL. Imagine trying to coordinate a similar system based on Oracle Forms. Use of HTML eliminates the version conflicts, SQL*Net conflicts, and configuration headaches that make being an application developer a real drag.

HTML provides some protection from constant change

> HTML is a non-proprietary, standards-based language. If a browser supports the base HTML language, it can display any HTML document, even if the document is 10 years old. This gives considerable freedom to you as a developer, because as long as browsers support HTML, a user can modify or change his machine however he wants, and your application will still work.

Despite all these advantages, HTML is not a panacea. There are some limitations that affect the way you design an application:

HTML is not a programming language

> HTML is a specification for marking up a document's content, not a programming language. It doesn't support variables, loops, conditionals, or have a robust event model, so you are forced to put all your program logic on the server. Scripting languages like JavaScript can help mitigate this problem (WebDB can even generate this type of scripting code for you automatically).

HTML applications are stateless
> HTTP, the underlying protocol of HTML, is a stateless protocol, meaning that it doesn't preserve information between connections. This seriously affects the way you must design web applications. We'll discuss this in later chapters.

HTML interfaces are not as sophisticated as client/server interfaces
> HTML is, at heart, a layout tool. Consequently, it doesn't support all the GUI widgets found in client/server development tools like Oracle Forms or Power-Builder. Again, JavaScript can help mitigate this problem.

Why PL/SQL?

Combining HTML with PL/SQL gives us all we need to develop useful web systems that are powerful, easy to design, and easy to develop. The language offers several benefits to overworked developers:

PL/SQL is easy to learn and use
> PL/SQL is an evolutionary, not revolutionary, step for most IS developers because it's a straightforward extension of standard SQL that's ideally suited for database processing.

PL/SQL fosters code reuse
> Packages (groups of procedures and functions) provide many of the benefits of object-oriented languages without the hassle of learning a brand new programming methodology.

PL/SQL integrates with other Oracle tools
> PL/SQL stored procedures are accessible from any SQL*Net or ODBC product, from Oracle Forms to Pro*C to Microsoft Access to Java. As a result, you can implement a business rule in the database as a PL/SQL procedure and use it in any frontend tool, rather than writing the same logic again and again for each development environment.

PL/SQL is portable
> PL/SQL is included with Oracle version 7 and above and is supported on all Oracle platforms.

PL/SQL is fast
> Oracle8 introduced, and Oracle8*i* refined, a host of performance improvements to PL/SQL. Additionally, packages are parsed, stored, and executed inside the database, providing superfast data access. Once loaded, these packages may be shared across multiple sessions, resulting in even better performance.

PL/SQL is proven
> Millions of lines of production PL/SQL code are quietly humming away in companies across the world. While it may not have the sex appeal of some other technologies, PL/SQL has proven itself a scalable, robust solution in thousands of mission-critical applications.

The major downside of PL/SQL is that it's a proprietary language supported only on Oracle systems. If you are concerned about locking yourself into an Oracle-only solution, you should consider using Java.

So why not Java?

You're probably wondering why, if Java is the future of Oracle, you should bother with PL/SQL at all. The answer is pretty simple: almost all IS developers are pre-pared to take advantage of PL/SQL and its many capabilities without a great deal of new training. Java, on the other hand, demands a solid understanding of object-oriented design and programming (a technique substantially different from the structured programming model used by languages like COBOL or C) before you can begin using it effectively. If you're worried that PL/SQL is doomed to go the way of Latin, consider the following:

- The millions of lines of production PL/SQL code provide a wonderful disin-centive against the wild-eyed radicalism of Java zealots.

- Oracle's strategy acknowledges that there is no "one-size-fits-all" solution for every problem, and has repeatedly emphasized that Java and PL/SQL will coexist in the database and play off one another in the future.

- The performance improvements for PL/SQL in Oracle8*i*, combined with the fact that WebDB is a PL/SQL application, bode well for Oracle's commitment to the language.

- Finally, and most importantly, Oracle has publicly committed that it will sup-port PL/SQL forever!

By the way, I'm not advocating Ludditism. Java is a very important and interesting language that you need to learn. In the interim, though, you can use PL/SQL to develop hundreds of useful web applications that will make your users very happy. Additionally, you won't have wasted any effort; these programs will con-tinue to work even after you've mastered Java and fully adopted Oracle8*i*. Finally, Oracle allows you to call PL/SQL procedures from inside a Java program and vice versa, allowing you to use the language most appropriate for the task at hand.

Start Learning XML

Other than Java, XML is probably one of the most important technological advances to hit the Web in a long time, especially in the arena of electronic com-merce, electronic data exchange, and integrating the various parts of ERP systems. In the last chapter of this book you'll learn how to create XML documents from inside the Oracle database, using PL/SQL.

2

Foundations

The ease with which you can develop applications on a PC has caused developers to pay far too little attention to the basic infrastructure in which the systems run. Developers often slap together a form, test it on a PC, and then roll it out to unsuspecting users. They fail to take into account that although they have tested the system on a LAN connection, users will use the system over a WAN connection. What seems fine in one setting is bad in another, and even the world's greatest application really stinks if it's deployed on an inappropriate infrastructure.

Understanding the implications of the infrastructure is even more important in web development, and your designs must account for differences between the major Internet networking protocols (especially statelessness, which we'll look at shortly) and their client/server counterparts. Web systems are centered on a network, so you must account for network traffic in your designs. Even the way you connect your database to the Web has an important impact. You haven't yet written a line of code and you've already got dozens of problems to work out.

This chapter lays the foundations for a WebDB or an OAS application. I'll talk about these applications more specifically in Chapter 3, *WebDB*, and Chapter 4, *Oracle Application Server (OAS)*.

Resources

An individual piece of content, whether it's a human resources manual or a phone list, is a *resource* in web parlance. There are two broad classes of resources: static and dynamic. *Static resources* are files in a certain format: HTML documents (HTML) created through a text or HTML editor, ASCII reports (TXT) created through a batch process, images (GIF, JPEG) created through an image editor, and even movies (AVI, MPEG) or sound (WAV, AU) created through a video or audio capture system. Almost any type of file becomes a static resource when placed in the proper directory on a machine running OAS or WebDB.

The second, much more interesting type of resource is a *dynamic resource*, a program that creates web content as it runs. For example, you could write a program to dynamically create a list of employee phone numbers from a human resources database. When a user visits this page, your program queries the database and builds the page as it runs. These sites are always up to date because they are built directly from the data's source, so they aren't subject to the vagaries of manual updating. OAS allows developers to use a number of languages, including PL/SQL, Java, Perl, and VRML (Virtual Reality Modeling Language), to develop dynamic resources; WebDB uses only PL/SQL. This book concentrates on developing dynamic resources using PL/SQL.

Server-to-Client Communication

The Internet (or an intranet) is a network that links different computers together. Before we can start writing web applications, we must understand how the output from these systems actually gets from the server to the browser, which means that we have to learn a little about how the Internet and the Web work.

OAS and WebDB use standard Internet conventions and protocols to send resources to a client. The most important parts of this interchange are:

- A TCP/IP network to connect the server to the client

- A software communication port to serve as a collection point for incoming requests

- A transfer protocol called HTTP to govern how server and client communicate

- A client program called a web browser to allow users to request and receive resources from the OAS or WebDB server

- A uniform resource locator (URL) to allow the browser to find a particular resource

- A MIME type to tell the browser what to do with resources once received from the OAS or WebDB server

The following sections briefly describe each of these parts.

The TCP/IP Network

Browsers connect to an OAS or WebDB server using the TCP/IP networking protocol. Although there are a number of different types of networking protocols, such as DECNet or IPX, web systems only work with TCP/IP. Fortunately, more and more operating systems have this functionality built in, including Unix, Windows 95, Windows 98, Windows NT, OS/2, and Linux.

Every machine on a TCP/IP network is identified by a four-part IP address. Each number in the address can range from 0 to 255, and the four numbers are separated by periods. For example, 253.4.99.17 might be the address for the machine running the human resources department's web server. Every machine on a TCP/IP network has a unique IP address.

Most TCP/IP networks have a special class of servers called Domain Name Servers (DNSs). Their job is to translate IP addresses into meaningful hostnames that are easy to remember. For example, assigning the address 253.4.99.17 to the name "HR" in the DNS allows users to refer to the human resources server as "HR," rather than its actual IP address.

The Communication Port

A *software port* (as opposed to a physical hardware port) is a common reference point on the server that is used to exchange messages. Each TCP/IP-based networking application, like OAS or WebDB, is assigned a specific port that it monitors for incoming requests. Client programs that need to communicate with the server connect to the server's assigned port. Once connected, the two systems exchange information according to a standard protocol (HTTP, FTP, etc.). Each port is identified by a port number, its ordinal position in the range of all ports. On Unix systems, for example, there are 64,536 different ports.

 As a security precaution, a user with root privilege must start programs that use the first 1024 ports. Less privileged users can use ports higher than 1024.

The HyperText Transfer Protocol (HTTP)

A transfer protocol is a convention that governs how systems exchange information. Take, for example, a phone conversation. When you call someone, you (hopefully!) don't start blurting out whatever comes to mind as soon as they pick up the receiver. Instead, your conversation follows a set pattern that civilized society has agreed upon to make communication more efficient:

1. I initiate a conversation by calling you.

2. You say "Hello."

3. I identify myself.

4. We exchange a message.

5. We say "Goodbye."

6. We hang up.

This sort of formalized exchange is the idea behind a protocol: it lets the sender and receiver know the order in which communications will occur. While computers use much more formalized systems than humans, the idea is basically the same.* OAS and WebDB follow a standard Internet protocol called HyperText Transfer Protocol (HTTP) to communicate with client web browsers. OAS supports HTTP 1.0 and HTTP 1.1, while WebDB supports only HTTP 1.0.

By convention, several special TCP ports are associated with specific protocols. For example, port 21 is usually used for FTP, port 25 is used for SMTP (a common email protocol), and port 80 is used for HTTP.

Protocols vary in complexity. Unlike client/server protocols, such as SQL*Net or Net8, HTTP is relatively simple because it is *stateless*, meaning that the client and server terminate their connection once their conversation is complete. Unlike client/server systems, which maintain state by keeping open a continuous connection to the database, HTTP systems are connected only in bursts and not for the duration of the session.

Because the client and server forget everything that happened during previous connections, developers must take explicit steps to maintain information, or *state*, from page to page. In other words, there are no global variables in a web application; they are all local. Anything you want to retain from screen to screen has to be stored and retrieved in every page. For example, if you're building a web-based threaded discussion list that begins with a login screen, you must manually program it to remember the login information. We'll discuss strategies for doing this in Chapter 7, *The PL/SQL Toolkit*, and Chapter 8, *Developing Applications*.

The Web Browser

Users request information from a WebDB or OAS server using a web browser such as Microsoft Internet Explorer or Netscape Communicator. The browser is responsible for presenting web content on these servers to the user. In the early days of the Web, a browser could handle only basic HTML and text documents, but the explosion of web content has turned the browser into an information kiosk, multimedia center, and minicomputer all rolled into one. For example, most modern browsers can display an HTML document filled with pictures, sounds, and even movies. With the advent of Java, the browser has become a *virtual machine*, a computer within a computer capable of running Java programs.

---

* Sometimes it's almost identical; SMTP communications begin when the client says "HELO" to the server!

There are a number of browsers on the market, and each one behaves slightly differently. For example, the appearance of any given HTML document often varies from browser to browser. To differentiate their product from the competition, browser vendors add features that work only with their browser. You should test your content on a number of different browsers, even if your company has adopted a standard, since many users refuse to give up browsers to which they are fanatically attached. Additionally, more and more people are dialing in from home, and they will often have older (or, depending on your company, newer) software than your company standard.

The Uniform Resource Locator

Uniform Resource Locators (URLs) are used to request a resource from an OAS or WebDB server independently of the operating system used on the machine. A URL abstracts the machine name, resource path, and resource name into a string with the following syntax:

```
protocol://server:port/path/resource?query_string
```

protocol
  Specifies the network protocol that the browser and the server use to communicate. The most common values are HTTP and FTP.

server
  Identifies the name of the machine that hosts the resource. Although you can use the machine's IP address, it's better to use the name defined in the DNS since it helps isolate the URL from the network reconfiguration.

port
  Specifies the TCP port used by the OAS or WebDB server. If the port is omitted, then port 80 is used by default.

path
  Specifies the virtual directory or schema containing the resource. The path usually maps to either a virtual directory mapping on the web server or, in Oracle web servers, to a Database Access Descriptor (DAD), a logical name used to map a procedure call in a URL to the database schema in which it resides.

resource name
  Typically specifies the actual name of the file to return. If the name is omitted, the listener returns a default file, if one is available. The name of the default file varies: *index.html* is used on many Unix systems, and *default.htm* is usually used on Windows NT systems. On Oracle web servers, the resource can also correspond to a PL/SQL procedure.

query string (optional)

> Optionally passes parameters to dynamic resources. The string begins with a question mark (?) and is followed by ampersand (&)-delimited sets of name/value pairs. Each name/value pair consists of a parameter name followed by an equals sign (=) and a value for the parameter. The parameter name must match a name in the procedure's formal parameter list. The parameter value must be encoded by converting its nonalphanumeric characters to their hexadecimal equivalents; converted characters are preceded with a percent sign (%). The exceptions to this rule are the underscore character, which is left alone, and the space, which can be converted to either a plus (+) sign or %20. For example, "w/in second(s)" converts to "w%2Fin+second%28s%29".

You can omit the server, port, and path sections from hyperlinks (links the user clicks to go to other locations) inside other documents, which allows you to create relative, rather than absolute, URLs. Relative URLs are like relative directories in a filesystem: they let you describe the location of one resource in relation to the current resource. Most resources don't stand on their own; they are part of a larger hierarchical site that usually begins with a "home" and branches out from there. There are practical as well as aesthetic reasons to define a site's structure using relative rather than absolute URLs. For example, if a site is moved to a new host, the server section on all the links in the site must be changed to the new hostname. This is very tedious work. If the site is defined using relative URLs, however, the relative structure of its pages is unaffected by the move.

You create a relative URL by omitting the server, port, and path section from the URLs for hyperlinks and for ACTION attributes in HTML forms. The omitted information is filled in with the server and path information for the current resource, just as the file path information in an operating system command can be assumed from the current directory. The "current directory" of a URL is called the *base URL*.

For example, if a page's URL is *http://betty/somepage.html*, links on that page to other resources on the site do not have to explicitly include "betty" in the URL. Instead, they can simply begin with the path and name of other resources. The server part, "betty," is implied by the base URL. You can even include new subdirectories off the base URL.

The Resource MIME Type

Every resource is associated with a *MIME type* that tells the browser what to do with the resource once the transfer is complete (e.g., display it in the main window, launch a file viewer, and so on). MIME, which stands for Multipurpose Internet Mail Extensions, is a standard for exchanging various types of files (such as images, text, and video) over the Internet so that each computer platform, whether NT, Unix, or VMS, will interpret and correctly handle the resource's contents.

MIME types describe the data format using two parts. The first part, the *type*, identifies the resource's general format, such as `text`, `image`, or `audio`. The second part, the *subtype*, identifies the resource's specific data format. For example, the subtypes for the `image` type include `gif` and `jpeg`. The type and subtype are delimited with a slash (`/`); for example, a picture's full MIME type could be `image/gif` or `image/jpeg`. The default for WebDB and OAS is `text/html`.

Browsers must be configured to handle each MIME type. Almost all browsers can display `text/plain`, `text/html`, and `image/jpeg` documents without any extra configuration. When a browser receives a document with a MIME type it doesn't recognize, it asks the user to select a helper program to display the document. This is similar to selecting a file association based on a file extension in Windows (i.e., mapping the *.doc* extension to the Microsoft Word application). Once the user makes an association, subsequent requests for that MIME type are opened using the associated application.

A Helpful Analogy

I've covered a lot of important material in this section. It might be useful to summarize it by making an analogy to the telephone system network, as shown in Table 2-1.

Table 2-1. An Analogy Between the Web and the Phone System

Term	Analogy
Resources	A resource is like the message you want to transmit during the call. It's the actual information you want to send or receive.
TCP/IP network	The TCP/IP network is like the standards used by the phone company to route your call from your phone to the person that you're calling.
Port	The port is like the circuit that's opened across the network. It is the conduit through which the message is sent.
HTTP	HTTP is like the "hello" and "goodbye" parts of your conversation, the agreed-upon convention that governs how the conversation takes place.
Web browser	The web browser is like the telephone, the component that allows you to place the call.
URL	The URL is like the phone number, the convention that associates a particular resource with an abstract location.
MIME type	The MIME type is like the "nature" of the conversation (i.e., business, pleasure, etc.). It is the specific classification of the message; additionally, it implies a specific action that must be taken based on the message.

Content Delivery Model

In this section I'll explain how the OAS and WebDB servers apply the ideas introduced in the previous section to deliver content from the server to the client (e.g., URLs, virtual directories, ports, etc.).

Although the specific details vary, OAS and WebDB follow the same basic process model to deliver web content and rely on a virtual schema mapping called a Database Access Descriptor (DAD) to access the database. A DAD is similar to a virtual directory mapping; it creates a name, used within a URL, that links the request to a specific schema in the database.

Figure 2-1 illustrates the basic parts of the model.

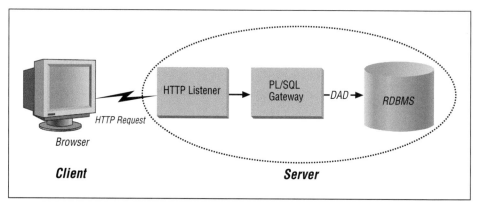

Figure 2-1. Basic components of OAS and WebDB systems

A request begins when a user submits a URL or an HTML form to an OAS or WebDB server. A server component called the *HTTP listener* intercepts the request and extracts its path section. This step, called *URL resolution*, determines what type of resource the request is for and how it will be processed. If the URL's path section matches a virtual directory mapping, then the request is for a static resource and the HTTP listener returns the requested resource (if found) to the user's browser. If the path section matches a DAD stored in the server's configuration files, the request is for a dynamic resource and the HTTP listener forwards, or *dispatches*, the request to the PL/SQL gateway.

The PL/SQL gateway reparses the URL (or HTML form `action` attribute), extracting the DAD name and the name of the procedure to execute, which is found in the resource name section of the URL. The gateway also extracts any parameters that might have been passed as part of the request. If the request was made with a URL, the parameters are stored in the query string. If the request was made with a form, the parameters are stored in the form's named data entry fields.

The gateway uses the DAD configuration information to connect to the appropriate database schema, then executes the specified procedure, passing any parameters included in the call. The procedure, which executes directly inside the database, usually calls procedures in a set of packages called the *PL/SQL toolkit*. These calls create the page's contents by "printing" HTML tags into a temporary buffer. When the procedure completes, the gateway signals the HTTP listener to send the contents of the buffer—now populated with the HTML output from the procedure—back to the user's browser. The user's browser displays the page, just as it would any other static resource.

Let's look at this procedure in more detail, especially the functions of the HTTP listener and the PL/SQL gateway.

The HTTP Listener

The HTTP listener is what we normally think of as the web server. Its job is to receive the requests users make with their browsers, determine how to process them, then return the requested resources (along with their MIME types) to the client machines that made the request. Most of the listener's life is spent monitoring a TCP port for requests made from a web browser. Although OAS and WebDB use port 80 by default, they can be configured to use other ports.

Only one application at time can listen on a port. To run OAS and WebDB on the same machine, you must configure them to listen on different ports. For example, if OAS is listening on port 80, you could configure WebDB to listen on port 81.

The HTTP listener makes static resources available by mapping physical directories on the OAS or WebDB server to a virtual alias. These aliases are used in the URL to request a static resource that resides in the corresponding directory. The goal is to give clients a uniform way to locate a resource that is independent from the operating system of the OAS or WebDB server. For example, on an NT server, you can map the directory *c:\files\public\web_stuff* to a virtual directory called *web*. URLs that need to access resources in the directory must use the alias "web", rather than the actual directory name, to retrieve static resources.

You can configure OAS to make subdirectories beneath a mapped directory accessible from the Web; WebDB maps subdirectories by default. The subdirectory name, as defined on the server's operating system, is appended to the "root" alias of the URL. For example, if *c:\files\public\web_stuff* had two subdirectories named *bob* and *sue*, the virtual mapping to them would be */web/bob* and */web/sue.**

Since they include operating system specific names, subdirectory mappings are not completely platform independent. On Unix systems, for example, directory names

---

* Since the Web originated mostly on Unix systems, URLs use the forward slash ("/") to denote directories, much to the chagrin of the DOS world, which uses the backslash ("\").

are case sensitive, so the directories *Junk* and *junk* are not the same. Consequently, a URL that accesses a subdirectory on a Unix server must be case sensitive as well. Other platforms have similar caveats. The spaces in Win9x directory
names cause all sorts of headaches, and the 3.x version has an eight-character
limit. The best advice on any platform is to keep subdirectory names simple.

The PL/SQL Gateway

The PL/SQL gateway is to the database what the HTTP listener is to the filesystem:

- Just as static resources are accessed with a URL, PL/SQL dynamic resources are
  accessed with a URL.

- Just as physical directories are mapped to virtual directories, physical database schemas are mapped to virtual schemas. These virtual mappings are used
  in a URL to select the database schema in which a particular dynamic resource
  resides.

- Just as static resources are identified by filenames, PL/SQL dynamic resources
  are identified by procedure names (packaged procedures are identified with
  both a package and a procedure name). These names are used in a URL to
  select the procedure to execute.

Both OAS and WebDB use the Database Access Descriptors to connect to a specific schema, which includes all the information necessary to establish a database
connection, such as a username, password, and connect string. In either case, the
DAD is mapped to a virtual alias that is used within a URL to select a schema.

OAS schema mappings have two parts: a DAD, which maps a schema, and agents,
which map to a DAD. The agent name, not the DAD, appears in the URL to make
the connection between the Web and the database. Both the URL and the ACTION
attribute of a form that requests a dynamic resource have the following general
format (optional sections are bracketed):

```
http://server[:port]/agent_name/plsql/[package.]procedure[?parm1=foo...]
```

Here are a few examples:

```
http://gandalf/agent_webtest/plsql/print_all_emps
http://gandalf/agent_webtest/plsql/show_emps?i_name=BOB
http://207.25.98.87:8181/secure_agent/plsql/show_users
http://betty/agent_webtest/plsql/forum.current_forum_list
```

WebDB has a slightly simpler mapping system that uses just the DAD in the URL;
WebDB does not use agents. The URL's format is as follows (optional sections are
bracketed):

```
http://server[:port]/dad_name/[package.]procedure[?parm1=foo...]
```

Here are some examples:

```
http://pcandrew.ora.com/WebDB/WEBDB.home
http://gandalf:8181/WebDB/show_emps?I_name=FRED+FLINTSTONE
http://www.travel.com/travelers_site/flights.show_list?country=FR
```

Database Integration

The HTTP listener and PL/SQL gateway are used to build web-enabled systems that provide tight integration with a backend Oracle database. PL/SQL-based OAS and WebDB applications are developed using a set of packages called the PL/SQL toolkit. In this section, we'll take a quick look at the toolkit and see an example procedure. The last section covers how to pass parameters.

The PL/SQL Toolkit

WebDB and OAS both include the PL/SQL toolkit. The toolkit contains a variety of PL/SQL packages written and supplied by Oracle that perform a range of tasks, including generating HTML tags, manipulating cookies (name/value pairs used to save information throughout an entire session), and creating complex HTML structures based on information in a database table. In general, procedures built with the toolkit will work in either product, although you may run into minor database privilege issues that the DBA can help you resolve.

The packages in the toolkit (described in detail in Chapter 7) are:

HTP and HTF
> HTP is a set of procedures that print syntactically correct HTML tags, which are returned to the user's web browser. HTF is an equivalent set of functions that return HTML strings whose output is returned to the program that called the function. In either package, procedures and functions correspond to specific HTML tags; their parameters correspond to tag attributes.

OWA_COOKIE
> A set of data structures, procedures, and functions used to create and manipulate cookies.

OWA_IMAGE
> A set of data structures, procedures, and functions used to manipulate image maps.

OWA_OPT_LOCK
> A set of data structures, procedures, and functions used to perform optimistic record locking. The package can either compute a checksum that's used to test for differences or compare each field of the old and new records (we'll look at this in detail in Chapter 7).

OWA_PATTERN

A set of data structures, procedures, and functions that perform advanced search and replace operations on text strings using regular expressions.

OWA_SEC

A set of data structures, procedures, and functions used to develop customized security and authentication procedures, such as GET_USER_ID (to return the user executing the procedure) or GET_CLIENT_IP (to return the IP address of the machine making the request).

OWA_TEXT

A set of data structures, procedures, and functions used to perform operations on large strings. Also used as the basis of many of the procedures in OWA_PATTERN.

OWA_UTIL

A set of data structures, procedures, and functions used to create advanced HTML structures, such as calendars or tables. Many of the WebDB components, such as forms or calendars, are based directly on this package.

A PL/SQL Example

The following example gives the flavor of how the toolkit creates web content. The example is a relatively simple PL/SQL procedure that displays rows in an employee table. The output is formatted into HTML using the procedures in the toolkit's HTP package:

```
/* Formatted by PL/Formatter v.1.1.13 */
PROCEDURE show_emps (
   i_job IN VARCHAR2 DEFAULT 'SALESMAN'
   )
AS

   CURSOR emp_cur
   IS
      SELECT *
      FROM scott.emp
      WHERE job LIKE i_job
      ORDER BY ename;
   emp_rec emp_cur%ROWTYPE;
BEGIN
   HTP.title ('Employees in the EMP table');
   HTP.tableopen (cattributes => 'border=1 width=100%');
   OPEN emp_cur;
   LOOP
      FETCH emp_cur INTO emp_rec;
      EXIT WHEN emp_cur%notfound;
      HTP.tablerowopen;
      HTP.tabledata (emp_rec.ename);
      HTP.tabledata (emp_rec.job);
```

```
            HTP.tabledata (emp_rec.hiredate);
            HTP.tabledata (emp_rec.sal);
            HTP.tablerowclose;
    END LOOP;
    CLOSE emp_cur;
    HTP.tableclose;
END;
```

Figure 2-2 shows the output from the procedure. For a more advanced discussion of the PL/SQL toolkit, see Chapter 7.

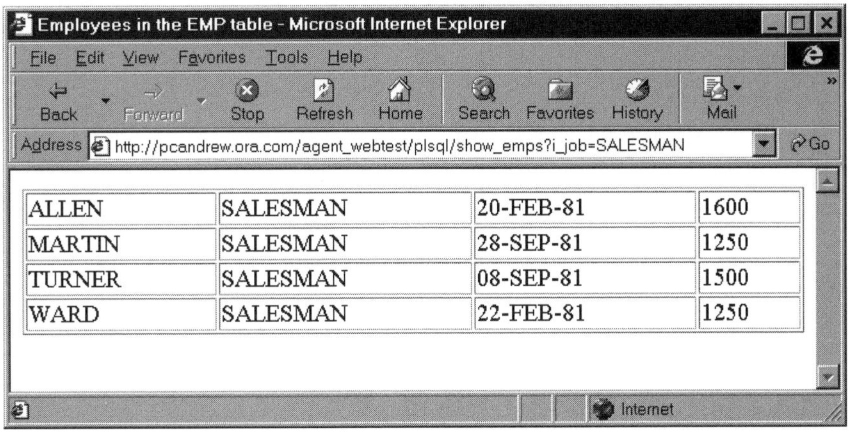

Figure 2-2. Output of the show_emps procedure

Calling the Example

You can pass parameters to a WebDB or an OAS PL/SQL procedure by including them either in the query string of a URL or as named elements on an HTML form. These parameters are mapped to the procedure's formal argument list using named notation. For example, let's suppose we want to develop a web page that inserts a new user into a table. The procedure we want to call is defined as:

```
/* Formatted by PL/Formatter v.1.1.13 */
PROCEDURE add (
    lname IN VARCHAR2 DEFAULT NULL,
    fname IN VARCHAR2 DEFAULT NULL,
    dpt_code IN VARCHAR2 DEFAULT NULL
    )
IS
BEGIN
    INSERT INTO emp_table (last_name,first_name,dept)
        VALUES (lname, fname, dpt_code);
    COMMIT;
    HTP.print ('User was inserted');
```

```
EXCEPTION
   WHEN OTHERS
   THEN
      HTP.print ('Sorry, could not insert user.');
END;
```

Using a query string

The first way to call the procedure is to embed the parameter values in the URL's query string. Recall that the query string is made up of sets of name/value pairs. When we call a PL/SQL procedure, the "name" part of the pair selects the formal parameter to which we are assigning a value. The "value" part specifies the actual value to pass. The URL to call the procedure is:

```
http://server/DAD/add?lname=odewahn&fname=andrew&dpt_code=MIS
```

Using an HTML form

We can call the same procedure with an HTML form. In this case, the form's **action** field specifies the procedure to execute, and the named input elements on the HTML form pass parameters. The name of an input element must match the name of a parameter to the procedure. Here are the HTML tags needed to create a form to call the add procedure:

```
<form action=http://wilma/hr/plsql/add>
   First Name: <input type=text name=fname><br>
   Last Name:  <input type=text name=lname><br>
   Department: <select name=dpt_code>
      <option value=HR>Human Resources
      <option value=MIS>Computer department
      <option value=ACCT>Accounting
   </select>
</form>
```

The PL/SQL gateway translates the information in the query string or on the form to a named notation procedure call:

```
add ( lname => 'odewahn', fname => 'andrew',
      dpt_code => 'MIS' );
```

Parameter arrays

Sometimes it is desirable to process multiple values for the same parameter, such as when you want to allow a user to enter multiple rows of data in a single form. In a query string, this is accomplished by giving the same name to multiple name/value pairs. In a form, it is accomplished by using the same name for multiple input elements. On the PL/SQL side, the corresponding parameter for the procedure must be declared as an array datatype. We'll see an example of this in Chapter 8.

Parameter gotchas

Calling a procedure from the Web circumvents the compiler safeguards that occur in normal procedure calls. When the gateway receives a URL to execute, it will try to do so whether the URL represents a syntactically correct call or not. If the call contains even the slightest error, the listener bombs out and presents an ugly error page to the user. Some of the most common sources of errors are:

Misspelling a formal parameter
  The named notation calling method uses the formal parameter name to match the corresponding actual parameter. The gateway generates an error if, for any reason, an actual parameter doesn't match one of the procedure's formal parameters.

Omitting a required actual parameter
  All procedure calls, regardless of notation, must provide an actual parameter for a formal parameter that does not have a default value. Failing to do so results in an exception.

Passing the wrong datatype as a parameter value
  An actual parameter value must match the declared type of its corresponding formal parameter. Unfortunately, users can create an exception by passing garbage data.

The following guidelines help minimize these and other errors:

* Follow a convention for naming formal parameters to reduce the chance of misspelling or misnaming a parameter.

* Provide default values for every formal parameter, even if it's only DEFAULT NULL, to reduce the chance that a required parameter is omitted.

* Declare parameters as a VARCHAR2 to protect against garbage data. Converting this value into the required type (i.e., VARCHAR2 to NUMBER) inside the procedure allows you to trap exceptions. You can also use the WebDB form wizard to automatically create JavaScript code to perform these checks (you can write your own JavaScript programs, but that's beyond the scope of this book).

Don't give a parameter the same name as a column in a table, as this can totally confuse the compiler. For example, in the **add** procedure presented in the previous section, naming the last name parameter `last_name` instead of `lname` would cause a subtle error in the INSERT statement because `last_name` has two different meanings: it's both a parameter and a table column. You can spend hours trying to track down this relatively simple problem.

Database Security Review

Even though security policies are developed and enforced by the DBA, you should still understand how database security issues can impact application design. For example, you should have a clear grasp of schemas and object privileges if you're going to secure your systems by allowing access only through a minimally privileged account.

 Depending on the application, you might need to create an application-specific security scheme (unless you create a DAD for every account, which is a maintenance nightmare) to differentiate between users. For example, in Chapter 8, we'll look at a threaded discussion list application in which we create our own username and password list to allow users to post messages.

This section is a security refresher, covering security relationships among database users, database objects, object privileges, and roles. If these terms are new to you, or you need to dust off a few cobwebs, read on. Otherwise, feel free to skip to the next chapter.

Database Users

A user account is the first line of defense in an Oracle database. Similar to an account on a Unix or NT system, each user account has an associated username and password. A user must log in to a particular account by providing the correct password before running scripts, inputting data, executing PL/SQL programs, or performing any other meaningful activity.

The term *schema* is often used synonymously with "user" or "account." Although the concepts are closely related, schema is slightly more specific and refers not only to the account itself, but also to the collection of objects (tables, indexes, packages, etc.) owned by the account.

Database Objects

The word *object* is one of the most overused in the computer world. Languages like Java and C++ create objects with wonderful properties like polymorphism, inheritance, and a slew of other four-syllable words. Object-relational databases like Oracle8*i* give us pseudo-objects that mimic the important properties of the objects in Java. Finally, life itself gives us everyday objects like buses, rutabagas, and human resources managers.

In Oracle, a *database object* is a general term for anything created and stored in an Oracle database, including tables, indexes, views, synonyms, and stored procedures. Each object is owned by the account in which it was created. To follow our Unix example, database objects are sort of like files; they belong to the user that created them and to no one else.

Each object has a unique name. A table may be named emp, a procedure may be named give_raise, and an index may be named emp_pk1. Once a name is given to an object, no other object within the schema—even if it is a different kind of object—can use the same name. Attempting to create an object with an existing name results in the error "ORA-00955: name is already used by an existing object."

Privileges

Just as every Unix account shouldn't have system administrator authority, every Oracle account shouldn't have DBA power. For example, Bob in accounting shouldn't be able to issue the DROP TABLE command just to see what will happen. Privileges allow us to control how much power a particular account can have.

There are two types of privileges: system and object. As a rule of thumb, *system privileges* let an account execute SQL Data Definition Language (DDL) commands, while *object privileges* let an account execute SQL Data Manipulation Language (DML) commands.

A privilege is granted to or revoked from a specific user account with the SQL commands GRANT and REVOKE. For example, the following two commands give the scott account the right to create a table and select from the emp table in the HR schema:

```
GRANT CREATE TABLE TO scott;
GRANT SELECT ON hr.emp TO scott;
```

The next two commands show how to remove a privilege using the REVOKE statement:

```
REVOKE CREATE TABLE FROM scott;
REVOKE SELECT ON hr.emp FROM scott;
```

System privileges

System privileges give an account the right to perform specific actions. For example, an account must be given permission, usually by the DBA, to create, alter, drop, or execute various database objects. An account can also be given permission to perform these actions in other schemas by including the ANY option.

There are a number of system privileges,* including:

CREATE TABLE
CREATE PROCEDURE
ALTER USER
EXECUTE ANY PROCEDURE
GRANT ANY PRIVILEGE

The most minimal system privilege is the CREATE SESSION privilege, which allows the account only to log in to the database. Unless granted other privileges, these accounts cannot do much damage. For this reason, they are often used as gateways to more privileged accounts, which selectively grant the account access to a limited number of objects.

Object privileges

Object privileges allow an account to make its objects available to other accounts. Each type of object has its own set of applicable privileges. After a privilege on an object is granted to another account, that account can perform a variety of operations that fall within the limits of the granted privileges. In WebDB, some of the most commonly used privileges (by object) include:

- Tables and views

  — SELECT: Select rows from the table.

  — INSERT: Insert rows into the table.

  — UPDATE: Update rows in the table.

  — DELETE: Delete rows from the table.

- Procedures, functions, and packages

  — EXECUTE: Execute a stored program.

- Sequences

  — SELECT: Select the sequence value.

 A stored procedure or function executes with the privileges of its owner, not those of the account that is executing it, unless overridden with the Oracle8*i* "invoker's rights" option.

An account may access an object once it has been granted the necessary privilege. If it tries to perform an action for which it does not have the necessary privilege, the RDBMS generates an error. The account references the object using its

---

* The SYSTEM_PRIVILEGE_MAP data dictionary table lists all the system privileges.

fully qualified object name, which is simply the object's name prepended with its owning schema. The two names are separated with a period. For example, suppose the accounts bob, sue, and cato each own a table named emp. Assuming we have the right privileges, we can use the fully qualified object name in the following SQL statement to get an aggregate list:

```
SELECT * FROM bob.emp
UNION
SELECT * FROM sue.emp
UNION
SELECT * FROM cato.emp;
```

For example, suppose Alice in accounting wants to dump some of her work on Bob, who was recently demoted to clerk for destroying a production database. She can use the SQL GRANT command to give Bob's account (bob) privileges on tables she owns so that Bob can run various scripts:

```
GRANT SELECT ON employees TO bob;
GRANT INSERT ON employees TO bob;
```

Once Bob has the proper privilege, he can execute SELECT commands on Alice's table by using the table's fully qualified name:

```
SELECT * FROM alice.employees
```

Notice that Alice has withheld the DELETE privilege; Bob will get an error if he tries the DELETE statement.

Roles

It would be a strange site indeed that let accountants control critical database objects. Instead, these objects are usually owned by a highly privileged account that is accessible to only the database administrator and a few trusted developers. The DBA creates less privileged accounts for average users and selectively grants them privileges based on their needs.

For example, an account named HR might own all the objects for the company's human resource management system. The DBA might create a view of the employees table and grant Bob's or Alice's account permission to query it. She might also create a separate account for data entry clerks with INSERT privileges on a few important tables. Finally, she might create an account for a web application that displays employee information stored in database snapshots. Ideally, each account has the minimum privileges it needs to fulfill its goal.

Managing these privileges by hand is a daunting task. Even a small company can have dozens of applications, hundreds of tables, and zillions of users. It is simply impossible for the DBA to manually grant the correct privileges to every user in a way that is convenient and safe. Remember, lurking in the back of every DBA's

Using Synonyms to Achieve Location Transparency

Occasionally, an object must be moved from one schema to another to accommodate new circumstances. For example, what happens if Alice is promoted and wants Cato (the new upstart in accounting) to own and maintain the employees table? Bob—and anyone else using the table—must update his scripts to reflect the table's new location. For this reason, it's a bad idea to embed an object's owner directly into a SQL or a PL/SQL statement.

Synonyms eliminate this problem. A *synonym* is simply an alias, or pointer, for another object. Used in place of a fully qualified object name, the synonym allows us to design systems that achieve *location transparency*. This is just a fancy way of saying that our programs do not depend on a particular account's owning a particular object. If an object is moved to a new owner, we can simply change the synonym in one place and everything will continue to work.

In the previous example, Bob could achieve location transparency by creating a synonym for the employees table:

```
CREATE SYNONYM employees_syn FOR
    alice.employees
```

He could then use the synonym name instead of making an explicit reference to the owning schema:

```
SELECT * FROM employees_syn;
```

When Alice moves the table to Cato, Bob can simply change the synonym to reflect the new location.

---

mind is the secret (and sometimes not so secret) fear that his or her users and developers are idiots who will drop critical tables just for kicks. It is crucial for both security and the DBA's sanity that each user have access to only what he or she needs.

This is where the concept of a database role comes to the rescue. A *role* is a collection of privileges grouped under a single name. Instead of granting privileges to individual users, the DBA grants them to a role. This role, in turn, is granted to the users that need the corresponding privileges. The DBA can add or revoke privileges from a role at any time, and these changes automatically flow to the users assigned to the role.

For example, the DBA might create a role called ACCOUNTANT and grant it selected privileges on tables and views owned by the HR account. The role reduces the maintenance on Alice's, Bob's, Cato's, and Xena's accounts to a single grant. Figure 2-3 shows a typical scenario in which roles are used to create access rights for various classes of users, such as pay clerks, managers, and receivables clerks.

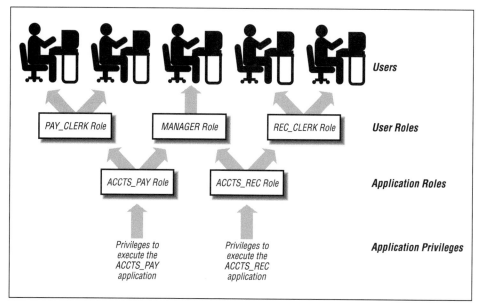

Figure 2-3. A common use for roles

 When writing stored PL/SQL program units, such as packages, note that the compiler ignores the privileges granted through roles. To work around this problem you must either create the program in the account that owns the object or explicitly grant the necessary privilege to the account that owns the stored procedure. However, users can still execute procedures granted through roles.

A role is a database object just like any other. Assuming you have the CREATE ROLE privilege, you create a role with the following syntax:

```
CREATE ROLE role_name;
```

You then grant privileges on various objects to the new role, just as you would to a normal user. For example:

```
GRANT SELECT ON customers TO accts_pay_role;
GRANT SELECT ON cust_orders TO accts_pay_role;
```

Finally, you grant the role to individual users, treating the role as though it were a new privilege. For example:

```
GRANT ACCTS_PAY_ROLE TO bob;
GRANT ACCTS_PAY_ROLE TO cato;
```

Revoking a privilege from the role automatically revokes it from all the users assigned to the role.

Additional Security Precautions

In addition to database security features, there are three other security precautions worth noting, although we won't cover them in any detail. These include:

Secure Sockets Layer (SSL)
> A standard for securing a web session by encrypting the traffic between a browser and a web server. The method relies on a *digital certificate,* a special file assigned to a site by a trusted source called a *certification authority* (CA). The CA generates the certificate and sends it to the web site. Browsers wishing to connect to the site must first download and accept the certificate, which is used in an encryption scheme to secure the subsequent traffic.

Firewall
> A machine placed between two networks that controls what traffic can cross the boundary. Companies almost always have a firewall between their internal network and, for instance, the Internet. The firewall can be configured to block traffic originating from certain areas, let through certain types of traffic (for instance, HTTP) and reject others (Telnet traffic), and force users to supply a username and password before they can go through the firewall.

Advanced Networking Option (ANO)
> A security server used to encrypt SQL*Net and Net8 traffic. This is useful in a web setting because (depending on the configuration of the firewall), users can establish a SQL*Net or Net8 connection over the Internet, allowing them to use tools like SQL*Plus. ANO secures the conversation.

Web security (and computer security in general) is a complex and broad subject that encompasses many different areas handled by different individuals. The DBA sets database security policies, system administrators check on operating system security, application developers build security features into their applications, and the network administrator designs hardware and software configurations to secure the network. Even the security guard at the front door has an important role in maintaining the physical security of your site.

> No matter how you secure your system, you are still vulnerable to an attack. One of the simplest and most effective hacking techniques, *social engineering,* simply tricks people into revealing otherwise secure information through deception. For example, it's much easier to call an internal help desk and sweet-talk someone out of a password than to penetrate a secured system.

As an application developer, your main security duty is to make sure that your applications do as little as possible to compromise the system (for example, writing a web system that reveals a password list). In general, though, you'll have very little direct involvement in the other areas. While you'll certainly work with the DBA to gain privileges to various objects, you will probably not work with the network administrator (other than to listen to complaints about how the administrator doesn't have enough bandwidth for your application).

3

WebDB

WebDB is a user-friendly tool for developing database-driven web applications and sites. You perform every WebDB task, from database administration to application development, using just a browser; everything in a WebDB site, from applications to content, can be stored inside a backend database.*

Every WebDB component, from development tools to the database administrator toolkit, has an HTML user interface, eliminating the need for complex tools like Oracle Forms or Oracle Enterprise Manager (OEM). Because browsers are equipped with standard Internet protocols, WebDB client machines do not need SQL*Net or Net8; this allows WebDB sites to be run or administered from "thin-client" machines. WebDB can also take advantage of JavaScript-enabled browsers.

Everything in a WebDB site can be stored directly inside an Oracle database. This allows the site to be professionally administered and maintained using the same tools and techniques as for any other production Oracle database. As an added benefit, the site's performance can be monitored and improved through well-understood database tuning techniques. WebDB's "database-centric" approach helps application developers and DBAs leverage their current skills, rather than acquiring an entirely new and unfamiliar skill set.

How you use WebDB depends on your job. Database administrators can use WebDB to manage database objects, check database logs, and perform other DBA tasks. Application developers can use WebDB to create HTML-based web applications using a set of *wizards* that automatically build application components, like forms or reports. End users can use the WebDB components you create to view reports, fill out data entry forms, or view the content published by other users.

---

* Oracle calls this concept "100% in the browser, 100% in the database," meaning that everything is accessed with just a browser and stored in just a database.

Additionally, almost any user can use WebDB to publish web content on their own personal home page, as well as view content made available by other WebDB users.

Given the nature of the Web, these tasks are rarely mutually exclusive. For example, a DBA might want to upload "tips and tricks" to a page of her personal WebDB site. An application developer might want to monitor application performance or create database objects such as tables. An end user might want to create a report based on a SQL query (stranger things have been known to happen!).

In this chapter, I'll give you an overview of the different things you can do with WebDB, then look at the architecture that makes this all possible. As you read this chapter, keep in mind that WebDB itself is written entirely in PL/SQL. In many ways, it's the ultimate example of the power of combining HTML and PL/SQL into a web application.

Overview of WebDB

WebDB is divided into three broad categories: database administration, application development, and content-driven web site management. In the next three sections, we'll briefly look at each area with an eye towards seeing what the product does, though not necessarily how you perform each task.*

Database Administration

You can use WebDB to perform many routine database administration tasks using just a web browser, rather than a "fat client" like the Oracle Enterprise Manager suite of database management tools. For example, suppose you've gotten a call from Bob in accounting insisting that "my Internet doesn't work." Befuddled by your patient explanation that his statement makes absolutely no sense, he demands that you walk over to his desk and help him fix his problem. Since customer service has been added to your list of job performance metrics, you comply. When you arrive at Bob's desk, you realize that he has simply forgotten his password.

Since no one in his right mind would install SQL*Plus (much less OEM) on Bob's machine, you would normally have to trek back to your desk to reset his password, confirming Bob's darkest suspicions that you really don't know what you're doing. Fortunately, you can use WebDB's security management options to save yourself the trip. While you can't do everything from WebDB, you can perform

---

* The appendix, *Resources for the Oracle Web Developer*, contains a list of resources that provide complete, step-by-step instructions.

many routine tasks, such as creating database objects, managing user accounts and security roles, and monitoring database performance. Since everything is accessible with just a browser, you can perform these tasks from almost any client, whether you're on-site or not.

The following sections briefly describe how you'd use WebDB to perform typical database administration tasks.

Browse database objects

You can use WebDB to view, or *browse*, the definitions for database objects. The browse capability of WebDB applies to all objects in a particular schema. Once you select the schema, WebDB displays a list of all the object types in the schema, such as tables, indexes, and views. Figure 3-1 shows the WebDB "Browse Database Objects" option.

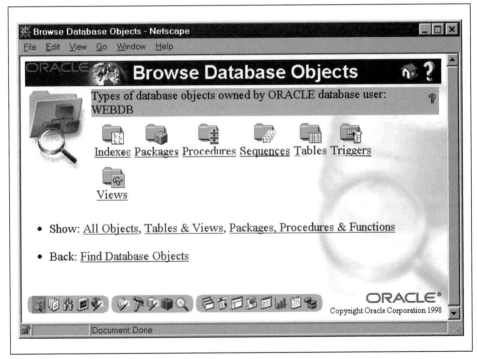

Figure 3-1. Browsing database objects with WebDB

Selecting a specific object type (for example, Tables) presents you with a list of all objects of that type owned by the specified schema (for example, EMP and DEPT). Selecting a particular object either displays its definition or takes you to the "Edit Objects" option.

Administer WebDB and database security

WebDB security is built with Oracle's standard security model. There are three security components:

Users

WebDB users, whether they are created in WebDB or exist in the database beforehand, are simply Oracle schemas. For example, the SCOTT (assuming it exists) and SYS accounts appear as WebDB users, even though they have nothing to do with WebDB. Consequently, WebDB users are like any other Oracle account: you can log into them with SQL*Plus, manage them with Oracle Enterprise Manager, and access their schema objects with third-party tools like ODBC.

Privileges

WebDB object privileges are Oracle object privileges. In addition to the native system and object privileges, WebDB introduces two additional, non-native privileges, build-in and browse-in privileges, that allow multiple users to access WebDB components. The *build-in* privilege, which is like the ANY option in a system privilege, allows a WebDB user or role to create user interface components in another user's schema. The *browse-in* privilege allows a user or role to access the user interface components owned by another schema. These privileges are implemented as rows in WebDB's data dictionary tables.

Roles

WebDB roles are database roles. These roles are used in conjunction with the build-in and browse-in privileges; when you assign a WebDB user a role, you not only assign a corresponding database role but also a WebDB-specific privilege. For this reason, you should assign roles using the WebDB interface, and not through OEM or SQL*Plus.

Figure 3-2 shows WebDB's "Create a New User" section of the "User Manager" option.

Monitor database and application performance

WebDB maintains both application and database logs to help you tune performance. The application logs contain information about the frequency with which WebDB is used. The database logs contain traditional database metrics, such as memory usage and the status of the redo logs.

Each kind of log is used to create a number of reports. Reports generated by the application log include application component response times, user requests per component, and user requests by hour. Reports generated by the database log include database parameters, redo logs, and rollback segments. Most of these

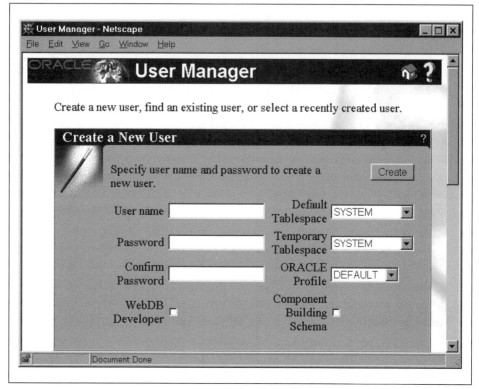

Figure 3-2. Creating a user with WebDB

reports can have several different formats, such as a chart or a table; you can even download them directly into a spreadsheet and create your own graphs! Figure 3-3 shows a chart of the size of a database's datafiles.

Application Development

WebDB applications consist of database objects, like tables and views, and user interface components, like forms and reports. For example, a simple application might consist of a database table, a data entry form to populate the table, and a report that queries the table and displays the results. Users use a web browser to access the form or report.

To simplify the development process, WebDB has a number of wizards that are analogous to the wizards in Microsoft Office. A *wizard* is a series of screens that create an application component based on information you provide. There are three kinds of wizards: database object wizards, user interface (UI) component wizards, and shared component wizards. In addition, since WebDB includes the PL/SQL toolkit, you can build your own custom components and applications. The following sections describe these wizard types.

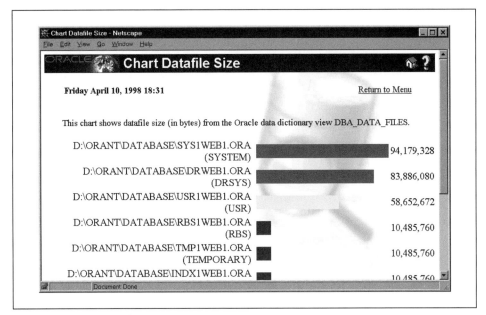

Figure 3-3. A WebDB chart

Building database objects

WebDB's "Object Wizards" option guides you through the steps needed to create a
database object. For example, the Table wizard option takes you through four
screens. On the first screen, you select the schema in which to create the table and
table name. On the second screen, which is reminiscent of Oracle Schema Manager (a GUI management tool included with Oracle Enterprise Manager that simplifies schema administration), you define each of the table's columns, providing
such information as a column name and datatype. On the third screen, you define
the table's storage parameters, such as its tablespace and number of initial extents.
The final screen allows you to confirm the table definition; clicking the "Ok" button creates the table.

WebDB has the following database object wizards:

Function wizard
> Template for the CREATE FUNCTION statement. A *function* is a group of
> instructions stored directly in the database. It returns a single value to the pro-
> gram that calls it. The function definition can contain parameters.

Index wizard
> Template for the CREATE INDEX statement. An *index* is used to improve per-
> formance in SQL queries.

Package wizard

Template for the CREATE PACKAGE statement. A *package* is a group of variables, procedures, and functions stored directly in the database. A package has two parts: a specification and a body. The specification lists the package's public variables, procedures, and functions. The body contains the actual program code for each procedure. Packages are used to mimic many of the design concepts found in object-oriented languages, such as overloading and encapsulation.

The database objects you create in WebDB are normal database objects; the wizard is simply filling in the different pieces of a SQL statement for you. If you're developing an application you can bypass the wizard entirely and create objects in SQL*Plus, Enterprise Manager, or any other tool. The "Object Wizards" option comes in handy, though, when you're off-site and can't get a SQL*Net connection.

Procedure wizard

Template for the CREATE PROCEDURE statement. A *procedure* is a group of instructions stored directly in the database that performs a specific task. The procedure definition can include parameters.

Sequence wizard

Template for the CREATE SEQUENCE statement. A *sequence* is a counter that is often used to provide primary key values.

Synonym wizard

Template for the CREATE SYNONYM statement. A *synonym* is used to provide an alias to another database object, usually to provide location transparency.

Table wizard

Template for the CREATE TABLE statement. A *table* is a collection of columns and rows that store data in the database.

Trigger wizard

Template for the CREATE TRIGGER statement. A *trigger* is a group of instructions that execute in response to a specific table event, such as an insert or a delete. Triggers are often used to set a row's primary key (based on a sequence) or update its timestamp.

Type wizard

Template for the CREATE TYPE statement. A *type* is a data structure much like a record stored directly in the Oracle database that provides object-like capabilities inside the database.

View wizard

> Template for the CREATE VIEW statement. A *view* is a stored SQL query that acts like a table. Views are used to simplify complex queries for end user reporting tools. They are also used for security purposes to restrict access to a subset of columns in an important table.

Figure 3-4 shows the table wizard.

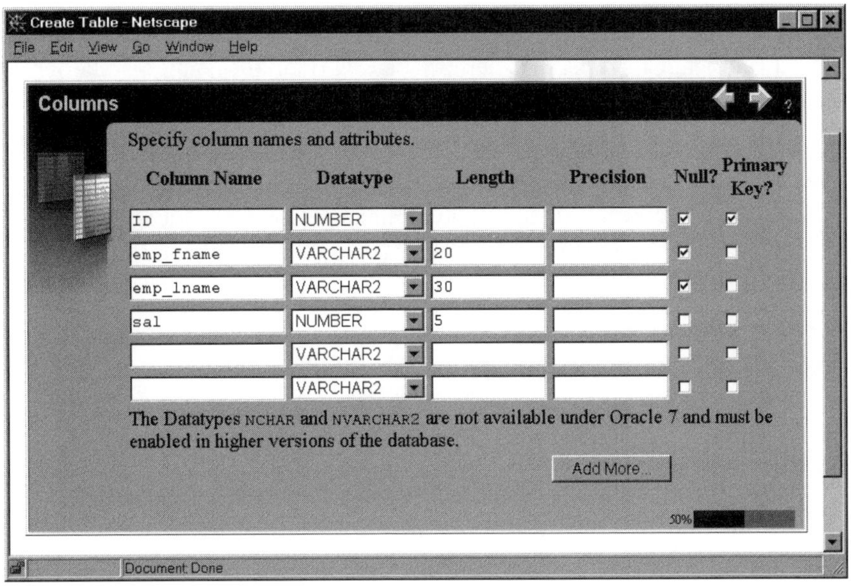

Figure 3-4. Creating a table with WebDB

Building user interface components

Once you've created a database object, you can use WebDB's user interface (UI) wizards to create user interface components such as data entry forms or reports. After you've stepped through a series of screens in which you define the components' properties, the wizard creates a PL/SQL stored package to implement the user interface.

There are eight user interface wizards:

Calendar wizard

> Creates an HTML-based calendar using information stored in a table. You could use the calendar wizard to create an HTML-based "to-do" list displayed in a format that looks like a monthly calendar.

Chart wizard

> Creates a bar chart based on information in either a database table or a SQL query.

Dynamic page wizard

> Allows you to create standard HTML pages that can contain SQL and PL/SQL commands embedded inside a special <ORACLE> tag, as in:

```
<ORACLE>SELECT * FROM emp</ORACLE>
```

Form wizard

> Creates several different kinds of HTML forms, such as forms that execute stored procedures, forms that perform standard table operations like inserts or updates, master detail forms, and Query by Example (QBE) forms.

Frame driver wizard

> Creates a split screen containing two HTML frames. The first frame (the "navigation" frame) contains a list of hyperlinks based on a query you provide. Clicking one of these links will display the page in the second frame (the "target").

Hierarchy wizard

> Creates a drill-down based on information on the parent-child relationships in a recursively defined table.

Menu wizard

> Allows you to create parent-child menu structures. The menu wizard is very similar to the hierarchy wizard.

Report wizard

> Creates a report based on a table or SQL query. You can display reports as HTML pages or ASCII files, or you can download them directly into an Excel spreadsheet. Figure 3-5 shows the report wizard in action.

Building shared components

After you've created your interfaces, you can use the shared component wizards to create a library of reusable components that ensure a consistent design across the application. A cardinal rule of interface design is that there should be a consistent look and feel across an application's screens and reports. Unfortunately, this goal is often very difficult to reach, especially for systems that have many developers. For example, suppose you and several other programmers are building a document management system. Each screen in the system must have a Search option that the user activates by clicking an icon. You, as an avid outdoors person, would like to use a pair of binoculars as the icon. Another person wants to use a magnifying glass, and yet another wants to use a picture of a blue-tick hound dog. How do you make sure everyone does the same thing?

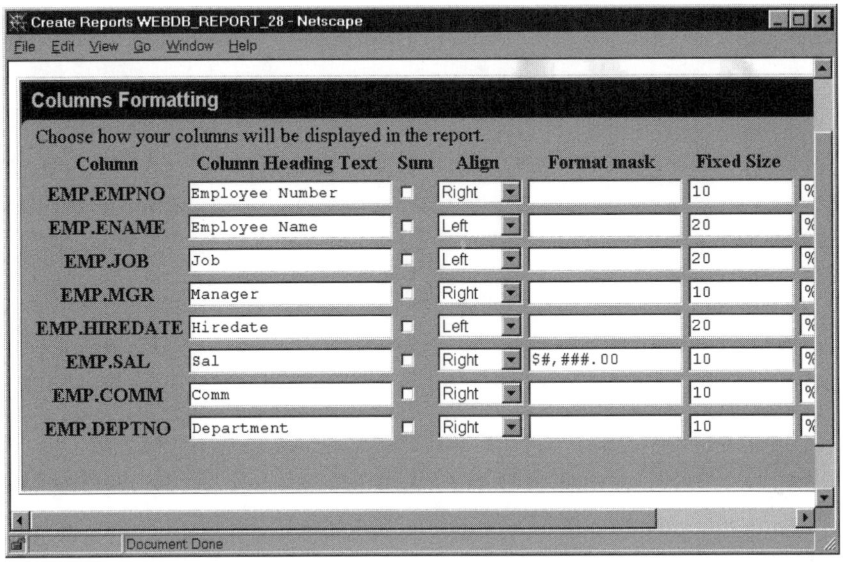

Figure 3-5. Formatting the columns of a WebDB report

Rather than leaving these sorts of choices to the vagaries of each developer, many companies use a library of standardized components. Each component has a name, such as SEARCH_BUTTON, that represents a real item, such as a picture of bloodhound. When a developer needs to put a search button on a form, she uses the named component, rather than a real icon. This guarantees a reasonable degree of consistency across a wide range of applications.

To simplify the often tedious process of standardization, WebDB allows you to create reusable application elements called *shared component libraries*. The basic idea of a shared component is that it associates a logical name with a physical object. Developers can include these shared components in their UI components. There are seven shared component libraries:

Colors library
> A named Red, Green, Blue (RGB; a common way to specify a color) color combination. For example, you can associate the RGB color #9F9F5F with the name Khaki.

Fonts library
> A named font. For example, you might want to associate the Arial font with the name INVOICE_FONT to enforce a consistent look across reports in an invoicing system.

Images library

A named image.

JavaScripts library

A named JavaScript script. You can use this component to build a library of client-side scripts that developers can reuse in their applications. For example, you might create a library of field validation scripts.

Links library

A named hyperlink. You can use this component to make sure that hyperlinks leading to the same location all use a consistent name. For example, you might want to create a named hyperlink to an online help system to guarantee that every application uses a consistent link name. Additionally, you use links to bind various WebDB components together into a single system. For example, in an employee data entry component of a human resources system, you might want to create links to employee educational history, salary history, and W2 information. Finally, you can use links to create hooks to PL/SQL procedures you develop with the PL/SQL toolkit.

Lists of Values library

A named List of Values (LOV). You can use this component to create a variety of styles of lists (such as radio buttons, select lists, and pop-up windows) based on an underlying database table, view, or SQL query. For example, you might want to create a list called ACTIVE_EMPLOYEES to allow a user to select from a predefined list of valid employees.

UI templates library

A named page layout template. You can use this component to create a standard page format for each page in an application.

Figure 3-6 shows the LOV wizard being used to create a pop-up List of Values.

Building custom components

While application generators are wonderful time savers, they almost always get just the first 80% of an application's requirements, leaving you to code the remaining 20% by hand. And what if you want to write an application for which WebDB doesn't have an associated wizard? For example, there is no shopping cart wizard, so if you want to create an electronic storefront application, you must write it from scratch.

WebDB includes the PL/SQL toolkit software development kit (SDK) to allow you to write your own web applications. This is the same set of packages that comes with OAS, so anything you develop in WebDB will also work in OAS, and vice versa. Subsequent chapters detail how to use these systems to develop your own applications.

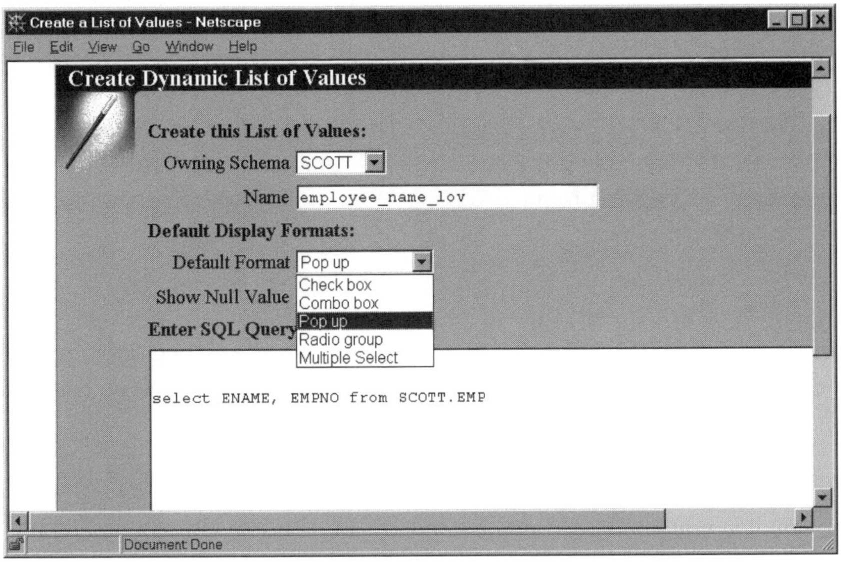

Figure 3-6. Creating a list of values in WebDB

Content-Driven Web Site Management

WebDB's third major function is creating content-driven web sites. The advantage of content-driven sites deriving from database information is that you can completely change and rearrange the sites and their content with a few mouse clicks. Filesystem-based sites, on the other hand, are much more difficult to modify because they have a more rigid structure. The most interesting thing about WebDB sites is that they not only allow users to view information already in the database, but also let users add their own content to the site. For example, a user could upload an Excel spreadsheet to his personal site and make it available without the webmaster's help.

Consistent with WebDB's "100% in the browser, 100% in the database" philosophy, every feature is accessed with a browser and all content is stored in an Oracle database (with a few exceptions, such as images, which can also be stored as files). WebDB uses this information to create a hierarchical view of the entire site, making user uploads available to users with the appropriate privileges. In this section, we'll look at three of WebDB's features for creating content-driven web sites: its options allowing users to publish their own content, its features for organizing and managing the content, and its methods for controlling who can access the content.

User-uploaded content

WebDB's most unique and innovative feature is that it allows users to add their own web content directly from their browsers, effectively eliminating the bottleneck of requiring the webmaster to manually add new content. Each user is assigned his or her own personal web *folder* to which he or she can add various kinds of content (depending on the privileges granted by the site administrator). Additionally, if given the proper privilege, users can contribute content to folders owned by other users.

Users add content from the WebDB *dashboard*. The dashboard is a set of options available at the top of every page that allows users to (among other things) add an item, create a new subfolder, change a folder's properties (such as its name and description), and allow other WebDB users to access a folder's content. Users can contribute the following items:

File

> A standard file, such as a Word or Excel document, that is uploaded to a database table. WebDB is integrated into the interMedia Text cartridge, which automatically indexes it for later searching.

Folderlink

> A hyperlink to another WebDB folder.

Imagemap

> A standard imagemap.

PL/SQL call

> A call to a PL/SQL procedure; for example, a call to one of the custom PL/SQL applications we'll develop later in this book.

Text item

> A plain text message that displays on the page. A user can use this item to quickly and easily post messages for the site.

URL

> A generic hyperlink to another site. For example, a user could enter a list of favorite sites on the Web.

WebDB component

> Creates a hyperlink to a WebDB user interface component. For example, a user could create a link to a report. Optionally, you can also configure WebDB to place the component on the page, rather than just a hyperlink.

Figure 3-7 shows the screen used to upload a file to a WebDB site.

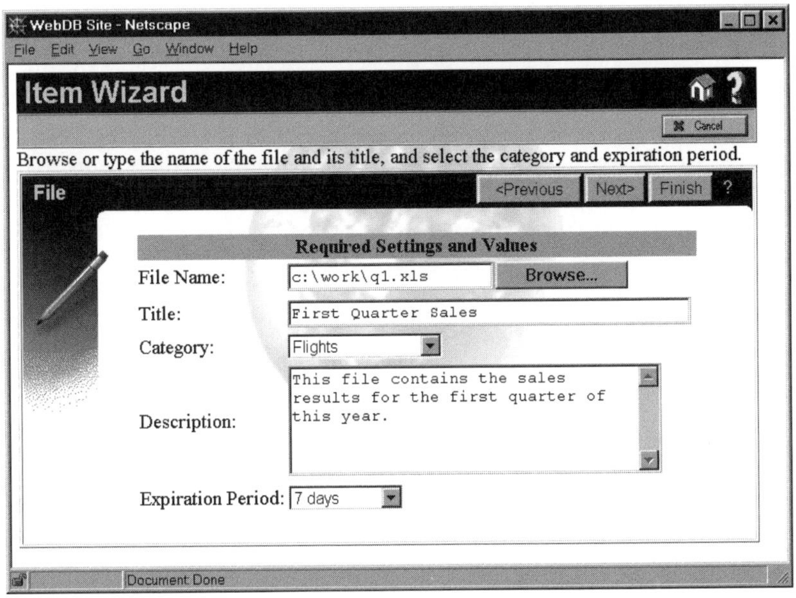

Figure 3-7. Uploading a file to a WebDB site

Managing content

Once users have added content to their site, you can manage it as you would any other information stored in an Oracle database. For example, you can create a backup schedule, see how much space each user consumes, and audit changes to the site's content. In short, you can apply all your organization's hard-won data management skill to Internet content.

In addition, you can organize site content so that it's easy for users to find. WebDB has three basic ways to do this:

Folders

As we've already seen, users can have individual folders to which they can upload content. You can also create project- or application-specific folders. For example, WebDB includes a demo application called "The Traveler," an example of a database-driven travel site. Behind the scenes, WebDB's folders are really just rows in a table; uploaded items include the primary key for the row in the folder table. The folder table is defined recursively (i.e., parent/ child rows) to represent subfolders.

Categories

Each item is assigned to a single category that identifies its general type. For example, the "The Traveler" demo uses travel-related categories, such as

Flights, Lodging, Restaurants, and Travel packages. These categories let users search for specific kinds of items, such as "Restaurants that serve seafood."

Perspectives

Users can also assign multiple perspectives to further categorize an item. Unlike a category, which defines what an item is, a perspective defines who might be interested in it. For example, "The Traveler" demo might have the perspectives Food Connoisseurs, Outdoor Enthusiasts, or History Buffs. Users can then search for items of interest to them, for example, "Restaurants that serve seafood of gourmet quality."

A user can rearrange a site on the fly by changing each item's categories and perspectives. Figure 3-8 shows WebDB's Site Map, a hierarchical list of all folders.

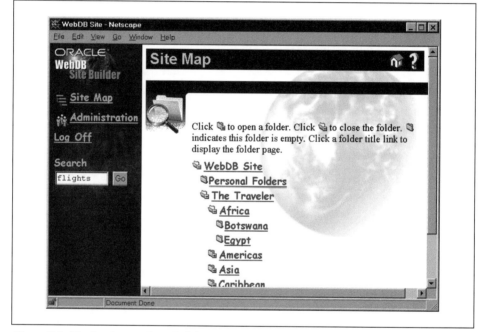

Figure 3-8. The Site Map, a list of all folders in WebDB

Controlling access to content

The WebDB *site administrator* assigns access privileges to information in the site. The administrator can manipulate the following WebDB settings:

Group

Allows the site administrator to define named groups of users, analogous to roles, that are used to easily assign web content to multiple users. Groups, however, are modeled in database tables and are not actual database roles.

Privilege

Allows the site administrator to add and manage WebDB site users. This is pretty much the same set of privileges used in the Oracle database, with some additional privileges for managing content. These include the ability to administer a site, add news items, and change the site's look and feel.

WebDB Architecture

Because WebDB uses the database's native components, it is a scalable, powerful development tool for building content-driven sites on Oracle. Since it's essentially written in the database's native language, it eliminates the need for cumbersome layers like ODBC or JDBC.

WebDB's dirty little secret is that its wizards are really just PL/SQL code generators that act on normal database objects. When you create a user with WebDB, you are really creating a corresponding database schema, just as you would for any other Oracle user. When you use the table wizard, you are really just filling in the pieces of a CREATE TABLE command. When you build a form, you are really creating a PL/SQL package. The options you enter into these wizards tell WebDB how to create the corresponding database objects.

WebDB is a standalone product that contains everything you need to create a complete application. Two built-in components—the PL/SQL gateway and the HTTP listener—make this possible. Figure 3-9 illustrates the relationships among the database objects, UI components, shared components, roles, users, the PL/SQL gateway, and the HTTP listener.

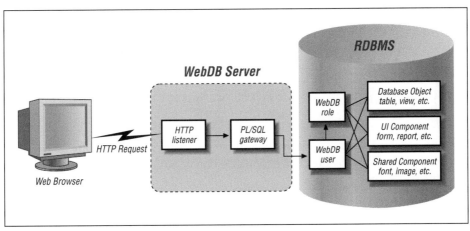

Figure 3-9. The components of WebDB

In the following sections, we'll look at WebDB's PL/SQL gateway and its integrated HTTP listener.

The PL/SQL Gateway

Once we've created our WebDB user interface components, we can use the PL/SQL gateway to execute them from the Web. The gateway is situated between the database and the HTTP listener. The HTTP listener forwards a request for a component to the PL/SQL gateway, which executes the procedure and stores its output in a buffer. The HTTP listener then sends the contents of this buffer, which now contains the HTML instructions that create the component, back to the user's browser.

Users call a procedure using a URL that specifies the name of the package (which has the same name as the component), the procedure to execute, and any parameters required by the procedure. The PL/SQL gateway uses this information to call the correct procedure. Each procedure begins with a security check to make sure the user attempting to access the component has the required permissions.

The gateway uses DADs to authenticate web users. A DAD is a unique name included as part of a URL. The appearance of a DAD name in the URL signals the HTTP listener that the URL is requesting a WebDB component. The PL/SQL gateway combines the DAD configuration information with the other parts of the URL—the package name, procedure name, and parameters—to execute the requested procedure. The URL syntax is:

```
http://webDB_server:port/dad_name/package.procedure?parm1=foo
```

Configuring a Database Access Descriptor (DAD)

The DAD configuration information specifies a unique name for the DAD and various other configuration information. Again, the name of the DAD is used in the URL to map to the database schema specified in the DAD. Figure 3-10 shows the WebDB interface used to manage these settings (in this case, WebDB appears in the path section of the URL to the WebDB server).

DAD parameters

The DAD parameters are:

Database Access Descriptor Name
> The unique DAD name. When it appears in a URL, the DAD name signals the HTTP listener to forward the request to the PL/SQL gateway. This parameter is always required.

Oracle User Name
> The Oracle schema that will execute the procedure. If this name is blank, the user is prompted for a username and password.

Oracle Password
> The password for the Oracle schema. If this is blank, the user is prompted for authentication information.

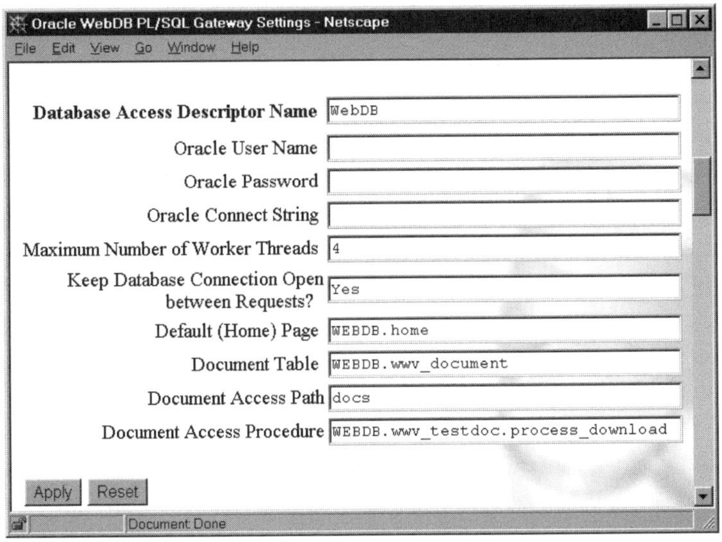

Figure 3-10. DAD administration in WebDB

Oracle Connect String

The connect string of the database running WebDB. The local database (ORA_ SID) is used as the default if the field is left blank.

Maximum Number of Worker Threads

The maximum number of threads the WebDB server will use to process requests.

Keep Database Connection Open between Requests?

If this parameter is set to "yes," the listener keeps the database connection open after the request is finished. The next time the user makes a request from the DAD, the listener can open the connection rather than establishing a new one. This improves performance dramatically, since establishing the initial connection is usually quite time consuming. However, this is not the same as a persistent connection; state information such as the values of PL/SQL variables is lost after the request. If the parameter is set to "No," the connection is closed after each request, resulting in poorer performance.

Default (Home) Page

The default procedure to execute when the URL omits a procedure name.

Document Table

The table used to store files uploaded to WebDB.

Document Access Path

The path element used to retrieve an uploaded file.

Document Access Procedure

The procedure to execute immediately after an uploaded file is retrieved.

> WebDB uses *basic authentication*, a standard HTTP mechanism in which the user must supply a username and password before accessing the site. The password is transmitted as plain text (unencrypted) across the Web, making it fairly insecure. A second method, *digest authentication*, is more secure because it encrypts the password before transmission. Unfortunately, while this method is supported in OAS, it is not (at least at the time of this writing) supported in WebDB.

Configuration file

The configuration information for the PL/SQL gateway is stored in the file *%ORACLE_HOME%/listener/wdbsvr.app*. Here's an example configuration file that underlies the entries in Figure 3-10:

```
[DAD_WebDB]
;connect_string   =
;password    =
;username    =
default_page    =  WEBDB.home
document_table   =  WEBDB.wwv_document
document_path    =  docs
document_proc    =  WEBDB.wwv_tcotdoc.process_download
;name_prefix   =
;always_describe   =
;after_proc   =
reuse    =  Yes
connmax    =  4
;
```

The HTTP Listener

The HTTP listener, the last major component of WebDB, is basically a miniature web server. It has the following characteristics:

- It supports HTTP 1.0.

- It can serve static files residing in mapped directories.

- It supports application-specific MIME type mapping.

- It is multithreaded to provide increased performance.

- It is specifically designed to integrate with the Oracle database via PL/SQL applications. Although the listener was added to make WebDB a standalone product, it can be used to develop any PL/SQL toolkit application.

- It does not currently (as of WebDB version 2.0.5) support HTTP 1.1, SSL, or CGI; Oracle is considering adding support for SSL, CGI, Java™ Servlets, Java Server Pages, and XML.

The HTTP listener configuration parameters fall into three general categories: server settings, virtual directory mappings, and MIME type mappings.

Server settings

The server settings govern the listener's general behavior. Parameters of note include:

Server Port
> The port setting determines the communications port on which WebDB "listens" for incoming requests. The default is 80. If you choose another value, URLs referencing the site must specify this value.

Default Mime Type
> The default MIME type returned for types that are not explicitly mapped.

Logging Level
> The listener maintains a number of logs that can track requests and errors. There are separate log files for the listener and PL/SQL gateway, as well as for each thread. Log files all end with a *.LOG* extension; log files for individual threads include the thread number as an index. Values for the logging level include:
>
> None
> > No logging
>
> Standard
> > Log requests using standard NCSA format
>
> Extended
> > Log requests using extended NCSA format
>
> Error
> > Log requests using NCSA format, including extended error information

Virtual directory mappings

The virtual directory mappings allow the listener to return static files by mapping physical directories to aliases used as part of a URL. Mappings are made using multiple name/value pairs consisting of:

Physical directory
> The physical directory on the machine running WebDB. Once mapped, all files and subdirectories are accessible from the Web.

Virtual directory

The corresponding alias for the physical directory. This alias is used as part of the URL to refer to a physical directory.

MIME type mappings

The MIME type mappings map a specific type of file to a MIME type. The listener is preconfigured with most of the standard mappings (e.g., `image/jpeg` to files with the *.JPG* extension). You can extend these defaults with your own mappings (e.g., `application/rpt` to files with the *.RPT* extension). Mappings are made using multiple name/value pairs consisting of:

MIME type

The MIME type returned for the specified set of corresponding file extensions.

File extension

The file extensions mapped to the MIME type. These mappings are case sensitive, so you will often find the same extension listed in various ways (e.g., *.jpg, .JPG, .jpeg, .JPEG*).

Configuration file

The configuration information for the HTTP listener is stored in the file *%ORACLE_HOME%/listener/wdbsvr.cfg*. The following listing is an example configuration file:

```
;
[SERVER]
;HomePage =
DefaultMimeType = application/octet-stream
LoggingLevel = Extended
;MaxFileCache =
MaxFileThreads = 3
MaxDispatcherThreads = 7
;
[DirMaps]
D:\ORANT\webdb\images\   /images/
;
[MIMETypes]
text/html   htm    html
image/jpeg  jpg    jpeg   JPG
text/plain  txt    ksh    lst
application/pdf   pdf
application/powerpoint  ppt    PPT
application/msword  doc    dot    DOC   DOT
application/x-tar   tar    TAR
application/zip  zip
text/edi    edi
application/excel   xls    XLS
text/xml  xml
;
```

WebDB is a big product with a huge set of features, and this overview has just scratched the surface of its many capabilities. WebDB comes with several manuals providing step-by-step instructions on configuring and using the product. Additionally, you can consult Rick Greenwald's *Oracle WebDB Bible* (IDG Books Worldwide) for a thorough treatment of the subject.

4

Oracle Application Server (OAS)

Oracle Application Server (OAS) is Oracle's enterprise web platform. While OAS performs all the functions of a normal web server, its main advantage is its tight integration with a backend Oracle database. After starting life with the name Oracle Webserver at version 1, then becoming Oracle Web Application Server at version 3, the Oracle Application Server, now at version 4, has steadily grown in size and features.

The resources required to run OAS have increased along with the new features. For example, the memory requirements (on NT, at least) went from 48 MB in version 3 to 128 MB in version 4.

In this chapter, we'll look at the architectural components of OAS as they relate to PL/SQL application development. Be sure that you've read Chapter 2, *Foundations*, which introduces the basic concepts behind the web infrastructure on which OAS is built. We'll start with a discussion of how OAS returns web resources to a user's browser. Then we'll look at the PL/SQL cartridge, an OAS component we can use to develop PL/SQL applications.

How OAS Returns Web Resources

OAS has three methods to return resources. The first simply uses a directory mapping system to send static files to the client's browser. The next two methods return dynamic resources: one executes resources using the standard CGI interface, and the other, the Web Request Broker (WRB), executes resources using a program called a cartridge.

As we saw in the previous chapter, the HTTP listener (renamed the Web listener in OAS) receives incoming requests either as URLs or as `action` attributes in an HTML form. If the virtual path maps to a CGI directory, the CGI interface is used. If it maps to a cartridge, the WRB method is used. Figure 4-1 shows the relationship between these components.

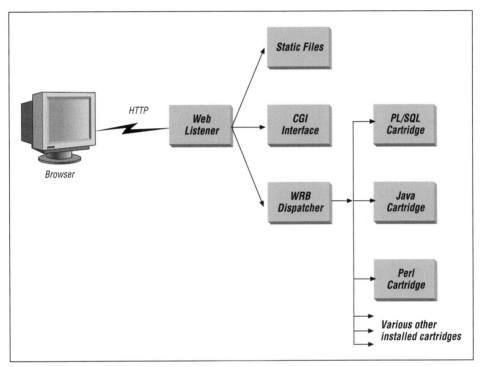

Figure 4-1. Overview of OAS components

In the next three sections, we'll look at how OAS handles requests for static files, CGI dynamic resources, and WRB dynamic resources.

Static Resources Mapped to a Virtual Directory

A static file is the simplest type of resource the OAS can deliver. A static resource is just a file that resides in a directory on the filesystem. To make the files accessible from the Web, OAS maintains a list of mappings between physical directories and symbolic aliases called *virtual directories*. A URL uses these aliases, along with the resource name, to retrieve the requested file. Figure 4-2 shows the virtual directory mapping screen for the OAS administration system.

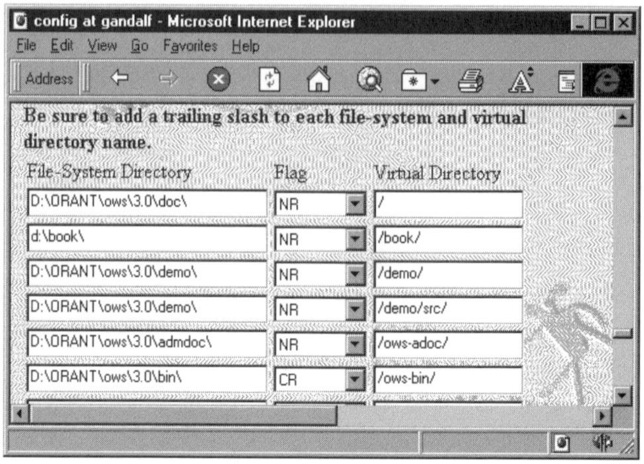

Figure 4-2. Virtual directory mappings

Dynamic Resources Mapped to the CGI Gateway

The *common gateway interface* (CGI), the earliest web technology for developing dynamic resources, allows you to execute any kind of server-side program, whether it's written in a third-generation language like C, a scripting language like Perl, or a database language like PL/SQL. One of the advantages of CGI is that you can use it to do almost anything: create gateways between the Web and an email system, build a help system based on Unix's manpages, or execute scripting programs to play tic-tac-toe. The execution of a CGI program follows these steps:

1. The web server spawns a new process under a separate user ID.

2. The program is started in the new execution space.

3. The program executes, sending its output to standard output. The listener sends this output back to the user's browser.

4. The program terminates, and the process is destroyed.

There are a number of uses for even simple CGI programs. Suppose, for example, you have a table that holds user complaints about your systems. Here is a technique that saves you valuable web-surfing time, allowing you to purge old complaints by clicking on a hyperlink. The system requires two parts. The first is a SQL*Plus script called *msg_maint.sql* that clears the table. The length of time new messages are kept is passed as a command-line argument:

```
set feedback off;
delete from tbl_user_complaints where
   date_created < (sysdate - &1);
commit;
```

The second part is a script named *clear_msg* that executes the SQL*Plus script and returns a status. The operating system script is necessary because you cannot directly execute a SQL script without SQL*Plus:

```ksh
#!/bin/ksh
#
# Print mandatory header info
#
print "Content-type: text/html\n\n"
print "<html>"
print "<title>All work and no play...</title>"
print "<body>"
print "<h1>Evaluating User Complaints</h1><p>"
#
# Execute sqlplus script msg_maint.sql
#
sqlplus scott/tiger @msg_maint.sql 2
#
# Print results
#
print "<h2>User Complaints Resolved</h2>"
print "</body>"
print "</html>"
```

The script is saved in a directory that is marked as containing CGI scripts and mapped to a virtual directory, typically named *cgi-bin*. Once these steps are completed, the user can execute the script with a URL. For example:

```
http://barney/cgi-bin/clear_msg
```

This extremely simplified example reveals some important limitations of the CGI interface:

CGI involves significant overhead

Before CGI programs can do any real work, the system must create and maintain processes, allocate resources, and perform a host of other housekeeping activities. Even worse, a CGI program must establish a new connection to the database every time it is executed. This severely affects performance, especially when a series of CGIs is linked together to form an entire application.

CGI programs can be very insecure

The previous example, which embeds a username and password directly into the script, is guaranteed to infuriate almost any DBA. Unless you have a set of library routines you can use in every program, securely connecting a program to the correct account is a thorny problem. In addition to username/password problems, many scripting languages have a complex and subtle syntax that makes it far too easy to unwittingly create insecure programs. A single misplaced character in a Perl program, for instance, can potentially compromise the entire system.

It is hard to process parameters passed to CGI programs

> As we've seen, parameters are passed to a CGI program using either the query string of a URL or input elements on a form. Additionally, any non-alphanumeric characters (in a query string, at least) must be encoded before they can be safely transmitted across the Web. Once they arrive at their destination, it is up to the CGI program to manually read and decode all of them before they can be used.

In the next section, we'll look at how OAS's Web Request Broker architecture alleviates the problems of CGI by using cartridges.

Dynamic Resources Mapped to the Web Request Broker

The Web Request Broker (WRB) is another way that OAS can return a dynamic resource, and it is a significant advance over CGI. The WRB architecture maintains a pool of processes that are already running and connected to the appropriate database, and WRB is therefore much faster than CGI. When a request to run a particular program comes in, the OAS simply hands it off to one of these processes, which executes it and returns the results.

Each process handles a specific type of dynamic resource, whether it's created with Perl, PL/SQL, or Java, or even less traditional languages like VRML. OAS plug-in cartridges allow developers to use these different development languages. The WRB consists of the cartridges themselves, the executable engines that run the cartridges, and the dispatcher that selects a particular cartridge to execute a request.

Cartridges

OAS uses cartridges to execute, or cause to be executed, specific kinds of resources. When OAS receives a request for a resource, it simply passes it to the appropriate cartridge. Several cartridges come with OAS, including the PL/SQL cartridge for executing PL/SQL stored procedures, the Java cartridge for executing server-side Java programs, and the Perl cartridge for executing Perl scripts. However, cartridges are not limited to serving as gateways to development languages. The ODBC cartridge, for example, executes OBDC statements and returns the results directly to a user's browser.

Each cartridge is installed on the web server and mapped to a virtual alias. When the web listener receives a URL that includes one of these virtual mappings, it knows that it must use that cartridge to execute the specified resource. As always, the path section of the URL specifies the virtual mapping, and the resource name section specifies the resource the cartridge is to execute. These two sections must be consistent: the PL/SQL cartridge cannot execute a Java program. Figure 4-3 shows how virtual directory names are mapped to the PL/SQL cartridge in the WRB configuration screen.

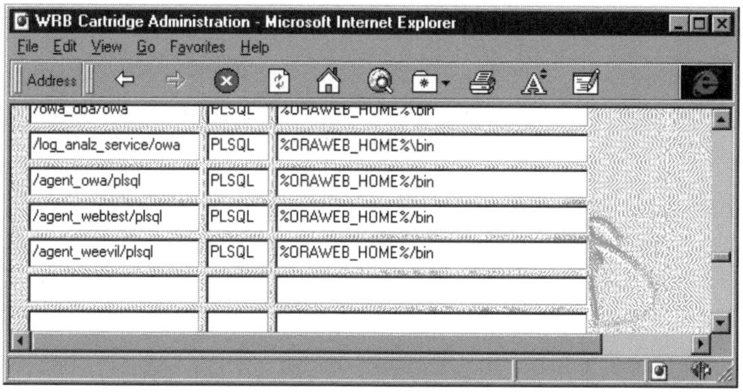

Figure 4-3. Virtual directory mappings for the PL/SQL cartridge

The number of commercially available cartridges is growing every day. Additionally, because cartridges are based on an open interface, you can develop your own custom cartridges if you cannot buy one from a vendor. For example, you could write a cartridge to Web-enable a backend COBOL system.

WRB Executable Engines

When OAS initializes, it starts a number of WRB Executable Engines (WRBXs), processes that run particular cartridges. OAS starts a relatively large number of each kind of process (which ones depends on a configuration setting) to make sure that individual WRBXs don't become bottlenecks.

For example, the pool of WRBX processes might consist of 20 PL/SQL cartridges, 10 Java cartridges, and 5 Perl cartridges. This way, if one cartridge is busy when a request comes in, another WRBX is ready to handle it. This pool of running processes accounts for most of the performance gains of the WRB architecture over CGI. However, a cartridge does not make your dynamic resource itself run any faster. It simply minimizes the time it takes for the resource to begin executing.

WRB dispatcher

The WRB dispatcher is the final element in the WRB architecture. It has two jobs: the first is to receive incoming requests from the web listener and assign them to free processes in the WRBX pool; the second is to manage the WRBX pool.

Like a dispatcher at a police station, the WRB dispatcher assigns incoming tasks to specific agents from a pool of available agents. Its main goal is to fill as many of these requests as possible in the shortest amount of time by managing the various WRBX processes. To do this efficiently, the dispatcher must maintain a list of available agents, what they are currently doing, and when they will finish their assigned tasks.

Additionally, the dispatcher conserves system resources by maintaining a proper mix among the different processes. For example, the dispatcher can create new processes or destroy existing ones based on the number and types of requests received by the web listener.

Figure 4-4 shows the relationship between the parts of the WRB architecture. The diagram illustrates how the dispatcher passes a request to just one of the many available WRBX processes.

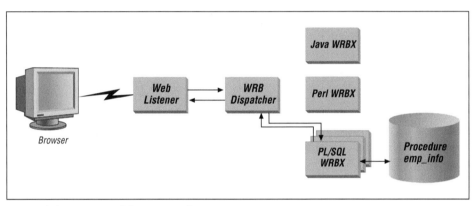

Figure 4-4. Overview of the WRB architecture

> OAS has a tendency to lose track of some of these cartridges over time, resulting in dead processes. You can work around this problem by periodically stopping and restarting the listener process using a command like at (in NT or Unix) or cron (Unix).

Creating Dynamic Resources

Now that we have a basic understanding of how the WRB uses cartridges to execute different kinds of resources, let's look at the PL/SQL cartridge in more detail.

The PL/SQL cartridge allows us to use PL/SQL procedures to create dynamic resources. As with the CGI interface, these resources are called with a URL. Unlike CGI, a PL/SQL cartridge maintains a persistent connection to a database, so it executes almost instantaneously. In addition to producing lightning-fast performance, the cartridge resolves the two thorny problems with the CGI interface: connection management and parameter passing.

Following our discussion of the advantage of this cartridge, we'll bring up a few security caveats to keep in mind when using cartridges.

Connection Management

WRBX processes connect to one particular account within a database upon initialization. The configuration for the connection is divided into two parts: the Database Access Descriptor and the PL/SQL agent.

Database Access Descriptor

A Database Access Descriptor (DAD) creates a unique alias for a database that is to be accessed over the Web. The DAD contains all the information needed to connect to the database, including the database name, its *ORACLE_HOME* directory, and its SQL*Net V2 service name. Figure 4-5 shows OAS's DAD configuration page.

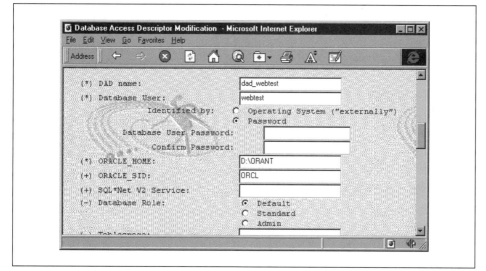

Figure 4-5. Configuration screen for a DAD

PL/SQL agent

The *PL/SQL agent* is a unique alias for a database account owned by a particular DAD that makes the account's procedures and packages accessible over the Web. This includes procedures and packages owned directly by the account, as well as those owned by other accounts that have granted EXECUTE permission to the schema.

The agent consists of:

- A unique name
- Account login information, including:
  - The DAD name for the database that owns the account
  - The account name and password
- Web-specific configuration information, including:
  - The URL for the error page that is displayed if the agent cannot execute a request
  - Authorized ports on which the agent accepts requests

Figure 4-6 shows OAS's agent configuration page.

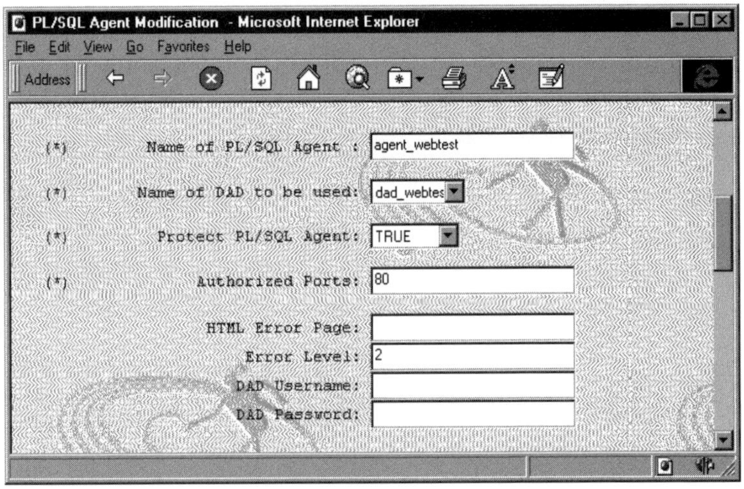

Figure 4-6. Configuration screen for a PL/SQL agent

Figure 4-7 illustrates the relationship between a database, a DAD, and a PL/SQL agent.

Parameter Passing

In addition to simplifying connection management, the PL/SQL agent also simplifies parameter passing by automatically associating each parameter with one of the procedure's formal parameters. As noted in the previous chapter, you can pass values in a query string of a hyperlink or as a named field in a form. In either case, the PL/SQL agent makes sure that these values are used to execute the PL/SQL procedure specified in the resource name section.

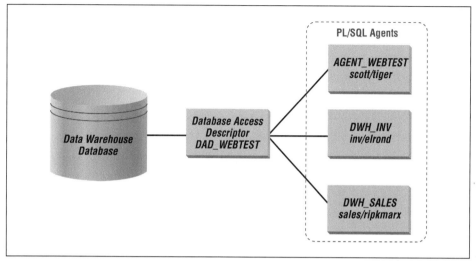

Figure 4-7. The relationship between the DAD and PL/SQL agent

Security Issues with the PL/SQL Cartridge

For all its benefits, the PL/SQL cartridge can open a major security hole. When you create an agent for an account, every procedure in the account is fair game for web execution. For example, if you create a DAD and agent on your HR schema so that you can write a phone list, you are also exposing procedures like give_ raise or fire_employee. Savvy (or downright evil!) users who understand how to execute these procedures can do so with impunity.

You can use database privileges to prevent this sort of abuse. The scheme is very similar to using database roles to limit access to privileged tables. Basically, you assign the DAD and PL/SQL agent to a minimally privileged account (maybe it only has CONNECT privilege). You then use a combination of the GRANT EXE-CUTE and CREATE SYNONYM commands to allow the schema to execute procedures owned by privileged accounts. Figure 4-8 illustrates how this works.

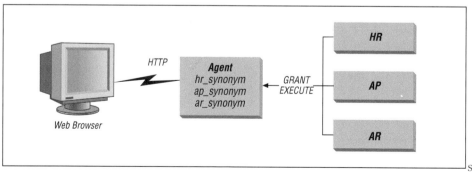

Figure 4-8. A minimally privileged PL/SQL agent

There are several advantages to this approach. First, it guarantees that the only code you have explicitly made available is accessible from a web browser. Second, the use of grants increases security because, as any DBA will tell you, the fewer publicly available privileges the better, especially if the schema contains sensitive information or is highly privileged. Finally, it reduces a lot of administrative overhead necessary to get an application up and running because you don't have dozens of agents to maintain.

To use the grant method, follow these steps:

1. Log into the account that owns the application code you want to execute.

2. Use the GRANT EXECUTE command to make the procedure or package available to the agent account.

3. Log into the agent account.

4. Create a synonym that points to the procedure in the other schema; the synonym does not have to have the same name as the original procedure or package.

5. Use the synonym name in the URL to execute the procedure.

5

HTML

Now that we've discussed WebDB and OAS, we're ready to begin building applications. As you learned in Computer Science 101, user applications have a user interface, whether it's a simple command line, like the one in DOS or Unix, or a full windowing system, like Windows or X. In this chapter you'll learn how to use HTML (HyperText Markup Language) to create an interface that's somewhere in between these two extremes.

This chapter, while by no means comprehensive, provides enough of an introduction to HTML to get you started building useful systems. We'll begin with the basics of HTML programming, covering how to best start learning the language (if you don't know it already) and how to use its tag- and attribute-based syntax. We'll then take a whirlwind tour of HTML, examining most of the major tags you'll use every day. You can find a listing of more complete reference works in the appendix, *Resources for the Oracle Web Developer.*

Programming in HTML

Your company's human resources department may have its personnel policy on an internal web site. You can go to a main page and click on policies that cover various things HR types find important: dress codes, organization charts, inter-employee dating rules, and so on. Almost invariably, these documents have been converted from existing documents, such as Word or WordPerfect documents, using an editor like Microsoft FrontPage, Adobe PageMill, or Netscape Composer. While these tools are certainly useful, we must understand the actual HTML they generate before we can create a user interface for our web systems.

Learning the Language

The first thing you need to know about HTML is that you don't need a fancy editor to create an HTML document. HTML is a text file format, so you can use any editor you want to create a document. The second thing to know is that, unlike many other Internet standards, HTML is fairly simple. You can learn much of what you'll need to know about HTML in an afternoon.

The best way to learn HTML is to create a skeleton document in your favorite editor, save it to a file, and view the results with a browser. You don't even have to be on the Web to see your creation; almost all browsers can open a file directly from your system. Once you get bored tinkering with the basic tags, you can justify hours of web surfing as an educational expense by using the "View Source" option to see the underlying HTML code (but not the source code of the dynamic resource that created the document) for the pages you visit. Of course, like any other language, HTML has a syntax you must master before you can use it. This is subject of the next section.

Syntax

HTML consists of plain ASCII text that is marked up using special instructions called *tags* that define the document's structure and format. It's a very forgiving language: errors that in other languages would be devastating (like misspelling a reserved word) are usually ignored. It's not case sensitive, the instructions can appear in practically any order or combination, and most browsers are now smart enough to fill in anything you might mistakenly omit.

The tradeoff for this simplicity is that HTML doesn't give you absolute control over the placement of each element, which makes it significantly different from a tool like Oracle Reports or Oracle Forms. For instance, rather than specify the exact X and Y coordinates for an input box, you simply tell the browser that you want a text field. The browser decides the best location for the box, based on the rules you've specified. You will constantly face the temptation to mangle the HTML syntax to bend the browser to your will. You should resist this urge. Letting the browser do the grunt work is well worth losing absolute control of the GUI interface, and is actually one of the most liberating aspects of this type of design.

The basic building blocks of HTML, tags and attributes, are described in the following sections.

Tags

Tags are instructions that look a lot like the formatting controls of older, pre-WYSIWYG word processors. A tag is descriptive: for example, the <b> tag makes a section of text appear in bold, and the <big> tag increases the size of the text. In addition to simply controlling the appearance and format of text, tags can create structural elements such as tables or data entry forms, as well as hyperlinks that create links between documents.

Each tag has a complementary *end tag* that ends the action it is performing. For the tags just cited, `</b>` stops the text from appearing in bold, and `</big>` returns the text to normal size. In an HTML list, individual items are denoted by enclosing them between `<li>` and `</li>` tags. Some tags don't require a corresponding end tag. For example, the `<p>` tag, which is used to create a line break in a string of text, doesn't require a corresponding `</p>`.

Because one item ends where the next one begins, some browsers allow you to omit some end tags. For example, in Microsoft Internet Explorer, you can leave off the `</li>` tag; its presence is assumed by the `<li>` which starts the next item. In Netscape, on the other hand, you must explicitly include the `</li>` tag. This is one reason why it's always a good idea to test your systems on at least the two major browsers, and stick to HTML standards as much as possible.

Tags are often nested to create effects. For example, the nested tags in the HTML sequence `<b><i>HTML</i> is great</b>` cause the text to appear as "*HTML* **is great**". You can also nest tags to create more complex structures, such as an input form formatted using an HTML table, or a list of hyperlinks.

Attributes

Most tags have optional parameters, called *attributes*, that provide more information about how they are to function. The tag `<font color=red size=3>` has two attributes, color and size. Not surprisingly, in this example the `color` attribute makes the text red, and the `size` attribute makes it appear as size 3. Attributes can appear in any order, so `<font size=3 color=red>` has the same effect as the previous example.

Attributes usually begin with the name of the attribute, followed by an equal sign, and then the desired value. If the value is not a single word or number, it must be enclosed in double quotes. Sometimes an attribute does not have any values. For example, the `<checkbox>` tag, used to create a checkbox in an HTML form, has a `checked` attribute. This attribute, unlike the `color` attribute, for example, has no associated values. Including the `checked` attribute is all that is necessary for the box to show up on the form with a check in it.

An end tag never has attributes.

A sample document

Here is a typical HTML document your company's human resources department might want you to develop. It asks users to enter their names and select whether they would like a raise.

```
<html>
   <head>
      <title>HR Salary Survey</title>
   </head>
   <body>
      <h1>Salary Survey</h1>
      <hr>
      <form action=/hr_dcd/plsql/survey>
         1. What is your name?
            <input type=text name=employee_name value="Enter Name">
         <p>
         2. Do you want a raise?
            <input name=answer type=radio> Yes
            <input name=answer type=radio checked> No
         <p>
         <input type=submit>
      </form>
   </body>
</html>
```

The survey begins with the <html> tag, which announces that the document is in HTML format. HTML documents have two parts: a head and a body. The header section, which begins with the <head> tag, contains descriptive information about the document, sometimes referred to as *metainformation*. In this document, the only descriptive information in the head is the title (denoted with the <title> tag) that appears in the browser's titlebar.

The body section comes after the head. The first item in the body is an instruction to the user. The <h1> tag (heading level 1) increases the size of the message to make it more noticeable. The <p> tag starts a new paragraph on the page. The <p> tag is needed because browsers ignore extra whitespace and line breaks. All the text in a document appears as one long string unless you explicitly use tags to insert breaks where you want them.

The next set of tags creates an input form. The form has three items: a text box in which the user can enter his name, a Yes/No radio button to answer the question "Do you want a raise?" (conveniently defaulted to "No"), and a button to submit the form.

The information on the form is processed when the user presses the Submit button. Submitting the form invokes the PL/SQL procedure specified in the **action** attribute declared in the <form> tag. This program might insert the information into a table, write it to a file, or call the fire_employee procedure if a user fails to give a satisfactory answer to the survey.

Figure 5-1 shows how a browser displays the document.

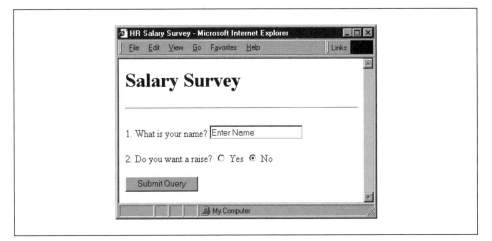

Figure 5-1. An HTML salary survey

A Whirlwind Tour

Although somewhat artificial, it's useful to draw a distinction between text and content when talking about HTML documents. For example, in HTML, you can create a list of items. These items might be simple text, but they can also be HTML tags, such as hyperlinks.

The following sections present some common tags you will need to build the content of your user interfaces. They are listed here with their functions:

Structural tags
> Delineate the part of an HTML document (head, body, comments) to which the content belongs.

Text formatting tags
> Change the size and appearance of the text within a document.

Content flow tags
> Delineate line and paragraph breaks within a document.

Anchor tags
> Create links within a document to other documents on the Web.

List tags
> Create a variety of useful formats for listing content more effectively.

Table tags
> Break the normal vertical flow of a document to present content information in a grid of columns and rows.

Form tags

> Create various types of input structures to facilitate user interaction with the
> site.

Structural Tags

All useful documents, whether large or small, have structures that organize the
information they contain. For example, a book begins with a table of contents that
provides an overview of the topics covered. These topics are divided into self-con-
tained chapters, each with its own structure, including headings and subheadings.
Finally, a book ends with an index that provides a much more granular view of
the book's content.

An ASCII report has a simpler structure. Each page begins with a header, is followed by some sort of structured data, and ends with a footer. An HTML document, which falls somewhere between these extremes, has three major structural
elements, described in the following list: head, body, and comment. The job of the
structural tag is to bring order to the otherwise unruly world of HTML.

Head

> Specifies general information about the document, such as its title, the default
> font size (basefont), and information about its contents. Unlike the Hydra of
> Greek mythology, each document can have only one head, which must come
> at the beginning. If a user prints out a web page that spans multiple printed
> pages (e.g., a table with a large number of rows), the head appears only on
> the first page.

Body

> What the user sees when viewing your document with a browser. It includes
> all text, forms, and images that make up the document. You set all aspects of
> the document appearance in the body, such as background color and back-
> ground image.

Comment

> Allows HTML authors to include notes to themselves, such as the last revision
> date or document version; these comments are not displayed by the browser.
> Unlike their third-generation language (3GL) counterparts, HTML comments
> are not ignored completely, and often contain (somewhat ironically, given that
> these are comments) the source code for scripting language functions.

The following list gives the main structural tags:

`<html>...</html>`

> Marks the beginning and end of an HTML document.

`<head>...</head>`
> Defines the head section of a document.

`<body>...</body>`
> Begins and ends the body of an HTML document; accepts the following attributes:
>
> `background` = URL of background image
> `bgcolor` = red, green, blue, etc.

`<title>...</title>`
> Specifies the browser's titlebar.

`<!-- ... --!>`
> Delineates a comment; information not displayed by the browser.

The following example is a skeleton HTML document that shows the structural tags in action. Note that each section is delimited by the corresponding start and end tags, including the `<html>` tags that enclose the entire document.

```
<html>
<head>
<title>You knew it was coming...</title>
</head>
<!--
This phrase is in every computer book on any subject.
--!>
<body bgcolor=blue>
    And here it is...Hello, World!
</body>
</html>
```

Text Formatting Tags

The text markup tags modify the appearance of the text in a document, between the start tag and the corresponding end tag. There is a wide variety of effects, ranging from the traditional to the bizarre and practically useless. Nesting the tags combines their effects; for example, you can create a bold, italicized word by nesting `<b>` and `<i>`. A list of text formatting tags follows:

`<b>...</b>`
> Sets the text between the tags to bold.

`<font>...</font>`
> Changes the font properties for the text between the start and end tags; accepts the following attributes:
>
> `size` = 8, 10, 12 . . .
> `color` = red, green, blue, etc.

`<hn>`...`</hn>`

Specifies font heading size *n*, which can range from 1 to 6, with `<h1>` the largest and `<h6>` the smallest.

`<i>`...`</i>`

Sets the text between the tags to italic.

`<small>`...`</small>`

Makes the intervening text smaller than the default font.

`<sup>`...`</sup>`

Superscripts the text; useful for creating footnotes.

`<tt>`...`</tt>`

Teletype; formats text using monospace font.

Content Flow Tags

HTML completely ignores whitespace and line breaks within a document. For example, the following document displays one line, even though the author obviously intends that each word appear on its own line:

```
<body bgcolor=white>
The
quick
brown
fox
</body>
```

The flow tags prevent a document from becoming one long, uninterrupted jumble of words. To fix the document above, the author would put a paragraph tag, `<p>`, at the end of each line. This is one of the few tags where the corresponding end tag is not required. The flow tags are summarized in the following list:

`<br>`

Break; creates a line break.

`<center>`...`</center>`

Center; centers the content between the tags.

`<hr>`

Horizontal rule; breaks content flow with a horizontal bar.

`<p>`

Paragraph; same as `<br>`, but with more space between the lines.

`<pre>`...`</pre>`

Preformatted; treat text as unformatted ASCII. The `<pre>` tag is most often used to force the browser to present the text exactly as written because it preserves whitespace and pagebreaks.

As mentioned earlier, the author of the previous example would have to include the <p> tag at the end of each line to create line breaks. The same effect can be achieved with the following line:

```
<p>The<p>quick<p>brown<p>fox
```

Anchor Tags

Anchor tags are used to create links within a document to other documents on the Web. When a user clicks an anchor tag, he or she is transported to the page specified in the underlying hyperlink. The anchor tag initially appears as blue, underlined text unless users have overridden its default appearance in their browsers' preferences. Following is a summary of the anchor tag:

`<a>...</a>`

Anchor; creates a hyperlink labeled with the text between the tags. This tag accepts the following attribute:

`href` = URL

List Tags

Almost any type of content, from plain text to hyperlinks, can be put into list format. A list begins with a tag that indicates if it is ordered or unordered, followed by a number of items enclosed between the list item tags. Though few in number, these tags can create a wide variety of useful formats. The following list summarizes the list tags and their common attributes:

`<ul>...</ul>`

Unordered list; all entries between the tags are bulleted.

`type` = disc, circle, square

`<ol>...</ol>`

Ordered list; all entries between the tags are lettered or numbered, depending on the settings of the `type` and `start` attributes:

`type` = 1, A, a, I, i
`start` = 1, 2, . . . , N

`<li>...</li>`

List item; this tag is always nested between either the `<ul>` tags or the `<ol>` tags. It puts each item in the list on a separate line.

The unordered list tag, `<ul>`, begins a list where the order of each item doesn't matter, such as a list of favorite web sites. Each element in the list is preceded by a specified bullet character. The bullet's shape is determined by the `type` attribute. Here's an example snippet of the HTML for an unordered list; the HTML code on the left produces the output on the right. Clicking on the underlined link will bring you to the URL:

```
<b>Cities in MA</b><p>
<ul>
   <li>
      <a href=www.boston.com>
         Boston
      </a>
   </li>
   <li>Cambridge</li>
   <li>Somerville</li>
</ul>
```

Cities in MA

- <u>Boston</u>
- Cambridge
- Somerville

The ordered list tag, `<ol>`, creates lists in which each item is preceded by one in a sequence of numbers or letters indicating its position in the list. A series of instructions, a "to do" list, and a top ten list are all ordered lists. The `<ol>` tag has two attributes to control the appearance of the sequence indicator. The value of the `type` attribute sets the type of sequence. The value "A" begins the sequence "A, B, C, . . .," while "a" begins "a, b, c, ..." "I" or "i" starts a list of Roman numerals based on the case of the value. Not specifying a value for `type`, or setting it to "1", will begin a numeric sequence. The `start` attribute sets the initial value of the sequence. Here's an example of an ordered list; the HTML code on the left produces the output on the right:

```
<b><i>SEC</i> Football Teams</b>
<p>
<ol>
   <!-- The end tag is implied --!>
   <li>Alabama Crimson Tide
   <li>Tennesse Volunteers
   <li>Auburn Tigers
</ol>
```

SEC **Football Teams**

1. Alabama Crimson Tide
2. Tennessee Volunteers
3. Auburn Tigers

The next example uses nesting to create a standard outline by creating a list within the `<li>` and `</li>` tags; the HTML code on the left produces the output on the right:

```
<ol>
<li>Introduction<li>
   <ol type=a>
      <li>CGI
      <li>HTML
      <li>PL/SQL
   </ol>
<li>OAS</li>
</ol>
```

1. Introduction
   a. CGI
   b. HTML
   c. PL/SQL
2. OAS

Table Tags

We can use an HTML table to break the normally vertical flow of a document into a grid of columns and rows. The cell at the intersection of the column and row can contain any type of content, including text, lists, forms, and even other tables. You can create almost any layout by breaking a complex document into smaller, simpler pieces that you place within the cell of a table. Following is a list of the four main table tags and some of their most commonly used attributes:

`<table>...</table>`
> Begins and ends an HTML table.
>
> `align` = right, left, center
> `bgcolor` = red, green, blue, etc.
> `border` = 1, 2, . . .
> `width` = 10%, 20%, . . .

`<tr>...</tr>`
> Creates a new row; used between `<table>` and `</table>`.
>
> `align` = right, left, center
> `bgcolor` = red, green, blue, etc.

`<th>...</th>` *and* `<td>...</td>`
> Create a header cell (`<th>`) or data cell (`<td>`); used between `<tr>` and `</tr>`.
>
> `align` = right, left, center
> `bgcolor` = red, green, blue, etc.
> `colspan` = 1, 2, 3, . . .
> `rowspan` = 1, 2, 3, . . .
> `width` = 10%, 20%, . . .

A table begins with the `<table>` tag, which always breaks the flow of the document by inserting a new line. If the `border` attribute is used, then the cells in the table are enclosed within a grid. The table stops at the `</table>` tag. The `<tr>` begins a new row within the table, so a table with a row for each state in the United States has 50 `<tr>` tags. The `<th>` and `<td>` tags divide each row into columns (cells): `<th>` indicates header cells and `<td>` indicates data cells. While any number of these tags can appear within a row, the total number of columns in the table is always equal to the maximum number of columns within any row.

A number of attributes are shared hierarchically by the table, row, and cell tags. The `align` attribute sets the text alignment for all the cells, and `bgcolor` sets their background color. The `width` attribute specifies the element's horizontal width as a percentage of the total width. For example, when used in the `<table>` tag, a width of 100% makes the table use the full width of the screen. The `colspan` and `rowspan` attributes, which are used only in the cell tags, allow you to create cells

that span multiple columns. For example, you could use the line <th colspan=5>
Here's some data</th> to put a heading row on a table with five columns.

Here is a simple table with five columns and four rows:

```
<title>Sales Data</title>
<center>
<table border=1 width=70%>
    <th colspan=6 align=center>Sales Data</th>
    <tr>
        <!-- Column Headers --!>
        <th>Office</th>
        <th>Q1</th>
        <th>Q2</th>
        <th>Q3</th>
        <th>Q4</th>
    <tr align=right>
        <!-- Row for the Boston office --!>
        <th><a href=/offices/boston.html>Boston</a></th>
        <td>1000</td>
        <td>1500</td>
        <td>1750</td>
        <td>1800</td>
    <tr align=right>
        <!-- Row for the New York office --!>
        <th><a href=/offices/nyc.html>New York</a></th>
        <td>2900</td>
        <td>2000</td>
        <td>2300</td>
        <td>2475</td>
</table>
</center>
```

The first row uses the <th> tag to create headers for each of the five columns. The
next two rows contain sales data by office, and have an identical structure. The first
column, created using the <tr> tag, creates a hyperlinked row header. The <td>
tag is then used to format the quarterly information by office into cells. Figure 5-2
shows how a browser displays the page.

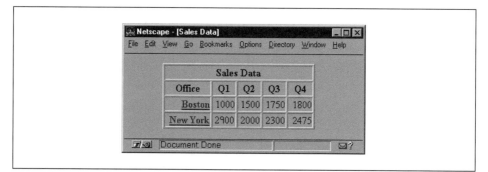

Figure 5-2. A simple table

Form Tags

Up to this point, we've looked at the output side of our HTML to format text, create lists of items, and put other HTML elements into tables. Now we're ready to use HTML form tags to create documents that can be used to put information into a database.

A *form* encompasses a set of tags, exactly like those we've been using, that create various types of input widgets that are displayed by the browser. These tags can be text boxes, radio buttons, and checkboxes that accept input from users. Once users have filled out the form, they submit it to the server for processing. A back-end program, which in this book will be a PL/SQL routine, parses their input and performs some type of processing.

When building HTML form applications, it's important to remember there is absolutely no communication with the database until the form is submitted. HTML forms are no replacement for traditional tools like Oracle Forms, and you should not treat them as such.* However, their portability and simplicity offer compelling advantages in many circumstances.

With HTML forms, as long as end users have a browser, they can enter data into your application without having any special configuration or software. Additionally, all the processing for your input form occurs at the server, allowing you to consolidate the business rules of your application into one place. Best of all, because these forms reside on a central server, any update you make is instantly distributed to all your users, eliminating the need for client-side upgrades or new installs. The form tags are displayed in the following list with their associated attributes, followed by a more detailed discussion of their properties. At the end of this section, I will offer some advice on how to improve the layout of a form or any other HTML document.

`<form>...</form>`
   Begins and ends a form.

   `action` = URL of PL/SQL procedure to execute
   `method` = GET, POST

`<input>`
   Creates an input element based on the `type` attribute. This tag has other attributes that are not listed here because they only apply for certain types.

   `name` = name of element
   `type` = text, password, checkbox, radio, submit, hidden

---

* This is because HTTP is a stateless protocol. Chapter 7, *The PL/SQL Toolkit*, and Chapter 8, *Developing Applications*, will suggest some ways to mitigate this problem.

`<select>...</select>`

Creates a drop-down list.

`name` = name of element
`size` = number of visible items

`<option>...</option>`

Creates an item in a `<select>` list; the string in the selected item's value field is passed as the parameter when the form is submitted.

`value` = string

`<textarea>...</textarea>`

Creates a free-form text entry box.

`name` = name of element
`cols` = number of columns (characters in a line)
`rows` = number of rows (number of lines)

The *<form>* tag

The most important parameter in the `<form>` tag is the `action` attribute, which specifies the program that will execute on the server when the form is submitted. In our case, this program is a PL/SQL procedure whose arguments correspond in name and number to each named input element in the form. When the user presses the Submit button, the values in the form are passed as parameters to the procedure, which then processes the user's input.

The `method` attribute determines how those values are passed. If GET is used, the names and encoded values of each element are appended and sent as one long string that is parsed and decoded at the server. Because the entire length of the string must be under 256 characters for some operating systems, this method should be used only for simple forms, but it is useful when you want to allow the user to include the values entered into a form as part of a bookmark. The POST method, on the other hand, is not limited in character length, but it does not allow for the bookmarking feature. Each element is processed individually by the server. In either case, OAS parses the parameters and passes them to the procedure.

The *<input>* tag

Form input elements are created with the `<input>` tag. The `name` attribute links the element to a parameter in the procedure specified by the `<form>` tag's `action` attribute. When the form is submitted, the value of the element is passed as the value of its corresponding parameter.

The `type` attribute determines what kind of input element appears on the screen. The following list displays the attributes for the `<input>` tag:

`type=text`

Single-line text input box.

`maxlength` = maximum number of characters that can be entered
`size` = character width of the field: 5, 8, 15, . . .
`value` = string (default value for the field)

`type=hidden`

Placeholder for a value; while it does not show up on the screen, it is passed as a parameter when the form is submitted. Hidden fields are often used to help pass information between multiple forms in a web application. Maxlength, size, and value are the same as `type=text`, but characters are masked using an asterisk.

`type=checkbox`

Checkbox for on/off values; the string in the value field is passed as the parameter value when the form is submitted.

`value` = string
`checked`

`type=radio`

Radio button; radio buttons with the same name form a single group in which the user can select one value. The string in the selected item's value field is passed as the parameter when the form is submitted.

`value` = string
`checked`

`type=submit`

Submit button; for named buttons, the string in the value field is passed as the parameter when the form is submitted.

`name` = action to take when the form is submitted
`value` = string (appears as the button's label)

The next example shows an HTML form with an input box, a set of a radio buttons, a checkbox, and a Submit button that, when pressed, executes a PL/SQL procedure called update_employee. This procedure has three parameters: emp_name, emp_office, and kissup_flag:

```
<html>
<head><title>Employee Info</title></head>
<body>
<form action=/hr/plsql/update_employee>
    Employee Name:
        <input type=text name=emp_name size=20 maxlength=10>
    <p>
    Office:
        <input type=radio name=emp_office checked value=BOS>Boston
```

```
        <input type=radio name=emp_office value=NYC>New York
        <input type=radio name=emp_office value=CHI>Chicago
    <p>
        <input type=checkbox name=kissup_flag value="Yes">
            Loves Job?
    <p>
        <input type=submit>
    </form>
    </body>
    </html>
```

Figure 5-3 shows how a browser displays the form.

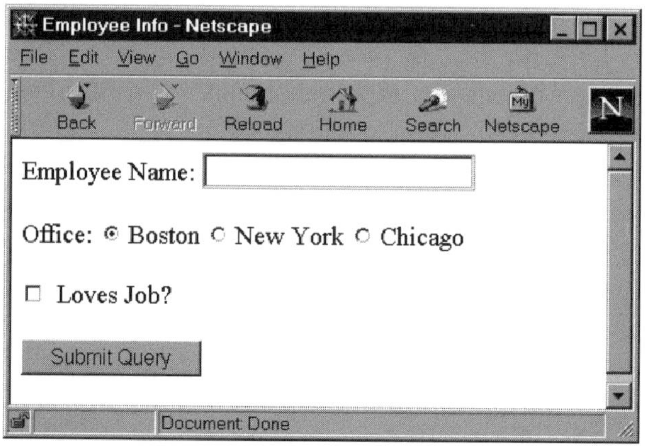

Figure 5-3. A simple HTML form

The employee text field passes the employee name as the emp_name parameter. The **maxlength** attribute limits the number of characters that can be entered to 10. The **size** attribute sets the name field's width to 20, so the size of the field is twice the size of the number of characters that can be entered. This prevents user input from scrolling within the field as text is entered.

A radio button allows the user to select one office from a list of three. The options in a set of radio buttons, related to one another by the **name** attribute, correspond to just one server-side parameter. In the previous example, there are three radio buttons named "office" that correspond to Boston, New York, and Chicago. If the user's gender were required, then the form would require two more radio buttons, named "gender," for male and female.

When the form is submitted, the string in the **value** attribute is used as the parameter when the user makes a selection. For example, "CHI" is passed when "Chicago" is the selected option.

A check in the kissup_flag checkbox indicates that the user loves his job. The default **checked** attribute here gives the user a subtle hint as to what the answer should be. If the box is checked, kissup_flag's value is "Yes" when the form is submitted.

The last input tag creates a Submit button that, when pressed, sends the information on the form to the server for processing. Each form must have at least one Submit button. Otherwise, you risk (perhaps purposefully) damning your users to a Kafkaesque hell of entering data that never gets processed. You can use the **value** attribute if you want to take an action based on what button the user presses. For example, if you want the user to click a button labeled "Add" to insert a record and "Delete" to remove a record, you can create two Submit buttons, both named "action." The value for one is "Add," and the value for the second is "Delete." When the user presses either button, its value is sent to the server as the "action" parameter. You can use this parameter to decide what to do with the information.

The <select> tag

You can use the **<select>** tag to create drop-down lists of items. The name of the **<select>** list, as specified in the **name** attribute, corresponds to the input parameter of the server process. The items in the list, which must be enclosed with the **<option>** tag, supply the value of that parameter. In the previous example, you can create a cleaner interface by replacing the three radio buttons with a single list of offices, as shown in the following example. The HTML code on the left produces the output on the right:

```
<select name=office>
   <option value=BOS>Boston
   <option value=NYC>New York
   <option value=CHI>Chicago
</select>
```

The **size** attribute transforms the drop-down list into a scrollable list. In this example, the number of items visible is equal to the size. The following example shows the effect of using the **size** attribute; the HTML code on the left produces the output on the right:

```
<select name=office size=3>
   <option value=BOS>Boston
   <option value=NYC>New York
   <option value=CHI>Chicago
   <option value=LA>Los Angeles
</select>
```

The <textarea> tag

The standard text input box is limited to a single line of input; to create multiline input areas to hold user comments, complaints, and the like, you must use the <textarea> and the </textarea> tags. Like all the other input tags, each text area must be named using the name attribute. The other main attributes, rows and cols, determine a field's character height and width. Unlike the other input fields, however, the textarea tag does not use the value attribute to set default values. Instead, any plain text between the start and end textarea tags appears as the default value for the field. The following snippet shows how to create a comment field that lets the user enter up to four lines of 40 characters each:

```
<textarea name=comments cols=40 rows=4></textarea>
```

Cleaning up the form

One of the best and worst aspects of HTML is its inability to precisely format a page. For example, when you are laying out an input screen in Oracle Forms, you have exact control, down to the X and Y coordinates, of the placement of each text box, label, and button. However, forcing the browser to display a document in such a highly specific way runs counter to the HTML philosophy. Remember, the browser's built-in rendering engine is meant to eliminate this grunt work. Standard HTML in a browser automatically compensates for changes in both window size and overall resolution.

This problem is especially noticeable in HTML forms. Input elements are either crammed up on one row, making the form look sloppy, or lined up one on top of the other, making the form scroll on and on forever. However, there are a few tricks that help overcome some of the inherent HTML limitations.

You can use any HTML constructs to improve a form's layout. This includes using flow tags to break the form into logical sections, formatting tags to emphasize labels, lists to create attractive radio buttons, and tables to align each item. The following example combines all these elements to create a nice-looking form:

```
<form action=/hr/plsql/update_employee>
  <table>
    <tr>
      <th align=right>Name:</th>
      <td><input type=text name=emp_name></td>
    <tr>
      <th align=right>Office:</th>
      <td>
        <select name=office size=3>
          <option value=BOS>Boston
          <option value=NYC>New York
          <option value=CHI>Chicago
        </select>
    <tr>
```

```
        <th align=right><i>Loves</i> Job?</th>
        <td><input type=checkbox name=kissup_flag value=Y></td>
    </table>
    <input type=submit value="Save Responses">
</form>
```

Figure 5-4 shows how this form is displayed in a browser.

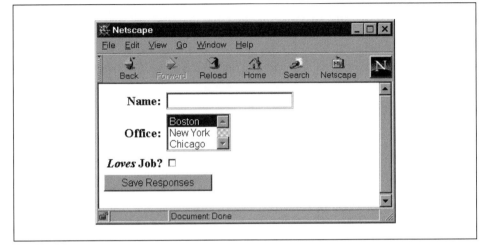

Figure 5-4. A form formatted with a table

Beware Browser-Specific Extensions

Browser vendors have created many browser-specific additions to the base HTML language. Some of these, like tables, are extremely useful and have been incorporated into nearly every major graphical browser. However, many "innovations" are simply pawns in the battle between Microsoft and Netscape to control the future of the web browser. You will find that your worst enemies are often browser vendors themselves; web technology is changing at a feverish pitch as each side tries to one-up the other with a new feature.

Although vendors are adding new extensions and features every day, it's probably safest to focus on the basic language and consider very carefully whether you should use a vendor-specific extension. If you are unwilling to constantly tweak your application to keep it compatible with the extensions as they change, you should probably avoid extensions altogether.

6

In this chapter:
• Structured
  Programming in
  PL/SQL
• Programming
  Constructs
• Packages
• PL/SQL Tools

PL/SQL

With HTML safely out of the way, we can turn our attention to the second half of our web development platform: PL/SQL, Oracle's proprietary extension to structured query language (SQL). The PL stands for Procedural Language, since PL/SQL is used to create procedural constructs (loops, variables, etc.) on top of the relational constructs of SQL.

Although it has some object-oriented features, PL/SQL is based largely on Ada, a structured programming language used heavily by the Department of Defense. As such, PL/SQL has more in common with languages like C, Pascal, or COBOL than it does with C++ or Java. Although it follows an older design model (structured versus object), PL/SQL has the advantages of being easy to learn, tightly integrated to the Oracle database, and extensible. If you know how to write a SQL script and know at least one 3GL language, you can learn to develop useful PL/SQL programs in just a few hours.

In the next three sections we'll cover what you need to know to start developing in PL/SQL: how to structure a PL/SQL program, how to fill in its major programming constructs, and how to create reusable modules called packages. In the last section we'll look at two third-party tools, TOAD and PL/Formatter, that make PL/SQL development much more enjoyable and productive.

There is much more to say about the PL/SQL language. For complete information, see Steven Feuerstein and Bill Pribyl's *Oracle PL/SQL Programming* (O'Reilly & Associates).

Structured Programming in PL/SQL

The idea behind structured, or modular, programming is that complex problems can be broken down into smaller, more manageable pieces. For example, I can break the daunting task of driving from Boston to New York into four simpler steps: find I-95 south in Boston, drive four hours, exit in New York, and find a parking space. I repeat this process on each of the previous steps, breaking each one into even smaller units until I eventually reach a level of complexity that I can reasonably handle. For example, I can break "find a parking spot" into the steps: drive around aimlessly, yell at somebody, honk my horn, and then turn around and go home.* Once I have identified all these simpler steps, I can solve the original problem.

The structure of a PL/SQL program reflects this underlying philosophy. A complex program is made up of units called *blocks* (as in building blocks) that can contain variables, SQL and PL/SQL instructions, error handling routines, and even other blocks. Each block may have four distinct parts: an optional header, optional variable declarations, executable instructions, and optional error handling code. These parts are described in the following list:

Header section
> This section, also known as the *specification*, comes at the beginning of a block. It defines the block's name, its type, and any parameters it requires. If the header is omitted, the block is called an *anonymous block* because it does not have a name. The header is required for procedures and functions, but is replaced with a simple DECLARE keyword for anonymous blocks. Anonymous blocks typically include just an executable section, and are often found as the executable portions of a conditional statement.

Declaration section
> This section contains declarations for all local variables and structures used in the block. Variables can include simple numbers and strings, as well as more complex structures, like cursors and arrays. The declaration section is optional; your program does not have to use any variables. However, PL/SQL is *strongly typed*, which means that you must declare every variable you plan to use (the one exception to this rule is the implicit loop index, which we'll discuss later).

Executable section
> This section, also known as the *body*, contains your actual code. This is the only required section; all blocks must have at least one executable instruction.† Sometimes you may want to just use the NULL instruction, which doesn't perform any action, as the entire executable portion of a block. This technique stems from the two approaches to modular design. The first approach, *bottom-up design*, begins by coding the simplest pieces and works up to more

---

* Sometimes these problems are maddeningly recursive. For example, "Turn around and go home" breaks into "Find I-95 north in New York, drive four hours, exit in Boston, and find a parking space."

† The exceptions to this rule are external procedures or specifications for Java methods (a way to call Java from PL/SQL). These, however, are beyond the scope of this book.

complex structures. The second approach, *top-down design*, begins at the highest level and works down. With the second method, you may know a particular module is necessary, but not yet know (or care) how it will be implemented, so you create a stub that serves as a placeholder until you are ready to fill in the details.

Exception section

This section handles problems (exceptions) that arise while the program is running. When an exception occurs (for instance, an attempt to insert a duplicate primary key into a table), the RDBMS immediately transfers control to the exception section, if it exists. Each error is associated, either by the system or the programmer, with a name like DUP_VAL_ON_INDEX or NO_DATA_ FOUND.

The exception section is a CASE statement that associates an error name with a *handler* that executes when the error occurs. Of course, it would be inconvenient to explicitly test for all the possible things that could go wrong with a particular program (how often do you test whether you have enough memory to execute a SQL statement?). The catch-all exception OTHERS traps exceptions not explicitly listed in the CASE statement.

If there is no handler at all for an exception, the block terminates and the error is passed back to the calling block to be resolved. If there is no handler for the error in any block, then the entire program terminates immediately, leaving the user staring at an ugly error message. Although the use of the exception section is optional, well-designed programs should always minimize the occurrence of unhandled exceptions.

Blocks allow you to build modularized programs. While anything between BEGIN and END is considered a block, the two most important blocks are procedures and functions.

Procedures

A *procedure* is a modular block of code with the following general structure:

```
PROCEDURE name (
    parameter1 IN | OUT | IN OUT AS datatype,
    parameter2 IN | OUT | IN OUT AS datatype,
    ... )
IS
    Local variable declarations
BEGIN
    Program instructions
EXCEPTION
    WHEN exception1 THEN
        Handler 1
    WHEN exception2 THEN
        Handler 2
```

```
       WHEN OTHERS THEN
            Default error handler
   END;
```

The name of the procedure should reflect the task it performs. The task should be fairly simple; a procedure shouldn't be more than a few hundred lines long. If it is, you probably haven't broken your problem down sufficiently. Here's a fairly simple procedure:*

```
   /* Formatted by PL/Formatter v.1.1.13 */
   CREATE OR REPLACE PROCEDURE give_raise (
       emp_id IN VARCHAR2 DEFAULT NULL,
       raise_pct IN VARCHAR2 DEFAULT NULL
       )
   IS

       monthly_salary   NUMBER DEFAULT 0;

   BEGIN
       -- Fetch current salary using a SELECT...INTO;
       SELECT   sal
          INTO  monthly_salary
          FROM  emp
          WHERE id = emp_id;
       -- Decide what to do
       IF monthly_salary > 10000
       THEN
           HTP.print ('You are rich enough already!');
       ELSE
           UPDATE emp
           SET    sal = sal * (1 + raise_pct)
           WHERE  id = emp_id;
           COMMIT ;
           HTP.print ('Your wish is my command');
       END IF;
       HTP.print ('All done.');
   EXCEPTION
       WHEN OTHERS
       THEN
           HTP.print ('Sorry, no raise for now.');
   END;
```

Functions

A *function*, the second kind of modular block, has the following general structure:

```
   FUNCTION name (
       parameter1 IN | OUT | IN OUT AS datatype,
```

---

* This listing, and the others throughout this chapter, begin with the line "CREATE OR REPLACE...," which is a SQL command and not part of the actual procedure. Since procedures (as well as functions and packages) are database objects, you must use SQL to CREATE and compile them. The REPLACE option allows you to run these scripts over and over without having to first drop the procedure.

```
    parameter2 IN | OUT | IN OUT AS datatype )

RETURN return_datatype IS
   Local variable declarations
BEGIN
   Function instructions
   RETURN return_value
EXCEPTION
   WHEN exception1 THEN
      Handler1
   WHEN exception2 THEN
      Handler2
   WHEN OTHERS THEN
      Default error handler
END;
```

A function computes and returns a single value (its return value) of the datatype defined in its header section. The RETURN command, which can appear in the executable or exception section (or both), sends the return value back to the program that called the function. The RETURN command terminates the function immediately.

You can use functions to perform common computations or return special values. For example, you might want to include some descriptive information at the end of each page, like your company's name and the date the page was created. You can write a simple function that you can call inside each program to avoid hardcoding. Here, for example, is such a function:

```
CREATE OR REPLACE FUNCTION get_web_tag_line
   RETURN VARCHAR2

   Ret_val VARCHAR2(500);

IS
BEGIN
   ret_val := 'Copyright ACME Incorporated, ';
   RETURN ret_val || TO_CHAR (SYSDATE, 'DD-MON-YY');
END;
```

Even this trivial example points out one of the main advantages of modularizing your code: it helps you avoid problems down the road. For example, what if a big German conglomerate buys your company? You certainly don't want to have to insert a bunch of umlauts into your programs. You probably also noticed that the date format shows only the last two digits of the year. Had you hardcoded the date format into each program, millennium fever would force you to change every occurrence to display the full four-digit year. Calling a function lets you change the code in just one place.

Parameters

You can include parameters in a procedure or function header to better control how it works. A *parameter* is similar to a local variable, but it acts more like a placeholder for a value that will be passed to the procedure by some future program. This allows a procedure to handle general situations, rather than specific instances of a given problem. These symbols are called *formal parameters*. The values provided by the calling program are called *actual parameters* because they represent actual, concrete values.

A procedure or function can accept any number of parameters, or even omit them entirely. For example, the give_raise procedure needed two parameters: one to pass the employee ID and one to pass the amount of the raise.

Parameter declarations follow this general format:

```
PROCEDURE/FUNCTION name (
   Name1 mode datatype DEFAULT defaul_val,
   Name2 mode datatype DEFAULT default_val,
   ...
   Name3 mode datatype DEFAULT default_val) IS
```

Each parameter must have a name, a mode, a datatype, and (optionally) a default value, as defined in the following list:

Parameter name
> The name for the parameter as it is used in the body of the block. Each name must be unique. Parameter names should be reasonably meaningful.

Mode
> There are three modes: IN, OUT, and IN OUT. The IN mode means that the parameter is read only; the block can see the value (i.e., reference) of the parameter but cannot change it. The OUT mode is write only; the block can set, but not reference, the value of the parameter. This mode is used to return values from the procedure back to the calling program. The IN OUT mode means the parameter can be both referenced and updated.

Datatype
> The datatype specifies the parameter's type. These types are unrestrained; the size of the formal parameter is determined by the size of the corresponding actual parameter.

Default value
> The default value specifies the value of the parameter if no corresponding actual parameter is provided.

Here are some sample declarations:

```
PROCEDURE give_raise (
   emp_id IN NUMBER,
```

```
      job_code IN VARCHAR2 DEFAULT 'CEO'
      );

PROCEDURE print_emp_info (
   dpt_name_parm IN VARCHAR2 DEFAULT 'HUMAN RESOURCES'
   );

FUNCTION get_emp_name (emp_id IN NUMBER)
   RETURN VARCHAR2;
```

The last example is worth commenting on. It's a function that, given a primary key, returns an employee's name. What if you wanted to modify the function to return more information, like the employee's job code and department? Since a function can return only one value, we can't modify the get_emp_name function to return several different things. Instead, we can convert it into a procedure and use OUT parameters to pass the new values back. Here's an example:

```
PROCEDURE get_emp_info (
   emp_id IN NUMBER,
   emp_number OUT VARCHAR2,
   emp_name OUT VARCHAR2,
   emp_dept_id OUT NUMBER
   )
```

Calling Procedures and Functions

You call a procedure or function by name. You must also pass actual parameters for its formal parameters (if a module does not have any parameters, then the name alone is sufficient). Here are some examples of how to call a procedure or function from inside another PL/SQL program:

```
delete_all_customers;

dbms_sql.put_line (todays_date);

today_string := todays_date;
```

The first example calls the delete_all_customers procedure. This is the simplest type of call, since no parameters are passed to the procedure. As you can see, the ability to represent a complex sequence of actions with a single command makes for much more readable programs. The second example prints the results returned by the todays_date function. You can use a function call anywhere you can use a literal or a variable, as long as its return type is appropriate. The third example assigns a local variable to the value returned by todays_date.

You must supply actual parameters to procedures or functions that have a formal parameter list. There are two notations for doing this: positional notation and named notation.

Positional notation

Positional notation uses an actual parameter's ordinal position to map it to a corresponding formal parameter. This is the notation used most frequently in languages like C or Pascal. The following examples show positional notation in action:

```
give_raise (101,'PROGRAMMER');

give_raise (105);

print_emp_info('ACCOUNTING');

emp_name := get_emp_name (current_emp_id);

get_emp_info ( 101, enum, ename, edpt);
```

The first call passes two literal values to the two formal parameters (emp_id and job_code) of the give_raise procedure. The values are assigned to the formal parameters based on their order in the list, so emp_id is assigned the value "101" and job_code is assigned "PROGRAMMER." The second example seems to violate these rules because it only provides one parameter. Remember, however, that we have assigned a default value ("CEO") to the job_code. You can omit an actual value for a formal parameter if it has a default value. The RDBMS generates an error if you omit a value for a parameter that does not have a default value.

The third example has only one parameter, dpt_name_parm, which is assigned the value "ACCOUNTING." The fourth assigns the result of the get_emp_name function to a local variable called emp_name. The fifth sample calls get_emp_info. As we would expect, the emp_id formal parameter is assigned the value procedure, and each of the OUT formal parameters is associated with a corresponding local variable: emp_number with enum, emp_name with ename, and emp_dept_id with edpt. When the procedure finishes, the values of the local variables will have the values assigned to formal parameters in the procedure.

Named notation

The second way to supply parameters to a function or procedure is *named notation*, which eliminates the call's reliance on parameter position by explicitly mapping formal parameters to actual parameters. This is done by using the formal parameter name to which an actual parameter corresponds directly in the call. The syntax of a named notation call is:

```
procedure_name (
   formal_parameter1 => actual_parameter1,
   formal_parameter2 => actual_parameter2,
   formal_parameter3 => actual_parameter3,
   ...)
```

Here are two of the positional notation examples we looked at in the previous section rewritten in this format:

```
give_raise ( job_code => 'PROGRAMMER', emp_id => 101 );

get_emp_info ( emp_dpt_id => edpt,
               emp_name => ename,
               emp_number => enum,
               emp_id = > 101 );
```

While named notation requires more typing, there are many situations in which this notation is preferable to positional notation. Let's take as an example a procedure that performs a logic test based on a large set of flags. Suppose you had a procedure called complex_test with 10 parameters and that each parameter governed the execution of a distinct step. If a parameter value is 'Y', then the step executes. Otherwise, it does not. Here is the specification:

```
PROCEDURE complex_test (
        step1_ctl IN VARCHAR2 DEFAULT 'N',
        step2_ctl IN VARCHAR2 DEFAULT 'N',
        ...
        step9_ctl IN VARCHAR2 DEFAULT 'N',
        step10_ctl IN VARCHAR2 DEFAULT 'N'
        );
```

Now suppose that you want to execute just the tenth step. The positional syntax requires a value for the parameter based on its ordinal position. Executing just the tenth step in complex_test requires this ugly command:

```
complex_test ('N','N','N','N','N','N','N','N','N','Y');
```

Using the named notation, we can replace the complex with a simple substitute:

```
complex_test ( step10_ctl => 'Y' );
```

Overloading

Overloading allows you to create multiple versions of a procedure or function. Each version has the same name but a different *signature*, the technical term for the full set of declarations in a parameter list. The compiler uses a procedure or function call's name and signature to find a corresponding overloaded function.

Overloading is a powerful technique that makes procedures and functions easier to use. Say you want to create a generic function that returns any passed date in DD-MON-YYYY format. The input should allow the caller to pass a date in a variety of formats. For example, he could pass a DATE variable, a VARCHAR2 string that represents a date, or even numbers that represent the month, day, and year of the date. Here is the example without overloading:

```
FUNCTION get_nice_date_date (dt IN DATE)
    RETURN VARCHAR2;
```

```
FUNCTION get_nice_date_vchar (dt IN VARCHAR2)
   RETURN VARCHAR2;

FUNCTION get_nice_date_month (
   m IN NUMBER,
   d IN NUMBER,
   y IN NUMBER
   )
   RETURN VARCHAR2;
```

With overloading, however, you can use the same function name over and over as long as each version has a unique signature. All the programmer has to do to call the function is supply the data in one of the overloaded formats; the compiler automatically does the dirty work of mapping the call to the correct signature. Here are the three specifications required by the get_nice_date function:

```
FUNCTION get_nice_date (dt IN DATE)
   RETURN VARCHAR2;

FUNCTION get_nice_date (dt IN VARCHAR2)
   RETURN VARCHAR2;

FUNCTION get_nice_date (
   m IN NUMBER,
   d IN NUMBER,
   y IN NUMBER
   )
   RETURN VARCHAR2;
```

Without overloading, you had to create three different versions of the same function and leave the programmer to call the correct version. This is a real nuisance because the programmer must know (or, more likely, look up) the applicable name. This flexibility helps ensure that the procedure and functions you develop are easy to use and understand.

Permissions

In this section we'll look at how to share procedures and functions among a number of different schemas. Like all database objects, procedures and functions (as well as packages, which are covered later in this chapter) are owned by a single schema. Consequently, only that schema can execute them unless other database schemas are explicitly granted EXECUTE permission. When you want to write generic modules that can be used by a large number of developers, you can use the GRANT EXECUTE command. This command should be executed within the owner's account, and it has the following syntax:

```
SQL> GRANT EXECUTE ON program_or_package_name TO schema;
```

This grant highlights an extremely important aspect of Oracle's security rules. By default, procedures and functions execute with all the permissions of their *owner*, and not those of the account in which they are executed. For example, you can execute a complex procedure that hits sensitive tables from a minimally privileged account by selectively using GRANT EXECUTE. Oracle8*i* has a second model, called *invoker's rights*, which requires that the user (the *invoker*) has the necessary underlying privileges.

Programming Constructs

Most programs are built out of a fairly standard set of programming constructs. For example, to write a useful program, I need to be able to store values in variables, test these values against a condition, or loop through a set of instructions a certain number of times. In this section, we'll see how to use these and other constructs in PL/SQL. Specifically, we'll cover comments, variables, conditionals, loops, cursors, and index-by tables (PL/SQL's version of an array).

Comments

Comments allow you to document your PL/SQL programs. These comments are stored in the database along with the rest of the PL/SQL code. PL/SQL has two types of comments: multiline and single-line.

Multiline comments are enclosed between the delimiters /* and */. Here's an example:

```
/*
|| The following procedure unconditionally deletes all
|| rows from the customer's table.
*/
PROCEDURE delete_all_customers is
  ...
```

Single-line comments are denoted by two consecutive dashes. The comment can appear either on its own line or after a PL/SQL instruction, as illustrated in the following example:

```
CREATE OR REPLACE PROCEDURE delete_all_customers
IS
BEGIN
   -- The delete statement blows away all customers
   DELETE
     FROM customers;
   COMMIT;   -- Confirm changes
END;
```

Variables

The second construct, variables, allows you to save values in memory. For example, you may want to keep a counter inside a loop, or store a string value for processing. In this section, we'll see how to declare a variable and assign it a value. We'll also look at how to turn a variable into a constant by permanently fixing its value.

Declaring a variable

The syntax for a variable declaration is:

```
name datatype(size) DEFAULT default_value;
```

You can also assign the default value using the := operator. In this case, the syntax is:

```
name datatype(size) := default_value;
```

The next three sections describe the name, datatype, and default value.

Name. The name may be up to 30 characters long, and may include letters, numbers, or underscores. Variable names must start with a letter. A good variable is descriptive; many programmers like to use one- or two-letter variable names like X or A1 because they are easy to type,* but this does not make for very readable code. If a variable represents an employee's monthly pay rate, then call it "monthly_pay_rate," not "mpr" or, even worse, "r." Let's face it—most of our time as developers is spent either fixing our old programs or helping someone else fix theirs, not writing new ones. You have only one chance to develop a program. You have the rest of your working life to support it. The few seconds you save by using a short, meaningless name are not worth the future maintenance hassle for either you or the poor sap who'll take your place when you become a consultant.

Datatype. The datatype specifies the type and amount of data a variable can hold. While there are a variety of different datatypes, in this section we'll look at the two most common: NUMBER and VARCHAR2.

The NUMBER type holds general numbers, such as 1, −457, or 3.14. You can assign a number variable a *precision* and *scale* to set its maximum size. The precision is the maximum number of digits allowed. The scale controls rounding. A positive number indicates the number of places to the right of the decimal place to round, and a negative number indicates the number of units to the left of the decimal. The size used in the declaration is written as a combination of the precision and the scale. For example, the number 1523.567 is rounded to 1523.6 if the datatype is NUMBER(4,1); it would be 1500 if the datatype is NUMBER(4, −2).

The VARCHAR2 datatype holds character strings, like 'Hello, world!', 'Saturday', or 'Buster Keaton'. In PL/SQL, the value of a string is enclosed by single quotation

---

* I once saw a program in which the variables were named after the developer's coworkers.

marks (ticks), not double quotes. The compiler can get very confused if you mistakenly use double quotes. Also, the declaration of the VARCHAR2 type must include the maximum size of the string, which can range from 1 to 32,767 characters.* For example, a string of 50 characters is declared as a VARCHAR2(50).

In addition to explicitly declaring a variable's type, you can implicitly declare it using an *anchored declaration*. The anchored declaration directly associates a variable's type with the type of a column in a database table. For example, suppose you want to use a PL/SQL variable to hold an employee's last name from an employee table. Rather than hardcoding the column definition in the program, you can simply anchor the variable to the last-name column in the employee table.

Anchored declarations have other benefits besides ease of use. They simplify long-term maintenance in two ways: first, they improve readability, because the relationship between a variable and a column is explicit; second, they minimize problems caused by changes in the database schema. How many times have you had to fix a program because a column was redefined? The syntax for an anchored declaration is:

```
variable_name table_name.column_name%TYPE;
```

Here are a few examples that help reduce the chance of "overflowing" a VARCHAR2 variable with too many characters:

```
Emp_name        EMP.ENAME%TYPE;
Emp_Dept_code   EMP.DEPT%TYPE;
Dept_name       DEPT.DNAME%TYPE;
```

Default value. A variable default value is the value a variable contains when it's referenced for the first time. If you don't know what this value is, then you're asking for trouble; it can be very difficult to track down bugs caused by uninitialized variables. Here are some sample variable declarations:

```
rec_count NUMBER default 0;

yearly_interest_rate NUMBER(5,4) := 0.08;

account_status_code VARCHAR2(10) default 'OPEN';

emp_last_name emp.lname%TYPE;
```

Assigning values

Once we've declared the variable, we can assign it a value in the body of our program. PL/SQL uses the := operator to assign a value to a variable.

---

* Be careful if you plan to use a PL/SQL variable to populate a VARCHAR2 column in a database table. The maximum size in the RDBMS is just 2000 characters.

Here are a few sample assignments:

```
count := 0;

emp_count := emp_count + 1;

annual_salary := hourly_rate * 2000;
```

You should make sure you declare the variables large enough to hold the full range of potential values. If the value you assign exceeds the maximum size declared for the variable, the RDBMS generates the VALUE_ERROR exception. For example, assigning the last name 'Pantanizoupolos' to a VARCHAR2(10) raises an exception.

Constants

A *constant* is a fixed variable, which means you can't change its assigned value inside your program. To turn a variable into a constant, you simply include the CONSTANT keyword in the variable's declaration. Note that, by convention, constant variable names are usually uppercase. Here are some examples:

```
PI CONSTANT NUMBER := 3.14159;

YEARLY_WORK_HOURS CONSTANT NUMBER := 2000;

LINES_PER_PAGE CONSTANT NUMBER := 60;

OPEN_STATUS CONSTANT VARCHAR(1) := 'O';
```

The main use for constants is to replace a program's *magic values*—numbers or strings meaningful only to the programmer or business—with more easily understood names. For instance, the last example in the previous section used the number 2000 to calculate an annual salary. While we can often deduce the meaning of a magic value (in this case, the number of hours in the work year), it's just bad coding practice to randomly sprinkle your program with literals.

The problem with sticking these values directly into the code is that—believe it or not—constants can change. Your employer might decide to adopt a six-hour workday (perhaps a German conglomerate buys your company) and reduce the number of hours in the work year to 1500. Using literals, you would have to go through your code line by line and replace all the 2000s with 1500s. Constants eliminate this tedious make-work. We can simply create a constant called YEARLY_WORK_ HOURS, assign it a value of 2000, or 1500, or whatever value we want, and use it to clarify our calculations. This is shown in the following example:

```
annual_salary := hourly_rate * YEARLY_WORK_HOURS;
```

Conditionals

In this section, we'll look at how to create conditional statements. A conditional statement executes a code segment based on a condition, such as an equality test (a = b), a comparison test (a > b), or a Boolean test. PL/SQL has three conditional structures: IF-THEN, IF-THEN-ELSE, and IF-THEN-ELSIF-THEN-...-ELSE.

The IF-THEN format executes a code block if the condition is TRUE. For example:

```
IF line_count > LINES_PER_PAGE
THEN
    line_count := 0;
    DBMS_SQL.PUT_LINE ('--------');
END IF;
```

The IF-THEN-ELSE format has two code blocks. If the condition is TRUE, the first block is executed; otherwise, the second block is executed. For example:

```
IF items_sold > get_employee_target (emp_id)
THEN
    over_quota_count := over_quota_count + 1;
    give_raise (emp_id);
ELSE
    give_talking_to (emp_id);
END IF;
```

The IF-THEN-ELSIF-THEN-...-ELSE, PL/SQL's equivalent of the CASE or SWITCH statement, can contain multiple conditions. The statement executes the code block associated with the first TRUE condition. Here's an example:

```
IF    is_number (current_char)
   OR is_letter (current_char)
THEN
    new_char := current_char;
ELSIF  current_char = ' '
THEN
    new_char := '+';
ELSE
    new_char := convert_to_hex (current_char);
END IF;
```

Be careful with conditional syntax. Every PL/SQL programmer has made at least one of the following two mistakes: using END instead of END IF, or adding an "E" in the "ELSIF" keyword. In either case, the compiler gets confused and generates an error.

Loops

Looping, or iteration, causes the block between the keywords LOOP and END LOOP to be repeatedly executed. The loop ends, or terminates, when an exit condition is met. Once a loop terminates, program control is returned to the first line after the END LOOP keyword. There are three looping structures: simple, WHILE, and FOR.

In the simple loop, the exit condition is embedded inside the loop body. The EXIT command terminates the loop immediately, and is usually embedded inside an IF…THEN statement. EXIT WHEN combines EXIT with a conditional to form a more compact syntax. Here are two constructions of a simple loop. The first example uses EXIT:

```
LOOP
    COUNT := COUNT + 1;
    IF COUNT > 10
    THEN
        EXIT;
    END IF;
END LOOP;
```

The second example uses EXIT WHEN:

```
LOOP
    COUNT := COUNT + 1;
    EXIT WHEN COUNT > 10;
END LOOP;
```

In the second kind of loop, the WHILE loop, the exit condition is outside the body of the loop. The code within the body of the loop iterates while the loop condition is true. The loop terminates when the condition is false, for example:

```
WHILE (COUNT <= 10)
LOOP
    COUNT := COUNT + 1;
END LOOP;
```

The last kind of loop, the FOR loop, iterates a predetermined number of times. For example, the number of loops needed to process each month in the year does not depend on a complex condition; it always requires 12 passes through the loop. A FOR loop is controlled by an index variable that ranges from a lower bound to an upper bound. The index variable begins at the lower bound. Each pass through the loop increments it. The loop terminates when the index reaches the upper bound, for example:

```
FOR month_index IN 1 .. 12
LOOP
    process_month_sales (month_index);
END LOOP;
```

There are a few things to be aware of when using FOR loops:

- The lower bound and upper bound are evaluated only once, on the first pass through the loop. Changes made to the bounds inside the body, assuming they are local variables, are ignored.

- It's generally considered bad practice to use the EXIT command to short cir-
  cuit the fixed nature of the FOR loop. If the number of loops depends on a
  condition, then a simple loop or WHILE loop is a clearer construct than a FOR
  loop.

Cursors

A *cursor* is a PL/SQL construct used to process a SQL statement one row at a time.
Each cursor is associated with a SELECT statement and a number of attributes. The
SELECT statement defines a virtual table called the *result set* that contains all the
rows of the underlying SELECT statement. The cursor's attributes provide information about the cursor's structure and current status.

The first step in the life of most cursors is a two-part declaration. The first part of
the declaration names the cursor and binds it to a SELECT statement. The second
part uses this name and a cursor attribute to create a PL/SQL data structure that
holds the rows of the result set. Once these two elements are declared, the cursor
is ready for processing, which requires three steps:

1. The cursor is opened by executing the query and building the result set.

2. Each row in the result is processed inside the body of a loop by fetching the
   current row of the result set into the PL/SQL data structure. Each fetch
   advances the current row pointer.

3. The cursor is closed and the memory taken by the result set is freed.

Let's look at declaring and processing a cursor in more detail.

Declaring a cursor

The declaration of a cursor binds a name to a SQL SELECT statement. In addition
to the cursor declaration itself, you'll also need to declare a variable that will hold
the information read from the cursor, since the cursor is only a pointer to a row,
not the row itself. This variable, declared as a *record*, holds data from the current
row of the cursor.

A record is similar to a row in a table; it is a single entity made up of named fields,
exactly as a row is composed of columns. Each field has its own datatype. The
syntax for referencing a field is similar to the syntax used for referencing a table
column; it requires the name of the record, a period, and the name of the field.

The simplest way to create a record is to anchor it to the cursor's structure using
the %ROWTYPE attribute. The following example shows the declaration for a cursor and a record variable to hold its results:

```
CURSOR emp_cur
IS
```

```
SELECT *
  FROM emp
  ORDER BY lname;
```

```
emp_rec emp_cur%ROWTYPE;
```

You can limit the rows returned in a cursor by using variables in the statement's WHERE clause. You can also include parameters as part of the declaration of a cursor itself. The syntax for declaring a parameter is the same as for procedures and functions. This is useful when you want to create a modular cursor declaration shared by a number of modules. For instance, to limit the previous example to a single individual, we could pass a primary key as a parameter (the record is still required, even if there is just one row in the result set):

```
CURSOR emp_cur (id IN NUMBER)
IS
    SELECT *
      FROM emp
      WHERE emp.emp_id = id;
```

```
emp_rec emp_cur%ROWTYPE;
```

Processing a cursor

You can process the rows of a cursor after you declare it. The first step in the process is the OPEN command, which executes the query and builds the result set. The OPEN command takes the name of the cursor to open, and must also provide values for any of the cursor's parameters. The syntax for passing cursor parameters is the same as that for procedures and functions:

```
OPEN emp_cur;
```

```
OPEN emp_cur(102);
```

Once the cursor is open, its individual rows can be processed. Usually, this happens within a loop. The FETCH statement pulls the current row from the result set into the PL/SQL record and advances the current pointer to the next record. The values of the FOUND and NOTFOUND cursor attributes indicate whether the most recent fetch returned a row and can be used as the exit condition for the loop. The cursor is positioned immediately before the first row when it is opened. Once the row is fetched into a record data structure, its individual columns can be used just like local variables. Once the records are processed, the cursor must be closed using the CLOSE command. For example:

```
/* Formatted by PL/Formatter v.1.1.13 */
CREATE OR REPLACE PROCEDURE print_emps
IS

    CURSOR emp_cur
    IS
```

```
      SELECT *
        FROM emp
        ORDER BY lname;

   emp_rec emp_cur%ROWTYPE;

BEGIN
   OPEN emp_cur;   -- open the cursor
   LOOP
      FETCH emp_cur INTO emp_rec;
      EXIT WHEN emp_cur%notfound;   -- exit condition
      /*
      || Print employee information. Note that the syntax for the
      || field names uses the record variable, not the cursor.
      */
      HTP.print (emp_rec.lname);
      HTP.print (get_department_name (emp_rec.dpt_id));
      HTP.print (emp_rec.lname);
   END LOOP;
   CLOSE emp_cur;
END;
```

As another example, here is a formal implementation of a slightly modified version of the get_emp_info procedure. In this example, only one fetch is necessary, so there is no need for a loop. However, the procedure must test to see if a matching record was found before it returns a value. This is done using the FOUND attribute:

```
/* Formatted by PL/Formatter v.1.1.13 */
/*
|| Procedure to return employee information
|| for the passed employee id
|| Parameters
|| ----------
||    e_id      IN  - employee to return (primary key)
||    e_num     OUT - employee number
||    e_name    OUT - employee name
||    e_dpt_id  OUT - employee'sn department name
*/
CREATE OR REPLACE PROCEDURE get_emp_info (
   e_id IN NUMBER,
   e_num OUT VARCHAR2,
   e_name OUT VARCHAR2,
   e_dpt_id OUT NUMBER
   )
IS

   -- Tests for the parameter value in the WHERE clause
   CURSOR emp_cur
   IS
      SELECT *
        FROM emp
        WHERE emp.emp_id = e_id;
```

```
      emp_rec emp_cur%ROWTYPE;

BEGIN
   OPEN emp_cur;
   FETCH emp_cur INTO emp_rec;
   IF emp_cur%found
   THEN
      e_num := emp_rec.emp_number;
      e_name := emp_rec.fname || ' ' || emp_rec.lname;
      e_dpt_id := emp_rec.dpt_id;
   ELSE
      e_num := NULL;
      e_name := NULL;
      e_dpt_id := NULL;
   END IF;
   CLOSE emp_cur;
END get_emp_info;
```

Implicit cursors

The previous examples were all *explicit cursors*. We declared the cursor, opened it, processed its rows, then closed it. There is a second type of hidden cursor called an *implicit cursor* that allows us to skip these steps. The SELECT...INTO command, which programmers use to save time, is the most common example of an implicit cursor. Here's an example that loads information from a table into a local variable, all in one step:

```
SELECT emp_rec.emp_number,
       emp_rec.fname || ' ' || emp_rec.lname,
       emp_rec.dpt_id
  INTO e_num, e_name, e_dpt_id
  FROM emp
 WHERE emp.emp_id = e_id;
```

Despite its brevity, there are three reasons to avoid SELECT...INTO:

* SELECT...INTO is slower than an explicit cursor because it makes two fetches instead of one. The first fetch determines how many rows the query returns, and the second fetch actually retrieves the data and assigns the columns to the variables.

* SELECT...INTO raises an exception if the underlying query doesn't return exactly one row. If it returns no rows, it raises the NO_DATA_FOUND exception. If it finds more than one row, it raises the TOO_MANY_ROWS exception. This behavior often results in unhandled exceptions, because the harried programmer, in a rush to finish, makes a wrong assumption about the query.

* SELECT...INTO makes you lazy. We should take positive steps to prevent foreseeable errors, not simply respond to them as if they're uncontrollable acts of God. The extra time it takes to implement a single-row SELECT using an explicit cursor almost always outweighs the short-term benefits of the SELECT... INTO command.

Index-by Tables (Arrays)

The last construct we'll look at is the index-by table, PL/SQL's version of an array (prior to Oracle8*i*, these were called PL/SQL tables). Like a true array, an index-by table is made up of elements indexed by unique integers. This, however, is about as far as the analogy goes. Table 6-1 summarizes the difference between real arrays and index-by tables.

Table 6-1. Differences Between Real Arrays and Index-by Tables

Real Array	Index-by Table
Multidimensional.	One-dimensional.
Contains a fixed number of elements.	Contains an "unlimited" number of elements.
Memory is allocated for every element in the array, even if it's never used.	Memory is allocated only when an element is added.
Elements are consecutive (i.e., a(1), a(2), a(3) . . . a(N)).	Elements are non-consecutive (i.e., a(1), a(5632), a(1013), a(999), . . .).

In reality, an index-by table is much closer to a linked-list or single-column table than to an array. Despite this (or because of it, depending on the application), it's an extremely useful construct with a wide range of applications. In this section, we'll see how to declare an array, assign values to its elements, and then retrieve the values.

Creating an index-by table

There are two steps in creating an index-by table. The first is to define a new datatype for the table. The second is to declare the actual table variable itself by assigning it to the new table datatype created in the first step.

You define a table's datatype by placing the following command in the declaration section of a procedure or function:[*]

```
TYPE table_type_name IS TABLE OF element_datatype
    INDEX BY BINARY_INTEGER;
```

The *table_type_name* is the name of the index-by table datatype (not the name of the table variable itself), and the *element_datatype* specifies the type of elements the table contains. These elements can be declared as simple scalar datatypes, such as strings, or as more complex types (in Oracle 7.3 and above), such as records. However, you can only pass scalar types from the Web. You can either define the type directly (for example, by declaring it as a NUMBER) or use an

---

[*] You can also declare the type in a package specification or body. We'll see how to do this in the next section.

anchored declaration to link it to a table in a column. Here are a few examples of declaring an index-by table datatype:

```
TYPE monthly_sales_type IS TABLE OF NUMBER
    INDEX BY BINARY_INTEGER;

TYPE ssn_array_type IS TABLE OF VARCHAR2(9)
    INDEX BY BINARY_INTEGER;

TYPE emp_array_type IS TABLE OF emp.lname%TYPE
    INDEX BY BINARY_INTEGER;
```

You can create a table variable after you've defined the table datatype. These are like normal variable declarations, except that they use the datatypes you defined in the previous step. Here are a few examples of creating a table variable:

```
sales_by_month monthly_sales_type;

ssn_array ssn_array_type;

emp_name_array emp_array_type;
```

You can begin adding elements to the table after you have created its type and an associated variable.

Adding elements to an index-by table

You assign values to an index-by table by associating its elements with unique integer indexes. The syntax is similar to that used in C or Pascal. Here are some examples for a table of string elements:

```
emp_name_array (16)   := 'albee';
emp_name_array (21)   := 'mcmanus';
emp_name_array (1043) := 'jenkins';
emp_name_array (1013) := 'harrington';
```

Unlike most 3GL languages, where the index is a fixed offset from the start of the array, the index of an index-by table is basically a primary key. Assigning an element for the first time is similar to inserting a record into a normal database table. Subsequent changes to the value are like UPDATE statements.

Retrieving elements from an index-by table

You retrieve the value for an element using the same syntax you would for a 3GL language. Here are a few examples:

```
HTP.print (emp_name_array (21));
HTP.print (emp_name_array (1013));
IF emp_name_array (1043) = 'jenkins'
THEN
    HTP.print ('Hi, Garry.');
END IF;
```

There is one major difference between the retrieval of an index-by table element and a 3GL array element: you can only retrieve elements to which you have previously assigned values. The retrieval process is a lot like the SELECT...INTO statement we looked at in the section on cursors: the RDBMS raises a NO_DATA_FOUND exception if the element doesn't exist. To prevent this, make sure you initialize your arrays before you use them.

Packages

Now that we've looked at PL/SQL's structure and its most common programming constructs, we're ready to group these elements into tidy little structures called packages. A *package* is a container (hence the name) for other PL/SQL elements, such as variables and constants, procedures and functions, and datatype definitions.

A package has two parts: a specification and a body. The specification is a sort of table of contents that lists the items in the package. The body contains the implementations for each item. For example, the specification tells us "This package contains a procedure named 'foo', which has the following parameters." The body of the package contains the actual implementation of foo.

Packages are the most powerful and useful PL/SQL constructs because they help us build standard code libraries with well-defined application programming interfaces (APIs). In a web environment, for example, you can create standard libraries to handle security, page formatting, or list of values (LOV) generation. Each time you build a new application, you can just plunk in calls to these standard libraries, rather than reinventing them for each new system. Packages are also excellent for building abstract data types (ADTs), a fancy terminology for structures like stacks, lists, and queues.

Prebuilt packages with clear APIs encourage software reuse, the Holy Grail of software engineering. In this final section, we'll learn how to use packages effectively. We'll start by looking at the structure of the specification and the body, and then move on to how to use a package within other programs. After that, we'll look at how to hide the implementation details of a package to create a "black box." Finally, we'll look at package persistence.

The Package Specification

The specification defines the package's API, which governs every aspect of how the package is used. The specification lists the headers of the procedures and functions in the API, as well as any variables, types, cursors, or constants necessary to interface with the package. These last items are global variables, accessible both from inside and outside the package. The headers and declarations in the specification are called *public* elements because they are the interface between the package and the outside world.

You might see the specification as an afterthought, if not a downright nuisance, that stands in the way of your real work. Nothing could be further from the truth. The success or failure of a package almost always depends on a clean, crisp interface that is simple to understand and use.

The Package Body

The package body contains the actual code for the modules in the specification. It must include a complete implementation of each of these modules. Additionally, it can also include procedures and functions not listed in the specification, as well as declarations for variables, types, cursors, and constants. These elements, invisible to the outside world, are *private* because they can be referenced only from within the body itself.

Example

Designing a good package takes practice. A package should be rich enough to support a wide variety of complex activities, yet simple enough to grasp quickly. As with any other art, the best place to learn package design is from the classics, so in this section we'll create a stack package based on an index-by table. Here's the specification:

```
/* Formatted by PL/Formatter v.1.1.13 */
CREATE OR REPLACE PACKAGE stack
IS

   /*------------------------------------------------------
   || Global type declaration
   */------------------------------------------------------
   TYPE stack_array IS TABLE OF VARCHAR2(2000)
      INDEX BY BINARY_INTEGER;

   /*------------------------------------------------------
   || Global API declaration
   */------------------------------------------------------
   -- Initialize the stack
   PROCEDURE init;

   -- Push an item onto the stack
   PROCEDURE push (item IN VARCHAR2);

   -- Return the first element on the stack
   FUNCTION pop
      RETURN VARCHAR2;
```

```
        -- Return a boolean if the stack is empty
        FUNCTION is_empty
           RETURN BOOLEAN;

        -- Copy the stack into an array
        PROCEDURE copy_to_array (
           s OUT stack_array,
           num_elements OUT NUMBER
           );

     END stack;
```

Our next step is to actually implement each of the procedures and functions listed in the specification. Here's the body of the stack package:

```
/* Formatted by PL/Formatter v.1.1.13 */
CREATE OR REPLACE PACKAGE BODY stack
IS

   /*-------------------------------------------------------
   || Local declarations
   */-------------------------------------------------------
   -- Declare stack data structure
   local_stack stack_array;
   -- Declare index to top of stack
   top NUMBER DEFAULT 0;

   /*-------------------------------------------------------
   || Implementation
   */-------------------------------------------------------

   /*
   || Initialize the stack
   */
   PROCEDURE init
   IS
   BEGIN
      top := 0;
   END init;

   /*
   || Push an item onto the stack.
   || Since PL/SQL arrays are unconstrained, we never have
   || to worry about pushing too many elements!
   */
   PROCEDURE push (item IN VARCHAR2)
   IS
   BEGIN
      top := top + 1;
      local_stack  (top) := item;
   END push;

   /*
   || Return a boolean if the stack is empty
```

```
*/
FUNCTION is_empty
   RETURN BOOLEAN
IS
BEGIN
   IF top = 0
   THEN
      RETURN TRUE;
   ELSE
      RETURN FALSE;
   END IF;
END is_empty;

/*
|| Return the first element on the stack.
|| Return NULL if the stack is empty.
*/
FUNCTION pop
   RETURN VARCHAR2
IS
   item_to_return VARCHAR2(2000);
BEGIN
   IF is_empty
   THEN
      item_to_return := NULL;
   ELSE
      item_to_return := local_stack (top);
      top := top - 1;
   END IF;
   RETURN item_to_return;
END pop;

/*
|| Copy the stack into an array
*/
PROCEDURE copy_to_array (
   s OUT stack_array,
   num_elements OUT NUMBER
   )
IS
BEGIN
   -- Set the number of elements
   num_elements := top;
   -- Load each element into the array
   FOR i IN 1 .. top
   LOOP
      s  (i) := local_stack (i);
   END LOOP;
END copy_to_array;

END stack;
```

Using a Package

After we've created the package specification and body, we can start using it in other procedures and functions. You use the following syntax to refer to a public element (variable, procedure, function, etc.) in a package:

```
package_name.public_element_name
```

The following sample illustrates how to use the stack package developed in the last section:

```
/* Formatted by PL/Formatter v.1.1.13 */
CREATE OR REPLACE PROCEDURE test_stack
IS
   stack_copy stack.stack_array;
   stack_size NUMBER;
BEGIN
   --Push some test data onto the stack
   FOR i IN 1 .. 10
   LOOP
      stack.push (i);
   END LOOP;

   -- Make a copy of the stack

   stack.copy_to_array (stack_copy, stack_size);

   -- Pop all elements off the stack
   WHILE NOT stack.is_empty
   LOOP
      DBMS_OUTPUT.put_line (stack.pop);
   END LOOP;

   -- Print the copied elements
   FOR i IN 1 .. stack_size
   LOOP
      DBMS_OUTPUT.put_line (stack_copy (i));
   END LOOP;

END test_stack;
```

Information Hiding

You might have noticed in the stack example that we declared the local_stack and the top variable inside the body, rather than in the specification. This is an example of *information hiding,* a technique that's used to hide a package's implementation details from its users.

A package should be a black box; input comes in one side and predictable output goes out the other. The details between these steps should be invisible to everyone except the package's developer. It's amazing how often knowing how something works can get us into trouble. How many times have you written one program to

take advantage of a bug in another? These shortcuts turn bugs into permanent fix-
tures. Information hiding eliminates the possibility of this problem by forcing everyone to use the package the way it was intended to be used.

Access to the internal workings of a package can cause problems even when the
workaround seems perfectly innocent. To return to our original example, if the
local_stack and top variables in the stack example were declared in the package
specification, and not hidden away in the body, a developer in a rush might be
tempted to write a program to bypass the stack directly, as you can see here:

```
/*
|| Quick procedure to print stack
*/
CREATE OR REPLACE PROCEDURE show_stack
   i NUMBER DEFAULT 0;
IS
BEGIN
   FOR i IN REVERSE 1 .. STACK.top
   LOOP
      DBMS_OUTPUT.put_line (STACK.local_stack (i));
   END LOOP;
END;
```

This shortcut depends on the stack being implemented as an index-by table. If we
decided to redesign the package to represent the stack in another way (for example, using an object type we can store directly in the database), it would break this
program and every other program that made a similar use of the package's public
data structures.

Variable Persistence Throughout a Session

Package variables, whether they are declared in the specification or the body,
maintain their values throughout a session. All values are initialized when a session begins and are lost when it ends. This is called *persistence* because the values remain, or persist, even when the package is not being directly used. Only
package variables declared as part of the specification or body persist. Variables
declared inside a procedure or function do not.

For example, suppose you log into SQL*Plus and push a few elements onto the
stack. After that, you execute a few SELECT statements, issue some updates, and
describe a table or two. Finally, before you're ready to log out, you call the test_
stack procedure. When it executes, not only does it print "1" through "10," it also
prints the elements you manually added at the beginning of the session. PL/SQL
remembered the previous elements, even though you've been doing other things.
However, if you logged out and reconnected before running the test_stack procedure, the previous elements disappear, because variables persist only throughout a
single session.

In Chapter 7, *The PL/SQL Toolkit*, we'll look at some strategies to mimic persistence in the web environment.

PL/SQL Tools

There are many tools you can use to improve your PL/SQL development productivity. Table 6-2 shows some of the more popular, along with the web sites where they can be found, so you can download and experiment. In the following subsections, we'll look at two of the most helpful tools, TOAD and PL/Formatter.

Table 6-2. Some Handy PL/SQL Development Tools

Tool	Web Site
CAST Workbench	*http://www.castsoftware.com*
FROG (Funky Resource for Oracle Gorillas)	*http://www.507pm.com/pcs*
Oracle Procedure Builder	*http://www.oracle.com*
PLEdit	*http://www.benthicsoftware.com*
PL/Formatter	*http://www.revealnet.com*
SQL/Expediter	*http://www.compuware.com*
SQL Navigator	*http://www.quests.com*
SQL*Object Builder	*http://www.idb-consulting.fr*
SQL Programmer	*http://www.sfi-software.com*
SQL Station	*http://www.platinum.com*
TOAD (Tool for Oracle Application Developers)	*http://www.toadsoft.com*

TOAD

In the bad old days, developers wrote their PL/SQL programs with a text editor like vi or Notepad, then compiled them with SQL*Plus. If the program failed to compile because of a syntax error, about the only tool you had to help track down the error was the SQL command:

```
SELECT * FROM user_errors
```

Even then, you got little more information than a generic Oracle syntax error and an approximate line number where the error might have occurred. You had to go back to the code and hunt and peck to find the problem. It could take hours to track down a misplaced quote mark or a misspelled keyword (ELSEIF instead of ELSIF was really hard to find).

Fortunately, third-party PL/SQL editors like TOAD (Tool for Oracle Application Developers) have changed all that. TOAD is a SQL and PL/SQL editor, object browser, query analyzer, and table data editor (finally, a tool that lets you enter data into a table in spreadsheet format!) all rolled into one. Figure 6-1 shows TOAD's PL/SQL editor.

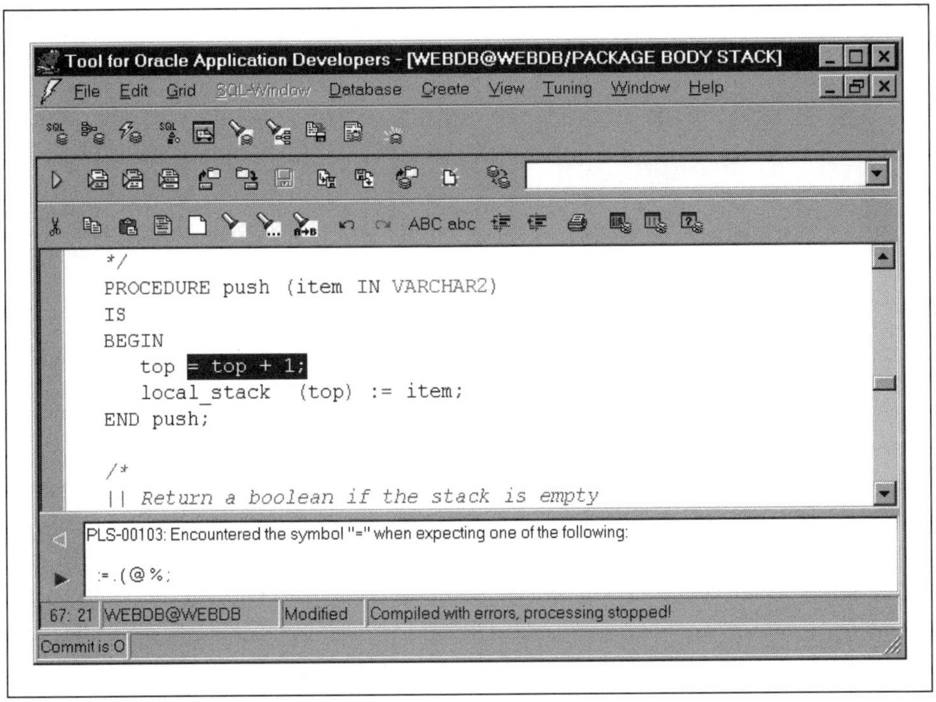

Figure 6-1. The TOAD PL/SQL Editor

Frankly, TOAD is awesome, and if you're doing any Oracle development, whether related to the Web or not, it's a must-have tool. Perhaps the most unbelievable thing about TOAD is that you can get it for free! Originally written by Jim McDaniel ("The Toadman") as freeware, TOAD is now fully supported by Quest Software, a maker of other Oracle tools. The downside is that the free version is no longer being updated with new features, so it doesn't support the new Oracle8/8*i* features. However, free is a very reasonable price! You can download the freeware version from *http://www.toadsoft.com*, and the commercially supported version from *http://www.quests.com/toad/toad_info.html*.

PL/Formatter

PL/Formatter, another productivity tool, is a PL/SQL code formatter from RevealNet (*http://www.revealnet.com*). PL/Formatter "pretty-prints" ugly, mangled code into the format recommended by Steven Feuerstein, the guru of PL/SQL development.

In addition to just satisfying your aesthetic sensibilities, well-formatted source code helps make your programs more readable and maintainable. Figure 6-2 shows PL/Formatter in action; the top half of the screen shows the original code and the bottom half shows the code after it's been reformatted.

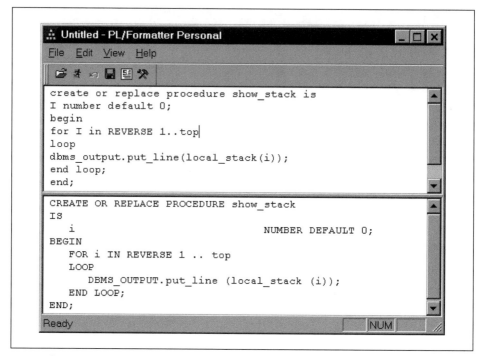

Figure 6-2. RevealNet's PL/Formatter

In this chapter:
• *Communicating with the Outside World*
• *Text Processing*
• *Maintaining State*
• *Improving Productivity*

7

The PL/SQL Toolkit

The PL/SQL toolkit is a set of PL/SQL packages supplied by Oracle for use in developing web applications. These packages are used to generate HTML dynamically, perform text operations, and improve developer productivity. Table 7-1 shows an alphabetical listing of the packages included in the PL/SQL toolkit, along with an explanation of their uses.

Table 7-1. PL/SQL Toolkit Packages

Package Name	Use
HTF	Parses HTML
HTP	Generates HTML
OWA_COOKIE	Stores cookies
OWA_OPT_LOCK	Performs record locking
OWA_PATTERN	Searches and replaces text
OWA_SEC	Manages security
OWA_TEXT	Represents text
OWA_UTIL	Improves productivity

The sections that follow group these packages in categories according to their functionality. HTF and HTP are used for communicating with the outside world; OWA_TEXT and OWA_PATTERN are used for text processing; OWA_COOKIE and OWA_OPT_LOCK are used for maintaining state. The last two packages, OWA_UTIL and OWA_SEC, are used for maintaining productivity and security.

In addition to learning how to use dozens of procedures, we'll keep an eye on what these packages can teach us about good design. After all, the developers who created these packages are some of the most talented PL/SQL programmers in the world. We would be wise to learn from their examples.

Communicating with the Outside World

When scripting languages like Perl are used to develop dynamic resources, their output is sent to the standard output (*stdout*) device, then funneled back to the browser. Because PL/SQL cannot communicate directly with *stdout*, the toolkit includes a package, called HTP, that mimics this behavior.

HTP: Generating HTML

The HTP package is a sort of web-enabled version of DBMS_OUTPUT, a built-in package that provides basic output capabilities such as printing text. Like DBMS_OUTPUT, HTP contains commands that store text in a buffer. When a procedure using the package terminates, the contents of the output buffer are "printed" and returned to the user. This buffering is one difference between PL/SQL toolkit programs and standard CGI programs, which immediately return output to the user. As such, the size of the buffer limits the size of a page. In most cases, this is not a problem; however, you should be aware that if you choose to dump a million-row table onto a single page, you will quickly encounter this limit. Table 7-2 shows the procedures included in the HTP package; HTP also includes a large number of wrapper procedures that correspond to various HTML tags.

Table 7-2. Various HTP Procedures

Procedure	Parameters	Description
ANCHOR	Depend on tag	Generates an anchor tag
PRINT	Any value	Outputs any value passed as a parameter
Various wrapper procedures (e.g., HTMLOPEN)	Depend on tag	Simplifies coding of an HTML tag

The HTP procedure PRINT, which is analogous to DBMS_OUTPUT.PUT_LINE, simply outputs the value that is passed as a parameter. Here, for example, is a procedure that generates a page that prints "Hello, World!":

```
CREATE OR REPLACE PROCEDURE hello_world
IS
BEGIN
   HTP.print ('<html>');
   HTP.print ('<head>');
   HTP.print ('<title>You knew it was coming...</title>');
   HTP.print ('</head>');
   HTP.print ('<!-- ');
   HTP.print ('This phrase is in every computer book.');
   HTP.print ('--!>');
   HTP.print ('<body bgcolor=blue>');
   HTP.print ('And here it is .... Hello, World!');
   HTP.print ('</body>');
   HTP.print ('</html>');
END;
```

More sophisticated tags require parameters to be included in the wrapper procedure. Each parameter corresponds to a particular tag attribute. As a general rule, a
parameter is named after the HTML attribute it represents and is used to complete
a template based on the tag's syntax. This parameter can take any valid PL/SQL
value, including a literal, variable, concatenation, or function. Optional attributes
are declared as DEFAULT NULL.

To make the HTML syntax more palatable to Oracle developers, HTP has a number of specialized wrapper procedures that correspond to individual tags. These
procedures hide HTML's ugly syntax from developers, who are more familiar with
PL/SQL and other 3GLs. For example, rather than embedding <html> directly into
a program, as we've done in the previous example, the HTP package provides a
more aesthetically pleasing procedure called HTMLOPEN to perform the same
function. Other HTP wrapper procedures include HTP.HTMLCLOSE for </html>,
and HTP.HEADOPEN and HTP.HEADCLOSE for <head> and </head>, respectively.

Although there are many benefits in using an API to isolate programs against
underlying changes, the wrapper procedures often cause more problems than they
prevent. During development, you may find yourself flipping through manuals to
figure out the order of a particular procedure's parameters or trying to match some
obscure tag to its toolkit equivalent. Once you locate the procedure, you often
find that there is no clear way to create the complex nesting required by many of
the most useful tags, such as those for forms or tables. In general, code is simply
much more readable if you can see the actual HTML, rather than hiding it away
behind a complex API.

By convention, the parameters for these attributes are preceded by a single character indicating the parameter's datatype. VARCHAR2 parameters, denoted by a "c,"
are by far the most common. "N" and "d" denote, respectively, the integer and
date datatypes, and appear mainly in overloaded or specialized procedures.

Here, for example, is the declaration—as it appears in the HTP specification—for a
wrapper procedure that generates an anchor (<a>) tag:

```
PROCEDURE anchor (
    curl IN VARCHAR2,
    ctext IN VARCHAR2,
    cname IN VARCHAR2 DEFAULT NULL,
    cattributes IN VARCHAR2 DEFAULT NULL
    )
```

The parameter values are used to complete a template based on the tag the procedure represents. The ANCHOR procedure has the following template:

```
<a href="curl" name="cname" cattributes>ctext</a>
```

Calling the ANCHOR procedure with the following values returns a link to the O'Reilly home page on the Web:

```
HTP.anchor (
   'www.oreilly.com',
   'O' || CHR (39) || 'Reilly Homepage',
   'oreilly_link',
   'target=_blank'
);
```

The URL for the link is *http://www.oreilly.com*, its name is *oreilly_link*, and its text (the part that shows up on the user's screen) is "O'Reilly Homepage." The call uses the cattributes parameter to cause the page to open in a new window. Since HTML has such a flexible syntax that a tag may have dozens of optional attributes, most of the procedures in the HTP package include the cattributes parameter as a sort of catch-all within the tag. Here is the URL returned by the call:

```
<A HREF='www.oreilly.com' NAME='oreilly_link' target=blank>O'Reilly Homepage</A>
```

Individually, these commands are of limited use. You can combine the various procedures, however, to create a complete page. Here is the "Hello, World" program written using the procedures from HTP:

```
CREATE OR REPLACE PROCEDURE hello_world2
IS
BEGIN
   HTP.htmlopen;
   HTP.headopen;
   HTP.title ('You knew it was coming...');
   HTP.headclose;
   HTP.comment ('This phrase is in every computer book.');
   HTP.bodyopen (cattributes => 'body bgcolor=blue');
   HTP.print ('And here it is .... Hello, World!');
   HTP.bodyclose;
   HTP.htmlclose;
END;
```

The other wrapper procedures in the package work in exactly the same way as the ANCHOR procedure. In the next section, we'll concentrate on how to make the best use of the wrapper procedures, rather than focus on the gritty details of their API.

WebAlchemy

As you can imagine, developing sophisticated interfaces by translating raw HTML into its PL/SQL equivalent is enormously tedious. Fortunately, there is a free tool that does much of this work: WebAlchemy, written by Alan Hobbs of Oracle Consulting, Australia, translates a static HTML file into a corresponding PL/SQL procedure. By combining WebAlchemy with any of the dozens of GUI-based HTML editors, you can create complex screens in PL/SQL quickly and easily.

WebAlchemy is simple enough to use that you probably won't even need any documentation. Figure 7-1 shows the main screen, whose menu options should be familiar to any user of PC software. Using the program is simply a matter of opening an HTML file and using the "Generate PL/SQL" option to generate a corresponding procedure. Figure 7-1 illustrates this procedure. The raw HTML file, *hello_world.html*, appears on the left panel; the right panel shows the PL/SQL procedure created by the "Generate PL/SQL" option.

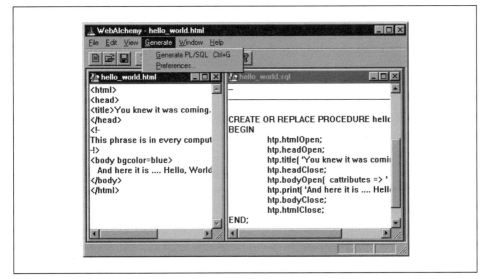

Figure 7-1. WebAlchemy main screen

You can download WebAlchemy from:

    http://www.users.bigpond.com/ahobbs/

At first blush, WebAlchemy inspires a sense of euphoria, because it promises to eliminate the need to know both HTML and the PL/SQL toolkit. However, although WebAlchemy is useful for creating static pages whose layout is known ahead of time, most programs generate documents dynamically from information stored in a table. There is simply no getting around the fact that you must understand how to manually construct an HTML document. Fortunately, this is not particularly difficult.

HTF: Parsing HTML

The HTF package turns HTP procedures into functions that return the HTML output as a formatted string. Table 7-3 summarizes the functions available in the HTF package.

Table 7-3. Various HTF Functions

Function	Parameters	Description
ANCHOR	Depend on tag	Stores anchor tag as a string
PRINT	Any value	Stores any value in a string

For example, the following procedure stores the results of the HTF.ANCHOR function in a string, and then uses the PL/SQL built-in SUBSTR function to print the result on two lines, using the DBMS_OUTPUT package:

```
CREATE OR REPLACE PROCEDURE htf_test
IS
   anchor_string VARCHAR2(500);
BEGIN
   anchor_string :=
      HTF.anchor (
         'http://www.ora.com',
         'O' || CHR (39) || 'Reilly',
         'ora_link',
         'target=_blank'
      );
   DBMS_OUTPUT.put_line (SUBSTR (anchor_string, 1, 29));
   DBMS_OUTPUT.put_line (SUBSTR (anchor_string, 30, 50));
END;
```

Text Processing

The enormous popularity of Perl is due in large part to its sophisticated text processing capabilities. A single Perl command can replace dozens of PL/SQL INSTR and SUBSTR operations. Additionally, Perl's pattern matching capabilities are well suited for processing and validating the text entered into HTML forms.

The PL/SQL toolkit has two packages that bring a subset of these capabilities to PL/SQL. The first, OWA_TEXT, manipulates large chunks of text. The second, OWA_PATTERN, allows developers to use sophisticated search patterns to perform many of the text operations found in Perl.

Beyond their mere utility, these two packages are interesting examples of good package design. OWA_TEXT is similar to the abstract datatypes described in Chapter 6, *PL/SQL*. OWA_PATTERN builds on OWA_TEXT to create dozens of variations of the search and replace procedure, each useful in particular circumstances.

OWA_TEXT: Representing Text

The largest PL/SQL string can contain 32,767 characters. Unfortunately, there are many cases where we might like to process larger chunks of text. A document indexing system, for example, must almost certainly process files much larger than

32K.* The OWA_TEXT package overcomes the 32K limitation by breaking text streams into smaller pieces that are stored as elements in a PL/SQL array.

Additionally, it is often useful to treat the components of a string as a single entity (e.g., a sentence as an array of words). OWA_TEXT is ideal for this type of application. In practice, though, you'll probably not use OWA_TEXT directly; instead, it's used to provide more flexibility to the OWA_PATTERN package discussed later in this chapter.

Data structures

OWA_TEXT's specification declares four data structures. The first two, vc_arr and int_arr, are PL/SQL arrays that are the building blocks of the more complex types. vc_arr is a 32K string array; int_arr holds indexes to the interesting rows of vc_arr. The declarations for these two datatypes are:

```
TYPE vc_arr IS TABLE OF VARCHAR2(32767)
   INDEX BY BINARY_INTEGER;

TYPE int_arr IS TABLE OF INTEGER
   INDEX BY BINARY_INTEGER;
```

The third data structure, called multi_line, is used to store information about an entire text stream. multi_line contains three fields: a vc_arr array to hold the individual rows of the stream, an integer to hold the number of rows in the vc_arr array, and a Boolean flag to indicate the presence of a partial row. Its declaration is:

```
TYPE multi_line IS RECORD (
   rows vc_arr,
   num_rows INTEGER,
   partial_row BOOLEAN
);
```

The fourth data structure, row_list, is used to represent pointers into the rows in a multi_line structure. This structure is generally used by other toolkit packages, such as OWA_PATTERN, discussed later in this chapter. The declaration for the row_list structure is:

```
TYPE row_list IS RECORD (
   rows int_arr,
   num_rows INTEGER
);
```

Procedures

The procedures in OWA_TEXT define a limited set of operations similar to those of a classic linked list. There are procedures to create a new multi_line structure,

---

* The human resources dress code guidelines at some companies probably exceed a megabyte.

to add a new row onto the end of an existing structure, and even to print its contents. Table 7-4 summarizes these procedures:

Table 7-4. Various OWA_TEXT Procedures

Procedure	Parameters	Description
ADD2MULTI	stream IN VARCHAR2 mline OUT multi_line continue IN BOOLEAN DEFAULT TRUE	Appends the passed stream to the multi_line structure. If the continue flag is TRUE, the stream is appended to the last line of the multi_line array. If FALSE, the stream is appended as the last row.
NEW_MULTI	mline OUT multi_line	Creates a new, blank multi_line. There is also a functionalized version that returns an empty structure.
NEW_ROW_LIST	rlist IN row_list	Creates a new row_list structure. The command can be used as either a procedure or a function.
PRINT_MULTI	mline IN multi_line	Prints the content of the multi_line data structure using HTP.PRINT.
PRINT_ROW_ LIST	rlist IN row_list	Prints the row_list using HTP.PRINT.
STREAM2MULTI	stream IN VARCHAR2 mline OUT multi_line	Converts a VARCHAR2 into a multi_line.

Example

Let's look at a quick example that illustrates OWA_TEXT in action. The following procedure, TOKENIZE, uses OWA_TEXT to break apart and print the individual words in a sentence:

```
CREATE OR REPLACE PROCEDURE tokenize (
    sentence IN VARCHAR2 DEFAULT NULL
    )
IS
    mline OWA_TEXT.multi_line;
    i NUMBER;
    n NUMBER := LENGTH (sentence);
    c VARCHAR2(1);
BEGIN
    OWA_TEXT.new_multi (mline);    -- Initialize the structure
    FOR i IN 1 .. n
    LOOP
        c := SUBSTR (sentence, i, 1);    -- Fetch current character
        IF c = ' '
        THEN
            -- Add a new row if the character is a space
            OWA_TEXT.add2multi (c, mline, FALSE);
        ELSE
            -- Otherwise, append the character to the string
            OWA_TEXT.add2multi (c, mline);
        END IF;
```

```
END LOOP;
/*
|| Print individual words in sentence
*/
FOR i IN 1 .. mline.num_rows
LOOP
    HTP.print ('Word ' || i || ' is ');
    HTP.print (mline.rows (i) || '<br>');
END LOOP;
END;
```

The following HTML form is used to test the procedure; note how the `<textarea>` tag is used to supply the value for the sentence parameter.

```
<html>
<title>Test tokenizer procedure</title>
<body>
    Enter the text to tokenize:
    <form action="http://gandalf/agent_webtest/plsql/tokenize">
        <textarea name=sentence>Enter sentence here</textarea>
        <p>
        <input type=submit>
    </form>
</body>
</html>
```

Figure 7-2 shows the results of the TOKENIZE procedure. The image on the left shows the form used to submit the sentence; the image on the right shows the corresponding output generated by TOKENIZE.

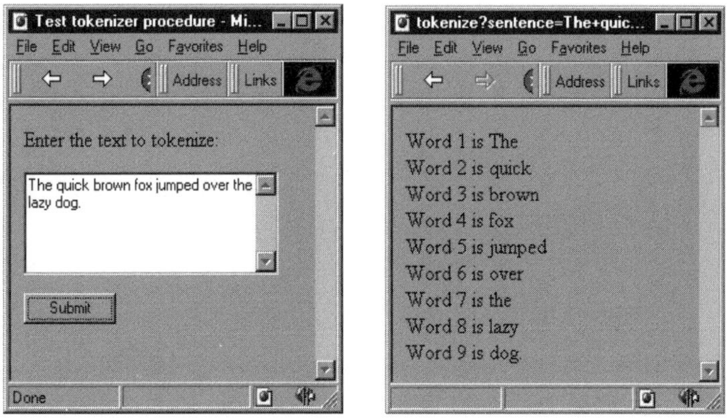

Figure 7-2. Results of the TOKENIZE procedure

Design note

In a classic ADT, such as the stack presented in Chapter 6, the datatypes would be hidden within the package body and would be accessible only through a programmatic interface. While this information hiding approach gives the developer strict control over how the package is used, it also makes it difficult to extend the package.

Although it seems like an obscure issue, the placement of the declaration has a profound impact on the life of the package. Declaring everything in the specification can make the package unwieldy and hard to maintain. The other extreme, declaring everything in the body and making nothing accessible, results in a package that is rigid and difficult to use in new circumstances.

OWA_TEXT resolves this tension admirably. By placing the declarations in the specification, the developers are consciously creating a general-purpose object that other packages can use. However, the package also contains a well-defined, private set of procedures that limit the operations that can be performed against its structures. In the next section, we'll see how the package is used to extend the toolkit's pattern searching capabilities.

OWA_PATTERN: Searching and Replacing Text

The OWA_PATTERN package is the second component of our text processing unit. As its name implies, OWA_PATTERN performs more complex text manipulation than is possible with PL/SQL's INSTR and SUBSTR functions. Regular expressions make this sophistication possible.

Regular expressions

A *regular expression*, or RegExp, is a compact description for a pattern of characters used to find matches within another string. Chances are you have used a simple RegExp to perform wildcard file searches using commands such as `dir *.sql` or `ls *.sql`. In these searches, instead of looking for a specific file, you are looking for any file that matches the *.sql* extension. In this case, the RegExp translates to the sentence "Any string of characters that ends in *.sql.*"

You can use regular expressions to create more sophisticated patterns. For example, suppose you want to take some action if any date appears within a string; you are only interested in its presence and do not know its value ahead of time. Clearly, the following INSTR test is not very effective:

```
IF   INSTR (some_string, '07/13/71')
  OR INSTR (some_string, '07/14/71')
  OR INSTR (some_string, '07/15/71')
  OR INSTR (some_string, '07/16/71') ...
```

What you are really after is a pattern consisting of three sets of two digits separated by slashes (for clarity, assume the date is always DD-MM-YY). A regular expression is a mini-language that uses a compact vocabulary to describe these patterns.

The first part of the RegExp vocabulary defines the different types of characters that can be matched, such as digits, letters, or tabs. These characters are sometimes called *atoms* because they form the basic building blocks on which the expressions are based. The atoms that can be used in OWA_PATTERN are shown in Table 7-5.

Table 7-5. Atoms Available in OWA_PATTERN

Atom	Description
.	Any character except newline (\n)
\n	Newline
\t	Tab
\d	Any digit (0 . . . 9)
\D	Any non-digit
\w	Any alphanumeric character (0 . . . 9, a . . . z, A . . . Z)
\W	Any nonalphanumeric character
\s	Any whitespace character (space, tab, or newline)
\S	Non-whitespace character
\b	Word boundary
\x$nn$	Character having the hexadecimal value nn (i.e., \x20 is a space)
\nnn	Character having the octal value nnn (i.e., \040 is a space)
\c	Any character matching c

The next part of the vocabulary defines how many characters must appear to constitute a match. For example, we may want to return a match only if there are exactly two consecutive digits. The characters in this set are called the *quantifiers*; the possibilities for them are shown in Table 7-6.

Table 7-6. Quantifiers Available in OWA_PATTERN

Quantifier	Description
?	Exactly zero or one occurrence of an atom
*	Zero or more occurrences of an atom
+	One or more occurrences of an atom
{n}	Exactly n occurrences of an atom
{n,}	At least n occurrences of an atom
{n,m}	At least n, but not more than m, occurrences of an atom

There are two possible *assertions*, or sets of characters used to fix the position of a match, as shown in Table 7-7.

Table 7-7. Assertions Available in OWA_PATTERN

Assertion	Description
^	Match must come at the start of the string.
$	Match must come at the end of the string.

Finally, the vocabulary of the regular expression contains a set of *flags* that are used to control the behavior of the search. Unlike the atoms, quantifiers, and assertions, these flags are not included as part of the RegExp itself. Instead, they are passed as a separate parameter to control how the various OWA_TEXT procedures behave. The two available flags are shown in Table 7-8.

Table 7-8. Flags Available in OWA_PATTERN

Flag	Description
I	The search is not case sensitive.
g	Used in the change procedure to specify a global search and replace.

There are additional special characters that remember the portions of the original string that was matched. The first special character, the ampersand (&), can be used during the replace phase of a search and replace operation. The & represents the original pattern found in a match; including it in a replace string recreates the original string of characters that matched the pattern. The second special character is a pair of parentheses. When a portion of a match sequence is enclosed in parentheses, the subsequent replace operation can remember each parenthesized match. These remembered strings are called *back references* (backrefs) and are stored in an array.

Data structures

You must supply a regular expression to each function in OWA_PATTERN. Initially, the pattern is stored as a simple VARCHAR2 string. In order to use the expression, however, OWA_PATTERN transforms it into a more useful format. This relatively time-consuming process converts the regular expression from a VARCHAR2 into a PL/SQL array, using the following declaration:

```
TYPE pattern IS TABLE OF VARCHAR2(4)
    INDEX BY BINARY_INTEGER;
```

Like many of the other data structures we've seen, pattern datatypes are initialized by calling a procedure. In this case, the procedure is called GET_PAT. There are two parameters to this procedure. The first is a VARCHAR2 string called arg that holds the regular expression to be parsed. The second is a pattern datatype (declared as an IN OUT mode parameter) to hold the resultant parsed pattern.

In the next section, we'll see once again how the toolkit's developers intentionally placed the declaration in the specification and not the body, even though it's a purely internal representation. This time, however, the intent is to improve the package's performance as well as its usability.

Procedures and functions

In addition to GET_PAT, the OWA_PATTERN package contains three other basic functions: MATCH, AMATCH, and CHANGE. In an attempt to match the enormous flexibility of Perl, each function has several overloaded versions that derive from the data structures found in OWA_TEXT. For example, the MATCH function can search either a simple VARCHAR2 string or the more complex multi_line data structure. This is a great example of the power and flexibility a good package can provide.

However, with 14 variations of just three functions, OWA_PATTERN reveals an API that just might be *too* complex. The next three sections describe the functions for this package, shown in Table 7-9. Keep in mind that some of these functions are like the finches on the Galapagos Islands: very specialized.

Table 7-9. Various OWA_PATTERN Procedures and Functions

Procedure/ Function	Parameters	Description
AMATCH	See Table 7-11 for details on overloaded versions.	Returns the position of the end of the first RegExp found within text
CHANGE	See Table 7-12 for details on overloaded versions.	Replaces matched pattern with a new string
GET_PAT	arg IN VARCHAR2 pat IN OUT pattern	Initializes a datatype
MATCH	See Table 7-10 for details on overloaded versions.	Returns a Boolean value indicating whether a RegExp was found inside text

The MATCH function. This function returns a Boolean value indicating whether a regular expression was found inside a chunk of text. There are six overloaded versions. The parameters for this function are:

line/mline

The text that is being searched, either a VARCHAR2 or an OWA_TEXT.MULTI_ LINE (in the latter case, the parameter is renamed mline).

pat

> The regular expression, either a VARCHAR2 or a pattern. If used as a pattern, the structure must be initialized with the GET_PAT procedure before it is passed as a parameter.

flags

> Controls the behavior of the search as described in Table 7-8; a VARCHAR2.

backrefs

> Optional parameter to hold back references when parentheses are used as part of the regular expression; an OWA_TEXT.VC_ARR.

rlist

> Identifies the rows in which a match was found; an OWA_TEXT.ROW_LIST (mandatory when the line parameter is an OWA_TEXT.MULTI_LINE).

Table 7-10 lists the formal parameters for each of the different versions of MATCH.

Table 7-10. Overloaded Versions of MATCH

Version	Parameters	Description
1	line IN VARCHAR2 pat IN VARCHAR2 flags IN VARCHAR2 DEFAULT NULL	The simplest of the versions; all parameters are VARCHAR2.
2	line IN VARCHAR2 pat IN OUT pattern flags IN VARCHAR2 DEFAULT NULL	In this version, the pat parameter is declared using the PATTERN datatype. This version optimizes multiple searches that use the same RegExp.
3	line IN VARCHAR2 pat IN VARCHAR2 backrefs OUT owa_text.vc_arr flags IN VARCHAR2 DEFAULT NULL	Version 1 with the optional backrefs parameter. When the function completes, the backrefs array contains the portions of the original string that matched the parentheses.
4	line IN VARCHAR2 pat IN VARCHAR2 backrefs OUT owa_text.vc_arr flags IN VARCHAR2 DEFAULT NULL	Version 2 with the optional backrefs parameter.
5	mline IN owa_text.multi_line pat IN VARCHAR2 rlist OUT owa_text.row_list flags IN VARCHAR2 DEFAULT NULL	In this version, the text string is a multi_line datatype rather than a VARCHAR2. The mline parameter must be initialized using the procedures described in the OWA_TEXT section.
6	mline IN owa_text.multi_line pat IN OUT pattern rlist OUT owa_text.row_list flags IN VARCHAR2 DEFAULT NULL	Same as version 5, but the pat parameter is declared as a pattern structure.

The AMATCH function. This function is similar to MATCH, except that it returns the position of the end of the first match found within the string.* The function returns 0 if no match is found. There are four overloaded versions; the parameters for each version are:

line

The text that is being searched; unlike the MATCH function, it is always a VARCHAR2.

from_loc

Starting position within the string for the search.

pat

The regular expression, either a VARCHAR2 or a pattern. If used as a pattern, the structure must be initialized with the GET_PAT procedure before it is passed as a parameter.

flags

Controls the behavior of the search as described in Table 7-8; a VARCHAR2.

backrefs

Optional parameter to hold back references when parentheses are used as part of the regular expression; an OWA_TEXT.VC_ARR.

Table 7-11 lists the four versions of AMATCH.

Table 7-11. Overloaded Versions of AMATCH

Version	Parameters	Description
1	line IN VARCHAR2 from_loc IN INTEGER pat IN VARCHAR2 flags IN VARCHAR2 DEFAULT NULL	The simplest of the versions; all parameters are VARCHAR2.
2	line IN VARCHAR2 from_loc IN INTEGER pat IN OUT pattern flags IN VARCHAR2 DEFAULT NULL	In this version, the pat parameter is declared using the PATTERN datatype.
3	line IN VARCHAR2 from_loc IN INTEGER pat IN VARCHAR2 backrefs OUT owa_text.vc_arr flags IN VARCHAR2 DEFAULT NULL	Version 1 with the optional backrefs parameter.
4	line IN VARCHAR2 from_loc IN INTEGER pat IN pattern backrefs OUT owa_text.vc_arr flags IN VARCHAR2 DEFAULT NULL	Version 2 with the optional backrefs parameter.

---

* INSTR, a similar function that's built into PL/SQL, returns the position of the first character of a match.

CHANGE. The CHANGE function or procedure searches a chunk of text for a pattern. When it finds a match, it replaces the matched substring with a new string. When used as a procedure, CHANGE simply updates the text with the appropriate matches. When used as a function, it makes the changes and returns the number of substitutions.

This second usage is questionable. When a function changes the value of a parameter, it violates the most important rule about functions: that a function should return exactly one value. By updating the parameters, CHANGE is essentially returning two values: one for the number of updates and another for the actual results of that update. Including an OUT mode parameter to the procedural version would probably have been a better design.

The parameters used in each version are:

line/mline
> The text that is being searched and replaced; either a VARCHAR2 or an OWA_TEXT.MULTI_LINE (in the latter case, the parameter is renamed mline).

from_str
> String to be replaced; always a VARCHAR2. Note that although the string represents a regular expression like the pat parameter in the MATCH and AMATCH functions, it cannot be used as a PATTERN datatype.

to_str
> The string that replaces from_str; always a VARCHAR2. An & character, when used anywhere in the string, is replaced by the original portion of the text line that matches the from_str pattern.

flags
> Controls the behavior of the search as described in Table 7-8; a VARCHAR2. If no value is specified (the default), only the first match is replaced. If the value "g" is used, it replaces all the matches.

Table 7-12 lists the four versions of CHANGE.

Table 7-12. Overloaded Versions of CHANGE

Version	Parameters	Description
1	line IN OUT VARCHAR2 from_str IN VARCHAR2 to_str IN VARCHAR2 flags IN VARCHAR2	Function that returns the number of substitutions made. After the function exits, the line parameter is updated with the results of the search and replace.
2	line IN OUT VARCHAR2 from_str IN VARCHAR2 to_str IN VARCHAR2 flags IN VARCHAR2	Procedural version of version 1.

Table 7-12. Overloaded Versions of CHANGE (continued)

Version	Parameters	Description
3	mline IN OUT owa_text.multi_line from_str IN VARCHAR2 to_str IN VARCHAR2 flags IN VARCHAR2	Function that returns the number of sub-stitutions made; the target text is declared as a multi_line structure.
4	mline IN OUT owa_text.multi_line from_str IN VARCHAR2 to_str IN VARCHAR2 flags IN VARCHAR2	Procedural version of version 3.

Example

As you can imagine, there are a lot of possible examples for the OWA_PATTERN package. However, it's not necessary to detail every one. Instead, let's focus on a single example, based on the CHANGE procedure, that allows you to test the effect of various regular expressions in search and replace operations.

The example procedure, regexp_test, accepts the parameters of version 1 of CHANGE and builds an HTML table that breaks the final page into two columns. The first column contains a data entry form with the fields necessary to test the CHANGE procedure. The second column displays the results of the CHANGE procedure when it is executed with the regexp_test procedure's parameters.

The interesting thing about this procedure is that it preserves the values entered when the user submits the form. This is accomplished by setting the form **action** attribute back to the regexp_test procedure. When the form is submitted, the procedure reconstructs the form using the input from the previous screen:

```
CREATE OR REPLACE PROCEDURE regexp_test (
    line IN OUT VARCHAR2 DEFAULT NULL,
    from_str IN VARCHAR2 DEFAULT NULL,
    to_str IN VARCHAR2 DEFAULT '<b>&</b>',
    flags IN VARCHAR2 DEFAULT NULL
    )
IS

BEGIN
    HTP.print ('<html><title>Pattern Test</title><body>');
    HTP.print ('<table border=1><tr><td>');    -- Used to format results
    HTP.print ('<form action=regexp_test>');
    HTP.print ('Line:<textarea name=line>' ||
                line ||
                '</textarea><br>');
    HTP.print ('From:<input name=from_str value="' ||
                from_str ||
                '"><br>');
    HTP.print ('To:<input name=to_str value="' ||
                to_str ||
                '"><br>');
```

```
      HTP.print ('Flags:<input name=flags value="' ||
                flags ||
                '"><br>');
   HTP.print ('<input type=submit>');
   HTP.print ('</form></td><td>');   -- Results print in second column
   -- Call the change procedure
   OWA_PATTERN.change (line, from_str, to_str, flags);
   HTP.print (line_copy);
   HTP.print ('</td></tr></html>');
END;
```

Figure 7-3 shows the output of the regexp_test procedure.

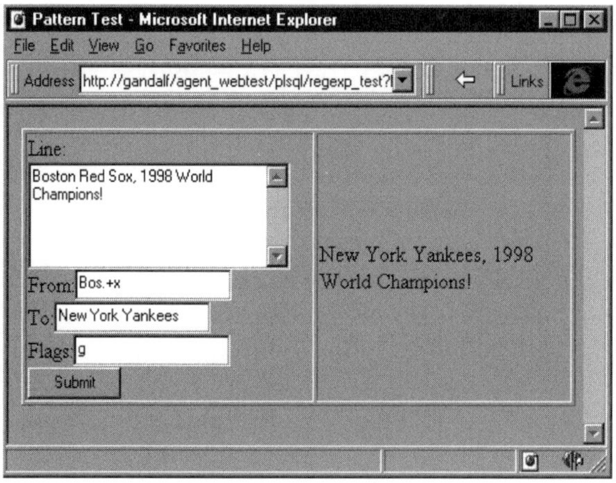

Figure 7-3. The results of the regexp_test procedure

Maintaining State

The inability to save information, or state, throughout a session is one of HTML's major limitations. HTML has no client/server type variables that remember things as the user moves from page to page. For example, if we want to use a piece of information entered by a user on the first page of a web system, we must save it somehow and be able to recall it later. There are four basic ways to do this: saving the information as part of a query string in a URL, saving it in a hidden field, saving it in a database table, or saving it in a cookie file by using the OWA_COOKIE package, described later in this section. In this section, we'll look at each method and discuss possible problems you may run into.

The first way to maintain state, using a query string of a URL, is the most straightforward: you simply build the string as you go, placing the information you want to pass from screen to screen in name/value pairs. These values are then passed to the procedure specified in the URL's `href` attribute when the user clicks on the hyperlink. The disadvantages to this approach include the following:

- Depending on the system, the maximum length of the URL is limited to 256 characters.

- Each value must be encoded to the CGI specification. It can be easy to forget to do this if you're in a rush.

The second way to save state information is to store it in hidden fields. A hidden field is simply an invisible input element that is part of an HTML form. Although the user cannot see the value on the screen, the hidden field is stored as part of the underlying HTML code. To maintain a value across multiple sessions, all we have to do is include the value as a hidden field on the form. You create a hidden field by setting the `type` attribute of an `<input>` element to "hidden," as in the following example:

```
<input type=hidden name=user_id value="10235">
```

The disadvantages of this approach include the following:

- Every procedure must include a corresponding parameter for the hidden value. While this might be okay for a small number of fields, it quickly becomes unworkable for larger numbers (this also applies when embedding the information in a URL).

- Each procedure must include the code to reproduce the hidden fields as part of its output.

- Hidden fields are insecure since almost all browsers have a "View Source" option that allows users to look at the underlying HTML code, making hidden fields of limited value when security is an issue.

The third method for maintaining state simply saves the information in a table and uses a SELECT statement to retrieve it later. However, there are two problems with this approach:

- It requires a hit against a table to both save and recall a piece of information.

- We need something to use as a primary key, carried across each page, to associate the state information with a particular session. The simplest way to do this is to store the client's IP address as part of a primary key. We can use this address, which is simple to obtain, when we want to recall the information later.

The fourth method is to save state information using *cookies*. Each cookie has a name and one or more associated values, and is saved either as a record on the user's machine or as an environment variable on the web server. In either case, it is accessible throughout (and sometimes even after) a user's session. You create a cookie on a user's browser by embedding HTML-like commands into the MIME header of a page. For example, the following set of instructions creates two cookies (notice that the second has multiple values):

```
Set-Cookie: username=odewahn
Set-Cookie: city=BOSTON; city=CHICAGO; city=NEW YORK
```

Some disadvantages of this approach are:

- Cookies were originally introduced by Netscape and are not part of the HTML standard. However, they have become a popular way to overcome statelessness and are now supported by most browsers.

- Cookies that are saved on a user's machine (and don't expire) tie the user to that specific machine. For example, many Internet storefronts use cookies to save your user information. When you visit the site, the server reads the cookies and thinks it's you. When someone else borrows or uses your computer, though, this information is still stored on the machine, which can lead to problems.

- Cookies can be turned off. Most browsers allow users to reject cookies, usually out of privacy concerns. Consequently, you can't save any state information to those users' machines.

In the next section, we'll look at the toolkit package for manipulating cookies.

OWA_COOKIE: Storing Cookies

The OWA_COOKIE package contains procedures that allow us to create, access, and even update cookies within PL/SQL.

Data structures

A cookie can have multiple values that can be as large as 4K. These are stored in an array named vc_arr:

```
TYPE vc_arr IS TABLE OF VARCHAR2(4096)
   INDEX BY BINARY_INTEGER;
```

 The vc_arr used in OWA_COOKIE is not the same as the one used in OWA_TEXT.

The cookie itself is represented with a record that holds its name, its values, and the number of these values:

```
TYPE cookie IS RECORD (
   name VARCHAR2(4096),
```

```
    vals vc_arr,
    num_vals INTEGER
);
```

Procedures and functions

The procedures and functions of OWA_COOKIE read, create, and remove cookies. The instructions to read cookies retrieve those cookies from the browser and store their values in a cookie variable. Creating or removing the cookies is slightly trickier. Table 7-13 shows the procedures and functions for OWA_COOKIE, along with their parameters.

Table 7-13. Various OWA_COOKIE Procedures and Functions

Procedure /Function	Parameters	Description
GET	name IN VARCHAR2	Generates instructions to retrieve a specified cookie from the browser and store its value in a cookie variable
GET_ALL	names OUT owa_cookie.vc_arr vals OUT owa_cookie.vc_arr num_vals OUT INTEGER	Generates instructions to retrieve the names and values of all unexpired cookies
SEND	name IN VARCHAR2 value IN VARCHAR2 expires IN DATE DEFAULT NULL path IN VARCHAR2 DEFAULT NULL domain IN VARCHAR2 DEFAULT NULL SECURE IN VARCHAR2 DEFAULT NULL	Generates instructions to create a cookie
REMOVE	name IN VARCHAR2 value IN VARCHAR2 path IN VARCHAR2 DEFAULT NULL	Generates instructions to delete a cookie

Like the procedures of the HTP package, the OWA_COOKIE procedures and functions generate instructions that are sent to the browser for processing. Unlike normal HTML tags, however, these instructions must appear outside the normal document in a section called the HTTP header. To place instructions in the header, we must use the MIME_HEADER and HTTP_HEADER_CLOSE procedures from the OWA_UTIL package. Please see the section "HTML and HTTP utilities," later in this chapter, for a detailed discussion of these procedures.

The following snippet shows how the OWA_UTIL procedures are used to create cookies:

```
/*
|| FALSE value in mime_header keeps the header open
|| so we can insert the cookie into the header section
*/
OWA_UTIL.mime_header ('text/html', FALSE);
OWA_COOKIE.send ('city', 'BOSTON');
```

```
OWA_COOKIE.send ('city', 'CHICAGO');
OWA_COOKIE.send ('city', 'NEW YORK');
OWA_UTIL.http_header_close;  -- Now close the header
HTP.print ('<html>');
...
```

The SEND procedure. This procedure generates the instruction to create a cookie. As noted, this instruction must appear inside the HTTP header. The parameters for the procedure are as follows:

name IN VARCHAR2
> Name of the cookie.

value IN VARCHAR2
> Value of the cookie.

expires IN DATE DEFAULT NULL
> Expiration date; the cookie is deleted after the specified date. If omitted, it never expires. Also note that the time zone must match the settings in OWA_ INIT.

path IN VARCHAR2 DEFAULT NULL
> If a path is specified, the server sends the cookie only when the URL of the request matches the path; this make the cookie available only to those requests that match the specified path.

domain IN VARCHAR2 DEFAULT NULL
> Like the path, the server sends the cookie only if the domain (i.e., *www. oreilly.com*) matches the URL of the request, allowing you to prevent a cookie from being sent if the domain (the server section of the URL) matches the specified path.

SECURE IN VARCHAR2 DEFAULT NULL
> If non-NULL, the keyword SECURE is added to the cookie; if added, the cookie is sent only if the client and server are connected through a secure protocol like HTTPS.

SEND produces a string based on the following template:

```
Set-Cookie: name=value expires=expires path=path domain=domain secure
```

The following procedure illustrates the use of the SEND procedure:

```
CREATE OR REPLACE PROCEDURE send_cookie (
   cookie_name IN VARCHAR2 DEFAULT NULL,
   cookie_val IN VARCHAR2 DEFAULT NULL
   )
IS

BEGIN
   -- Cookies must be set within the header
   OWA_UTIL.mime_header ('text/html', FALSE);
```

```
    -- Send a cookie if a name was entered
    IF cookie_name IS NOT NULL
    THEN
        OWA_COOKIE.send (cookie_name, cookie_val);
    END IF;
    OWA_UTIL.http_header_close;
END;
```

The REMOVE procedure. This procedure causes a cookie to immediately expire and, like SEND, must be used inside the HTTP header. The parameters are:

name IN VARCHAR2
> The name of the cookie to remove.

value IN VARCHAR2
> The value of the cookie to remove.

path IN VARCHAR2 DEFAULT NULL
> The path of the cookie to remove.

REMOVE produces the following template:

```
Set-Cookie: name=value expires=01-JAN-1990 path=path
```

The GET function. This function retrieves the value for the specified cookie and returns it as a cookie datatype. Unlike SEND or REMOVE, GET is not limited to the header and may appear anywhere within a procedure. It has one parameter:

name IN VARCHAR2
> Name of the cookie to retrieve.

The following example illustrates the GET procedure:

```
CREATE OR REPLACE PROCEDURE get_cookie (
    cookie_name IN VARCHAR2 DEFAULT NULL
    )
IS

    target_cookie OWA_COOKIE.cookie;

BEGIN
    target_cookie := OWA_COOKIE.get (cookie_name);
    -- Print message if the cookie was not found
    IF target_cookie.num_vals = 0
    THEN
        HTP.print ('<h1>Cookie not found!</h1>');
    ELSE
        HTP.print ('<h1>Values for cookie ' ||
                    cookie_name ||
                    '</h1><hr>');
        FOR i IN 1 .. target_cookie.num_vals
        LOOP
            HTP.print (target_cookie.vals (i) || '<p>');
```

```
        END LOOP;
     END IF;
  END;
```

The GET_ALL procedure. This procedure retrieves the names and values for all nonexpired cookies. Its parameters are:

names OUT owa_cookie.vc_arr
  Array of cookie names.

vals OUT owa_cookie.vc_arr
  Array of cookie values.

num_vals OUT INTEGER
  Total number of cookies retrieved.

The following procedure illustrates the GET_ALL procedure:

```
CREATE OR REPLACE PROCEDURE print_cookies
IS

   -- Note that vc_arr is in owa_cookie, not owa_text!

   current_cookie_names           OWA_COOKIE.vc_arr;
   current_cookie_vals            OWA_COOKIE.vc_arr;
   n                              INTEGER DEFAULT 0;

BEGIN
   -- Fetch and print the current cookies
   OWA_COOKIE.get_all (
      current_cookie_names,
      current_cookie_vals,
      n
   );
   FOR i IN 1 .. n
   LOOP
      HTP.print ('<b>' || current_cookie_names (i) || ':</b>');
      HTP.print ('<b>' || current_cookie_vals (i) || '<p>');
   END LOOP;
END;
```

OWA_OPT_LOCK: Record Locking

Developing data entry forms with HTML is closely related to the problem of maintaining state. As discussed in Chapter 2, *Foundations*, forms are processed in two steps. In the first, the form is displayed and the user is allowed to make changes. In the second, once the user has made all desired edits, the form is submitted to another program for processing. This program adds, deletes, or updates the original record. As any client/server developer knows, forms must be able to handle situations in which multiple users attempt to update the same record simultaneously.

There are two different approaches to handling the simultaneous update problem: pessimistic locking and optimistic locking. With *pessimistic locking,* the record is locked as soon as the user attempts to edit it. If the lock succeeds, other users are unable to make changes until the original user releases the lock.

With *optimistic locking,* no locks are issued, in the hope (hence the term "optimistic") that someone else won't come along in the interim and make changes to the record. A user makes edits on the screen, and only when the user has finished editing does the system attempt to lock the record and apply the changes. Unfortunately, because the record was not initially locked, other users are free to make changes while the first user is still staring at his screen. If this occurs, the first user must be given a choice about how to proceed; he can choose to overwrite the other user's updates with his own, or choose to discard his changes in favor of the other user's.

HTML's inability to maintain state makes it extremely difficult, if not impossible, to implement pessimistic locking. However, it is relatively straightforward, although a little clumsy, to implement optimistic locking. With this approach, a snapshot is taken of a record before the user makes any changes. When the user submits the form, the original record is requeried and compared to the snapshot. If they are identical (i.e., no one has made intervening changes) the user's edits are saved. Otherwise, the user is asked how to proceed.

The OWA_OPT_LOCK package provides two ways to simplify optimistic locking in HTML forms. With the first method, the record's columns are saved in hidden fields within the form. When the form is submitted, these hidden fields are passed to the new procedure in an array, where they are then compared with the original record. The second method computes a checksum of the original record. This value is compared to a recomputed checksum to determine if the record has been updated.*

Data structures

The vcArray array holds the hidden fields that are passed from the data entry form:

```
TYPE vcarray IS TABLE OF VARCHAR2(2000)
    INDEX BY BINARY_INTEGER;
```

Procedures and functions

The procedures and functions in OWA_OPT_LOCK implement the two strategies for optimistic locking. Table 7-14 shows the procedures and functions, along with

---

* A checksum is a mathematical function that computes a single, unique value for any input. For example, the sum of a record's bytes is probably unique to that particular record. Real checksum functions, however, are complex enough that even tiny changes to the record result in a different value.

their parameters. Note that the hidden fields and checksum approaches are two different methods, each with its own distinct set of operations.

Table 7-14. Various OWA_OPT_LOCK Procedures and Functions

Procedure/ Function	Parameters	Description
CHECKSUM	p_owner IN VARCHAR2 p_tname IN VARCHAR2 p_rowid IN VARCHAR2	Generates a checksum (rather than a hidden field) for each sensitive column of the row being updated
GET_ROWID	p_values IN owa_opt_ lock.vcArray	Returns the ROWID from fields generated by store_values
STORE_VALUES	p_owner IN VARCHAR2 p_tname IN VARCHAR2 p_rowid IN VARCHAR2	Generates a hidden field for each column of the row being updated
VERIFY_VALUES	p_old_values IN owa_opt_ lock.vcArray	Compares old and new values

The STORE_VALUES procedure. This procedure generates a hidden field for each column of the row that is to be updated. Its parameters are:

p_owner IN VARCHAR2
   The schema that owns the table that is to be updated; you can use the reserved word USER to default to the current schema.

p_tname IN VARCHAR2
   The table to be updated.

p_rowid IN VARCHAR2
   ROWID of the record in the table that is to be updated; the procedure always uses the ROWID of the row that is to be updated, regardless of the primary key of the table.

Like the HTP procedures, STORE_VALUES generates HTML tags that are returned to the browser. These tags must appear as part of the data entry form that is being used to update a record. The hidden fields generated by STORE_VALUES have the same name: "old_" followed by the name of the table passed in the p_tname parameter. This passes the old values in a single array parameter to the procedure that processes the form.

Here is a sample program that creates a simple data entry form based on the EMP table. The `<form>` tag's `action` attribute points us to the procedure that performs the update:

```
CREATE OR REPLACE PROCEDURE opt_lock_fentry (
    iempno IN VARCHAR2 DEFAULT NULL
    )
IS
```

```
      emp_rec scott.emp%ROWTYPE;
      rec_row_id ROWID;

BEGIN
   -- Fetch the record and rowid the employee with the given id
   SELECT *
      INTO emp_rec
      FROM scott.emp
     WHERE emp.empno = iempno;
   SELECT ROWID
      INTO rec_row_id
      FROM scott.emp
     WHERE emp.empno = iempno;
   -- Create a simple data entry form
   HTP.print ('<form action=opt_lock_fupdate>');
   HTP.formhidden (cname => 'iempno', cvalue => iempno);
   HTP.print ('Employee Name:');
   HTP.formtext (cname => 'iename', cvalue => emp_rec.ename);
   HTP.print ('Job:');
   HTP.formtext (cname => 'ijob', cvalue => emp_rec.job);
   /*
   || Store the current values for the row that is to be updated
   */
   OWA_OPT_LOCK.store_values ('SCOTT', 'emp', rec_row_id);
   HTP.print ('<input type=submit>');
   HTP.print ('</form>');
END;
```

The following listing shows what happens when the procedure is executed. The first three fields simply reproduce the original parameters: the schema name, the table name, and the ROWID of the record that is being updated. After these fields, all the columns in the target row are listed:

```
<FORM action=opt_lock_fupdate>
<INPUT TYPE="hidden" NAME="iempno" VALUE="7934">
Employee Name:
<INPUT TYPE="text" NAME="iename" VALUE="MILLER">
Job:
<INPUT TYPE="text" NAME="ijob" VALUE="CLERK">
<INPUT TYPE="hidden" NAME="old_emp" VALUE="SCOTT">
<INPUT TYPE="hidden" NAME="old_emp" VALUE="emp">
<INPUT TYPE="hidden" NAME="old_emp" VALUE="AAAAeFAACAAAAEbAAN">
<INPUT TYPE="hidden" NAME="old_emp" VALUE="7934">
<INPUT TYPE="hidden" NAME="old_emp" VALUE="MILLER">
<INPUT TYPE="hidden" NAME="old_emp" VALUE="CLERK">
<INPUT TYPE="hidden" NAME="old_emp" VALUE="7566">
<INPUT TYPE="hidden" NAME="old_emp" VALUE="23-JAN-82">
<INPUT TYPE="hidden" NAME="old_emp" VALUE="1300">
<INPUT TYPE="hidden" NAME="old_emp" VALUE="">
<INPUT TYPE="hidden" NAME="old_emp" VALUE="10">
<input type=submit>
</form>
```

The VERIFY_VALUES function. This function, used when a form is submitted, compares the old values from the row to the current values. If they match, the function returns TRUE; otherwise, it returns FALSE. Its one parameter is:

p_old_values IN owa_opt_lock.vcArray
      The array of field values created by the STORE_VALUES procedure.

The VERIFY_VALUES procedure is meant to work in tandem with the STORE_VAL-UES procedure. The following example performs the record update started in the earlier example. In addition to a parameter for each input element on the form, we must also include a parameter that receives the values from the STORE_VALUES procedure. The parameter, declared as a vcArray, must have the same name as the hidden fields created by STORE_VALUES:

```
CREATE OR REPLACE PROCEDURE opt_lock_fupdate (
    iempno IN VARCHAR2 DEFAULT NULL,
    iename IN VARCHAR2 DEFAULT NULL,
    ijob IN VARCHAR2 DEFAULT NULL,
    old_emp IN OWA_OPT_LOCK.vcarray
    )
IS
BEGIN
    IF OWA_OPT_LOCK.verify_values (old_emp)
    THEN
        -- Perform the update
        UPDATE scott.emp
           SET emp.ename = iename,
               emp.job = ijob
         WHERE emp.empno = iempno;
        COMMIT;
        HTP.print ('<h1>Change Successful</h1>');
    ELSE
        HTP.print ('<h1>The record has been changed!</h1>');
    END IF;
END;
```

The GET_ROWID function. This function accepts a vcArray, and returns the ROWID (always in the third element in the array) from the fields generated by the STORE_VALUES procedure. Like VERIFY_VALUES, GET_ROWID is used in the procedure that handles form submission. The function is included as a convenience to save us from having to pass the original primary key of the record we are attempting to update. For example, in the previous procedure, we had to include the empno field both in the data entry form and as a parameter to the submission form (again, due to statelessness) to retain the original primary key. We could have saved a step by omitting empno and using GET_ROWID to retrieve the ROWID of the target record, as illustrated in the following code snippet:

```
-- old_rowid is a local variable declared as a rowid

old_rowid := OWA_OPT_LOCK.get_rowid (old_emp);
```

```
UPDATE scott.emp
   SET emp.ename = iename,
       emp.job = ijob
 WHERE ROWID = old_rowid;
```

The CHECKSUM function. This function provides an alternative to the hidden field method that is useful when the underlying table contains sensitive information that might be compromised with the "View Source" browser option. Additionally, for tables with a very large number of columns, a checksum results in a more compact HTML form. This can be an important factor in improving download times, particularly when users are connecting with a modem or a WAN.

The CHECKSUM function has the same parameters as the STORE_VALUE procedure discussed earlier. The function returns a unique value for the values in the target row, and this value is stored as a hidden field within the data entry form. When the form is submitted, the checksum for the target row is recomputed and compared to the old value. If they are the same, then the procedure can apply the user's updates.

The following procedure illustrates how to use the CHECKSUM function when creating a data entry form. Unlike STORE_VALUES, which automatically passes the ROWID or the target record, we must manually include it as a hidden field when using the CHECKSUM approach:

```
CREATE OR REPLACE PROCEDURE opt_lock_centry (
    iempno IN VARCHAR2 DEFAULT NULL
    )
IS

    emp_rec scott.emp%ROWTYPE;
    rec_row_id ROWID;
    csum NUMBER;

BEGIN
    SELECT *
      INTO emp_rec
      FROM scott.emp
     WHERE emp.empno = iempno;
    SELECT ROWID
      INTO rec_row_id
      FROM scott.emp
     WHERE emp.empno = iempno;
    -- Create a simple data entry form
    HTP.print ('<form action=opt_lock_cupdate>');
    HTP.formhidden (cname => 'iempno', cvalue => iempno);
    HTP.formhidden (cname => 'irowid', cvalue => rec_row_id);
    HTP.print ('Employee Name:');
    HTP.formtext (cname => 'iename', cvalue => emp_rec.ename);
    HTP.print ('Job:');
```

```
HTP.formtext (cname => 'ijob', cvalue => emp_rec.job);
/*
|| Save the row's checksum in a hidden field
*/
csum := OWA_OPT_LOCK.checksum ('SCOTT', 'emp', rec_row_id);
HTP.formhidden (cname => 'iold_checksum', cvalue => csum);
HTP.print ('<input type=submit>');
HTP.print ('</form>');
END;
```

Here is the output of the procedure, showing the hidden field for the checksum of the target row:

```
<form action=opt_lock_cupdate>
<INPUT TYPE="hidden" NAME="iempno" VALUE="7934">
<INPUT TYPE="hidden" NAME="irowid" VALUE="AAAAeFAACAAAAEbAAN">
Employee Name:
<INPUT TYPE="text" NAME="iename" VALUE="MILLER">
Job:
<INPUT TYPE="text" NAME="ijob" VALUE="CLERK">
<INPUT TYPE="hidden" NAME="iold_checksum" VALUE="7925">
<input type=submit>
</form>
```

The next procedure illustrates how the function is used to process the form data; notice that the parameter name for the checksum must match the name used for the hidden field:

```
CREATE OR REPLACE PROCEDURE opt_lock_cupdate (
   iempno IN VARCHAR2 DEFAULT NULL,
   iename IN VARCHAR2 DEFAULT NULL,
   ijob IN VARCHAR2 DEFAULT NULL,
   iold_checksum IN VARCHAR2 DEFAULT NULL,
   irowid IN VARCHAR2 DEFAULT NULL
   )
IS

   new_checksum NUMBER;

BEGIN

   new_checksum :=
      OWA_OPT_LOCK.checksum ('SCOTT', 'emp', irowid);
   IF  (iold_checksum = new_checksum)
   THEN
      -- Perform the update
      UPDATE scott.emp
         SET emp.ename = iename,
             emp.job = ijob
       WHERE emp.empno = iempno;
      COMMIT;
      HTP.print ('<h1>Change Successful</h1>');
   ELSE
      HTP.print ('<h1>The record has been changed by another user.</h1>');
```

```
    END IF;
END;
```

There is a second version of the CHECKSUM function that computes a value for an arbitrary VARCHAR2 string. The following example shows its return value on two strings that differ by just one character:

```
OWA_OPT_LOCK.checksum ('Hello, World');   -- (csum = 21074)
OWA_OPT_LOCK.checksum ('Hello, Wordl');   -- (csum = 23114)
```

Improving Productivity

The final two packages, OWA_UTIL and OWA_SEC, let you perform a variety of administrative and security-related tasks that help improve overall productivity.

OWA_UTIL: Creating Complex HTML Structures

The OWA_UTIL package is a grab-bag of useful procedures and functions that simplify many complex tasks. It contains procedures to query the web server environment, simplify debugging, change the default HTTP header, and simplify HTML development.

Table 7-15 shows the various functions and procedures contained in the OWA_UTIL package, which are grouped in categories in the following sections according to their uses.

 I've attempted to classify the OWA_UTIL procedures into broad, general categories (debugging, querying the environment, representing dates, etc.). These classifications reflect my own experience and are not intended to limit other possible uses.

Table 7-15. Various OWA_UTIL Procedures and Functions

Procedure/Function	Description
BIND_VARIABLES	Creates complex HTML structures
CALENDARPRINT	Creates complex HTML structures
CELLSPRINT	Creates complex HTML structures
CHOOSE_DATE	Represents dates
DATETYPE	Represents dates
GET_CGI_ENV	Queries the environment
GET_OWA_SERVICE_PATH	Queries the environment
GET_PROCEDURE	Performs debugging
HTTP_HEADER_CLOSE	HTML and HTTP utilities

Table 7-15. Various OWA_UTIL Procedures and Functions (continued)

Procedure/Function	Description
IP_ADDRESS	Queries the environment
LISTPRINT	Creates complex HTML structures
MIME_HEADER	HTML and HTTP utilities
PRINT_CGI_ENV	Queries the environment
REDIRECT_URL	HTML and HTTP utilities
SHOWPAGE	Performs debugging
SHOWSOURCE	Performs debugging
SIGNATURE	HTML and HTTP utilities
STATUS_LINE	HTML and HTTP utilities
TABLEPRINT	Creates complex HTML structures
TODATE	Represents dates
WHO_CALLED_ME	Performs debugging

Debugging

OWA_UTIL has a number of procedures useful for debugging, many of which are built on top of the DBMS_UTILITY built-in package. These debugging procedures are listed in Table 7-16.

Table 7-16. OWA_UTIL Procedures and Functions Used for Debugging

Procedure/ Function	Parameters	Description
GET_PROCEDURE	None	Returns the name of the procedure being executed by the PL/SQL agent
SHOWPAGE	None	Prints the HTML generated by the HTP package
SHOWSOURCE	None	Prints the PL/SQL source code for a particular procedure, function, or package
WHO_CALLED_ME	owner IN VARCHAR2 name IN VARCHAR2 lineno IN NUMBER caller_t IN VARCHAR2	Returns information about the procedure that called the currently executing procedure

The SHOWPAGE procedure. This procedure allows you to print the HTML generated by the HTP package. As mentioned earlier, output from this package is stored in a buffer. The SHOWPAGE procedure lets you view the contents of this buffer in SQL*Plus. To use SHOWPAGE:

1. Use SQL*Plus to log into the account that owns the desired procedure.

2. Use the SQL*Plus command SET SERVEROUT ON to turn on server output.

3. Execute the procedure, making sure to provide necessary parameters.

4. Execute OWA_UTIL.SHOWPAGE to print the results.

The SHOWSOURCE procedure. This procedure prints the PL/SQL source code for a given procedure, function, or package.

The GET_PROCEDURE function. This function returns the name of the procedure that is being executed by the PL/SQL agent.

The WHO_CALLED_ME procedure. This procedure returns information about the procedure that called the currently executing procedure. This information is particularly useful when you are trying to trace a program's execution. The parameters to the WHO_CALLED_ME procedure, which are all defined as OUT variables, are the following:

owner IN VARCHAR2
> The owner of the calling program unit.

name IN VARCHAR2
> The name of the calling unit (procedure name, function name, or ANONYMOUS).

lineno IN NUMBER
> The line number of the call within the calling unit.

caller_t IN VARCHAR2
> The type of call made. Here is an example:

```
-- Parameters to who_called_me must be declared as local variables
OWA_UTIL.who_called_me (cowner, cname, clineno, ccaller);
HTP.print (cowner || '<p>');
HTP.print (cname || '<p>');
HTP.print (clineno || '<p>');
HTP.print (ccaller || '<p>');
```

Querying the environment

Like any web server, OAS maintains environment variables. Several procedures within OWA_UTIL allow you to query these settings, as shown in Table 7-17.

Table 7-17. OWA_UTIL Procedures, Functions, and Datatypes for Querying the Environment

Procedure/Function	Parameters	Description
GET_CGI_ENV	param_name IN VARCHAR2	Returns the value of an environment variable
GET_OWA_ SERVICE_PATH	None	Returns the full path of the PL/SQL agent that executed the request

Table 7-17. OWA_UTIL Procedures, Functions, and Datatypes for Querying the Environment (continued)

Procedure/Function	Parameters	Description
IP_ADDRESS	None	Datatype to hold the TCP/IP address of the client machine that executed a procedure or function
PRINT_CGI_ENV	None	Generates a list of the names and values for all environment variables

The PRINT_CGI_ENV procedure. This procedure generates a list of names and values for all the environment variables. The procedure is used like the HTML procedures. As a general rule, it is not a good idea to allow casual users to view these settings, which provide detailed information, such as path settings, that can be exploited by malicious deviants. Figure 7-4 illustrates the output of this procedure.

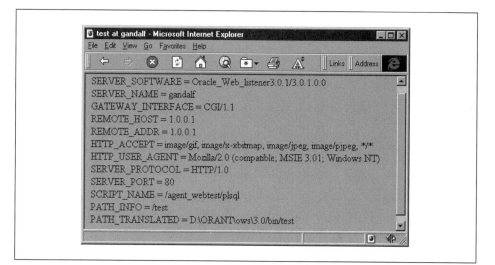

Figure 7-4. The output of OWA_UTIL.PRINT_CGI_ENV

The GET_CGI_ENV function. This function returns the value of an environment variable. It accepts a single VARCHAR2 parameter, param_name, and returns the value as a string. If the environment variable is not defined, the function returns NULL. For example:

```
-- Fetch the server name into a local variable
server := OWA_UTIL.get_cgi_env ('SERVER_NAME');
HTP.print ('The server is: ' || server);
```

The IP_ADDRESS datatype. The TCP/IP address of the client machine that executed a procedure or function is a particularly useful environment variable. For this reason, OWA_UTIL declares a special data structure just to hold this address.

Inexplicably, however, this structure seems to be used only by the OWA_SEC package's GET_CLIENT_IP_ADDRESS function. Go figure!

```
TYPE ip_address IS TABLE OF INTEGER
    INDEX BY BINARY_INTEGER;
```

The four elements of the ip_address array correspond to the four components of the address.

The GET_OWA_SERVICE_PATH function. This function returns the full path of the PL/SQL agent used to execute the request. This string is typically the name of the PL/SQL agent followed by "/plsql/" (depending on the agent's configuration).

```
-- SP is a local VARCHAR2 variable
sp := OWA_UTIL.get_owa_service_path;
HTP.print (sp);
```

Representing dates

With dozens of possible formats, dates are troublesome in almost every development environment. OWA_UTIL can help simplify date entry by providing a standard input format for the day, month, and year. The procedures used to do this are shown in Table 7-18.

Table 7-18. OWA_UTIL Procedures for Representing Dates

Procedure/Function	Parameters	Description
CHOOSE_DATE	p_name IN VARCHAR2 p_date IN DATE DEFAULT SYSDATE	Generates input elements for date, month, and year
DATETYPE	None	Datatype for day, month, and year from choose_date
TODATE	None	Converts a datetype into a normal date variable

The CHOOSE_DATE procedure. This procedure generates input elements for the day, month, and year that are used as part of a data entry form. Since each element has the same name, the date is passed as an array. Its parameters are as follows:

p_name IN VARCHAR2
    The name of the form element.

p_date IN DATE DEFAULT SYSDATE
    The value of the date.

The following procedure creates a nicely formatted form for entering a hire date:

```
HTP.print ('form action=proc_date');
HTP.print ('Date Hired:');
OWA_UTIL.choose_date ('date_hired','31-OCT-98');
```

Figure 7-5 shows the output from this procedure.

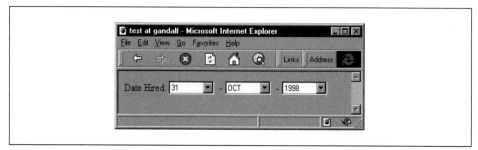

Figure 7-5. A form that uses OWA_UTIL.CHOOSE_DATE

The DATETYPE datatype. The day, month, and year created with the CHOOSE_
DATE procedure are held as three elements in an array:

```
TYPE datetype IS TABLE OF VARCHAR2(10)
   INDEX BY BINARY_INTEGER;
```

The specification also includes a DATETYPE variable called empty_date that is
used as the default value for parameters that receive a DATETYPE value.

The TODATE function. This function is used in the procedure that processes a
form and converts a DATETYPE into a normal date variable:

```
CREATE OR REPLACE PROCEDURE proc_date (
   date_hired OWA_UTIL.datetype DEFAULT OWA_UTIL.empty_date
   )
IS

   dhire DATE;

BEGIN
   dhire := OWA_UTIL.todate (date_hired);
   HTP.print (TO_CHAR (dhire, 'Month DD, YYYY'));
END;
```

HTML and HTTP utilities

OWA_UTIL contains a number of specialized HTTP and HTML procedures that
don't fit cleanly into the HTP package. These are shown in Table 7-19.

Table 7-19. OWA_UTIL Procedures Used for HTML and HTTP

Procedure	Parameters	Description
HTTP_HEADER_ CLOSE	ccontent_type IN VARCHAR2 bclose_header IN BOOLEAN DEFAULT TRUE	Manually closes a web page header
MIME_HEADER	ccontent_type IN VARCHAR2 bclose_header IN BOOLEAN DEFAULT TRUE	Signals the PL/SQL agent to change the default header for a document

Table 7-19. OWA_UTIL Procedures Used for HTML and HTTP (continued)

Procedure	Parameters	Description
REDIRECT_URL	curl IN VARCHAR2 bclose_header IN BOOLEAN DEFAULT TRUE	Sends a user to a URL (passed as a parameter)
SIGNATURE	cname (optional; not recommended)	Generates a single document signature showing the date the page was last updated
STATUS_LINE	nstatus IN INTEGER creason IN VARCHAR2 DEFAULT NULL bclose_header IN BOOLEAN DEFAULT TRUE	Sends a numerical code to the browser indicating the status of a request

The SIGNATURE procedure. A signature is a standardized line that usually appears at the end of a document. For example, an email signature often lists the sender's company, position, and phone number. Similarly, an HTML signature appears at the end of a web page. The SIGNATURE procedure generates a simple signature that gives the date the page was last updated:

```
<b>This page was produced by the PL/SQL Agent on sysdate</b>
```

You can also provide the name for a procedure or function in an optional parameter called cname. This adds an additional hyperlink to the signature that, when clicked, displays the PL/SQL code for the procedure or function specified in the parameter. This is a dangerous practice you should probably avoid.

The MIME_HEADER procedure. Every resource is identified as a particular type of content. This classification, called the MIME (Multipurpose Internet Mail Extension) type, is based on a set of standards used for transmitting ASCII and binary files across the Internet.

This MIME type is set in a section called the HTTP header that is separate from the actual content.[*] The header section begins with a header that (like normal HTML) must be closed by another instruction. By default, the PL/SQL agent automatically sends `text/html` as the MIME type and closes the header. To perform certain tasks, such as creating a cookie or activating a content handler on the user's browser, we must interrupt this normal flow of events.

For example, suppose we want to place the results of a query in a spreadsheet, rather than in an HTML document. To accomplish this, we must tell the browser that the content is not a normal HTML document, then generate a data stream, such as a tab-delimited set of columns, that is funneled to the spreadsheet program. We need to change the default `text/html` type to something like `text/tab` (the

---

[*] Although they have similar names, the HTTP header is *not* the same as the HTML header created by the `<head>` tag.

MIME type for tab-delimited content) to signal the browser to start a new content handler.

This is done with the OWA_UTIL procedures that change the default HTTP header. These procedures are not normal HTML; instead, they are special instructions that cause the browser to act in a particular way, and each must be used before any of the normal HTP procedures.

The MIME_HEADER procedure signals the PL/SQL agent to change the default header that is normally sent with the document. It has two parameters:

ccontent_type IN VARCHAR2
    The new content type.

bclose_header IN BOOLEAN DEFAULT TRUE
    Flag indicating if the header should be immediately closed; a value of FALSE leaves it open so that more instructions (like these to set cookies) can be included as part of the header.

The STATUS_LINE procedure. This procedure sends a numerical code to the browser indicating the status of a request. There are three parameters to the procedure:

nstatus IN INTEGER
    The numeric status code.

creason IN VARCHAR2 DEFAULT NULL
    Code description.

bclose_header IN BOOLEAN DEFAULT TRUE
    Flag to close the HTTP header.

The Internet community has developed a standard set of number/message result codes, the most common of which are:

    200: Success
    401: Unauthorized
    403: Forbidden
    404: Not Found

The REDIRECT_URL procedure. It is often necessary to transparently send users from one web page to another. Most often, this is done when a page is moved to another location. Rather than having users reenter the new location, we simply redirect them to the new page.

Sometimes we want to direct users to a static page from within a PL/SQL program. For example, suppose you need to make some changes to a popular PL/SQL web application and you want to keep users out for a while. You can use redirection to send users who attempt to use the application to a new page that explains why the application is closed and when it will be available again (assuming, of course, that you haven't shut the database down entirely). This basic courtesy can save you lots of calls from irate users.

The REDIRECT_URL procedure sends a user to the URL passed as a parameter. This URL can refer to a static page or another PL/SQL program; you can even pass parameters using the query string. Like MIME_HEADER and STATUS_LINE, REDIRECT_URL places its output within the HTTP header and must appear before any other HTP calls. It has two parameters:

curl IN VARCHAR2
   The new URL.

bclose_header IN BOOLEAN DEFAULT TRUE
   Flag to close the HTTP header.

The following procedure illustrates how you could redirect a user to a static page if you wanted to shut down an application temporarily:

```
PROCEDURE popular_app_main
IS
BEGIN
   IF popular_app_is_closed
   THEN
      -- Redirect to static page
      OWA_UTIL.redirect_url ('http://server/alert/status.html');
   ELSE
      HTP.title ('The application you know and love...');
      popular_app.show_main_page;
   END IF;
END;
```

The HTTP_HEADER_CLOSE procedure. This procedure is used to manually close the header when the bclose_header flag to any of the previous procedures is FALSE. It does not have any parameters.

Creating complex HTML structures

The OWA_UTIL procedures and functions listed in Table 7-20 help you create more complex HTML structures. They are described in the following sections.

The TABLEPRINT function. This function produces a formatted HTML table based on a SQL query whose appearance is similar to that of a SELECT statement in SQL*Plus. The function's return value indicates if all the rows in the underlying table have been displayed. Its parameters are:

ctable IN VARCHAR2
   The database table that is being reported on.

Table 7-20. OWA_UTIL Procedures and Functions for Creating Complex HTML Structures

Procedure/Function	Parameters	Description
BIND_VARIABLES	theQuery IN VARCHAR2 DEFAULT NULL bv*n*Name IN VARCHAR2 DEFAULT NULL bv*n*Value IN VARCHAR2 DEFAULT NULL	Provides an interface to the built-in package DBMS_SQL
CALENDARPRINT	p_theQuery IN VARCHAR2 OR NUMBER p_cname IN VARCHAR2 p_nsize IN NUMBER p_multiple IN BOOLEAN DEFAULT FALSE	Creates an HTML-based monthly calendar
CELLSPRINT	theQuery IN VARCHAR2 OR NUMBER p_max_rows IN NUMBER p_format_numbers IN VARCHAR2 DEFAULT NULL p_skip_rec IN NUMBER DEFAULT 0 p_more_data OUT BOOLEAN	A stripped-down version of TABLEPRINT
LISTPRINT	p_theQuery IN VARCHAR2 OR NUMBER p_cname IN VARCHAR2 p_nsize IN NUMBER p_multiple IN BOOLEAN DEFAULT FALSE	Creates a list of values (LOV) on an HTML form
TABLEPRINT	ctable IN VARCHAR2 cattributes IN VARCHAR2 DEFAULT NULL ntable_type IN INTEGER DEFAULT HTML_TABLE ccolumns IN VARCHAR2 DEFAULT '*' cclauses IN VARCHAR2 DEFAULT NULL ccol_aliases IN VARCHAR2 DEFAULT NULL nrow_min IN NUMBER DEFAULT 0 nrow_max IN NUMBER DEFAULT 0	Produces a formatted HTML table based on a SQL query

cattributes IN VARCHAR2 DEFAULT NULL

> Free-format attributes to be included as part of the table tag (i.e., `<table cattributes>`).

ntable_type IN INTEGER DEFAULT HTML_TABLE

> The output type; can be either an HTML table or a text table; two numeric constants, HTML_TABLE (value = 1) and PRE_TABLE (value = 2) are defined to represent these types.

ccolumns IN VARCHAR2 DEFAULT ''*

> The columns to include in the output; the list is delimited with commas.

cclauses IN VARCHAR2 DEFAULT NULL

A WHERE or ORDER BY clause used to select specific rows from the underlying table; the clause must be syntactically correct and include all necessary keywords (such as WHERE...).

ccol_aliases IN VARCHAR2 DEFAULT NULL

The column aliases used for each column; this list is comma-delimited and should correspond to the columns specified in the ccolumns parameter.

nrow_min IN NUMBER DEFAULT 0

The ordinal position of the first row in the result set to display; not the same as rownum.

nrow_max IN NUMBER DEFAULT 0

The ordinal position of the last row in the result set to display; not the same as rownum.

The tprint procedure, shown in the following code, uses the TABLEPRINT procedure to page through the EMP table five rows at a time. The i_page_num parameter is used to calculate corresponding values for the nrow_min and nrow_max parameters. The output is shown in Figure 7-6.

```
CREATE OR REPLACE PROCEDURE tprint (
    i_page_num IN VARCHAR2 DEFAULT '1'
    )
IS

    more_rows BOOLEAN;

    cur_page NUMBER
        := TO_NUMBER (i_page_num);
    min_row NUMBER;
    max_row NUMBER;

    i_num_rows CONSTANT NUMBER := 5;

BEGIN
    min_row :=  (cur_page - 1) * i_num_rows + 1;
    max_row := min_row + i_num_rows - 1;
    more_rows :=
        OWA_UTIL.tableprint (
            ctable       => 'scott.emp',
            cattributes  => 'border=1',
            ntable_type  => OWA_UTIL.html_table,
            ccolumns     => 'job, ename, hiredate, sal',
            cclauses     => 'order by job, ename',
            ccol_aliases => 'Job, Employee Name, Date Hired, Salary',
            nrow_min     => min_row,
            nrow_max     => max_row
        );
    -- Put a "Prev" hyperlink if min_row > 1
```

```
        IF cur_page > 1
        THEN
           HTP.anchor (
               'tprint?i_page_num=' || (cur_page - 1),
               'Previous'
           );
        END IF;
        -- Put a "Next" hyperlink if there are more rows in the query
        IF more_rows
        THEN
           HTP.anchor (
               'tprint?i_page_num=' || (cur_page + 1),
               'Next'
           );
        END IF;

    END;
```

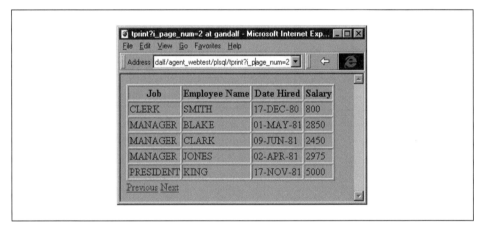

Figure 7-6. The output of the tprint procedure

The BIND_VARIABLES procedure. This procedure puts a friendly face on DBMS_SQL, one of the most flexible and powerful of all the built-in packages. DBMS_SQL allows you to dynamically construct and execute SQL statements as your program executes. The queries constructed by BIND_VARIABLES can even contain variables that are bound to values entered on the HTML form.

The BIND_VARIABLES procedure accepts a SQL statement and up to 25 name/value pairs of bind variables. It returns a cursor handle (not an actual cursor) that can be passed to other OWA_UTIL procedures to create complex HTML structures. This handle is also used by the various procedures in DBMS_SQL to fetch, parse, and close dynamic queries. For an excellent discussion of DBMS_SQL, see *Oracle Built-in Packages* by Steven Feuerstein, Charles Dye, and John Beresniewicz (O'Reilly & Associates, 1998).

The parameters to the BIND_VARIABLES procedure are:

theQuery IN VARCHAR2 DEFAULT NULL
The select query to use in creating the dynamic cursor; it can contain up to 25 bind variables.

bvnName IN VARCHAR2 DEFAULT NULL
The name of the *n*th bind variable (i.e., bv1Name, bv2Name, . . . bv25Name); there must be a bind variable parameter for each bind variable in the SELECT statement.

bvnValue IN VARCHAR2 DEFAULT NULL
The value of the *n*th bind variable (i.e., bv1Value, bv2Value, . . . bv25Value); there must be a corresponding value for each bind variable name.

Here is a simple code snippet illustrating the use of the BIND_VARIABLES procedure. The SELECT statement is built and stored in a string:

```
stmt :=
    'select emp.ename, emp.job, emp.sal, dpt.dname, dpt.loc';
  stmt := stmt || ' from scott.emp emp, scott.dept dpt';
  stmt := stmt || ' where emp.deptno = dpt.deptno and';
  stmt := stmt || ' dpt.dname like :bvDept and';
  stmt := stmt || ' emp.job like :bvJob and ';
  stmt := stmt || ' emp.sal > :bvSal';
  stmt := stmt || ' order by emp.ename';
  --
cur_handle :=
    OWA_UTIL.bind_variables (
        TheQuery => stmt,
        bv1Name  => 'bvDept',
        bv1Value => 'RESEARCH',
        bv2Name  => 'bvJob',
        bv2Value => '%',
        bv3Name  => 'bvSal',
        bv3Value => 1000
    );
```

The CELLSPRINT procedure. CELLSPRINT is a stripped-down version of TABLE-PRINT. The main difference between the two procedures is that CELLSPRINT can accept a dynamic query generated with BIND_VARIABLES in addition to a simple VARCHAR2 query string. This is especially useful when the underlying query contains a number of bind variables. Its parameters are:

theQuery IN VARCHAR2 OR NUMBER
The query on which to build the table; it can be a simple string or a cursor handle returned by BIND_VARIABLES.

p_max_rows IN NUMBER
The maximum number of rows allowed in the HTML output; this parameter is not optional.

p_format_numbers IN VARCHAR2 DEFAULT NULL
> If this value is non-null, numbers in the table are right-justified and formatted to two decimal places.

p_skip_rec IN NUMBER DEFAULT 0
> Optional offset; sets the first row of the result set that is displayed; similar to the nrow_min parameter of TABLEPRINT.

p_more_data OUT BOOLEAN
> Optional flag used in conjunction with p_skip_rec that indicates if there are more rows in the underlying table; similar to the return value of the TABLE-PRINT function.

Here is a simple example based on a VARCHAR2 query string:

```
OWA_UTIL.cellsprint (
   'select * from emp where job like ' || iename || '%',
   10,
   'Y'
);
```

We could use CELLSPRINT to quickly print the results of the SELECT statement defined in a call to the BIND_VARIABLES procedure:

```
OWA_UTIL.cellsprint (cur_handle, 10, 'Y');
```

The LISTPRINT procedure. This procedure is handy for creating lists of values (LOVs) on an HTML form. Like traditional LOVs, the elements in the list come from an underlying query. However, since HTTP is stateless, the entire contents of the query must be downloaded to the HTML form, which can present a problem for very large numbers of elements. It has the following parameters:

p_theQuery IN VARCHAR2 OR NUMBER
> The underlying query on which the LOV is based; can be either a VARCHAR2 string or a cursor handle to a dynamic query created with the BIND_VARI-ABLES procedure.

p_cname IN VARCHAR2
> The name of the HTML input element.

p_nsize IN NUMBER
> The size of the input list; setting this value to "1" creates a drop-down list; otherwise, it creates a scrollbox with the specified number of items visible.

p_multiple IN BOOLEAN DEFAULT FALSE
> Flag indicating that the select list can contain multiple selections; if TRUE, the input element must be treated as an array of elements when the form is processed.

The underlying query must have the following layout:

Column 1
> The value returned when the element is selected from the list (e.g., empno, deptno, etc.).

Column 2
> The value the user sees on the form (e.g., ename, deptname, etc.).

Column 3
> A non-NULL value in the third column marks the row as "selected" on the form.

The following procedure call creates an input element we can include within an HTML form:

```
OWA_UTIL.listprint (
    'select empno, ename, null from scott.emp order by ename',
    'iempno',
    1
);
```

The procedure generates the following HTML:

```
<SELECT NAME="emp_no" SIZE="1">
<OPTION value="7876">ADAMS
<OPTION value="7499">ALLEN
<OPTION value="7698">BLAKE
....
<OPTION value="7844">TURNER
<OPTION value="7521">WARD
</SELECT>
```

The CALENDARPRINT procedure. This procedure creates an HTML-based monthly calendar. The procedure has the following parameters:

p_query IN VARCHAR2 OR INTEGER
> The underlying query for the calendar; can be either a simple VARCHAR2 string or a handle to a dynamic cursor created with the BIND_VALUES procedure.

p_mf_only IN VARCHAR2 DEFAULT 'N'
> Flag to exclude Sunday and Saturday from the calendar; an "N" (the default) includes them, a "Y" excludes them.

The underlying query must have the following layout:

Column 1
> A date; CALENDARPRINT generates a one-month calendar for each unique month/year combination in this column. The query should be ordered by this column.

Column 2

> The text printed on the calendar for the date.

Column 3

> If non-NULL, this column turns the text into a hyperlink. The column must contain a valid URL.

For example, suppose we want to print a calendar based on a to-do list stored in a database table with the following columns and data:

```
DUE_DATE    DESCRIPTION                       HYPERLINK
---------   --------------------------------  -----------------------
20-OCT-98   Give cat pill                     http://www.sickcat.com
22-OCT-98   Research Dev2K                    http://www.oracle.com
28-OCT-98   Check out new O'Reilly books      http://www.oreilly.com
30-OCT-98   Buy Costume
31-OCT-98   Trick-or-Treat!
```

We can use the following line to create the calendar:

```
str := 'select due_date, description, hyperlink ';
str := str || 'from to_do order by due_date';
OWA_UTIL.calendarprint (str);
```

Figure 7-7 shows the output of this call.

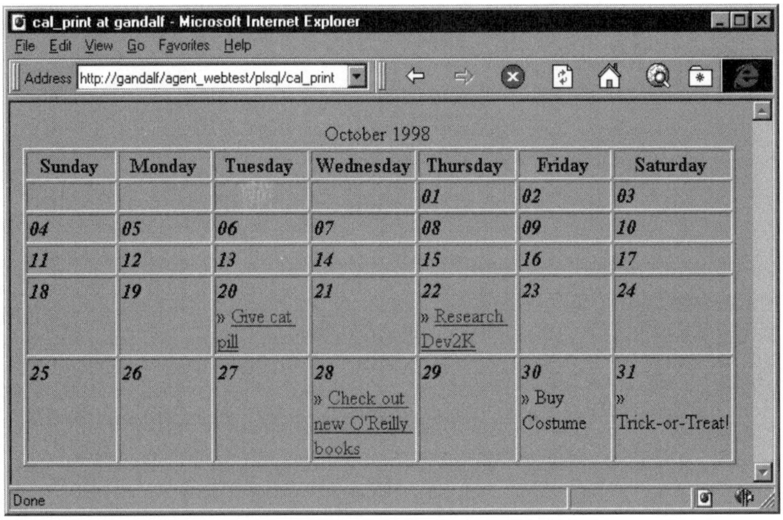

Figure 7-7. A calendar based on a to-do list

OWA_SEC: Managing Security

The toolkit includes a package, OWA_SEC, that is used to query and set various security options, such as realms, domains, etc. Most of these procedures are conceptually similar to the procedures of OWA_UTIL that query the environment variables. Table 7-21 summarizes the various security procedures and functions.

Table 7-21. Various OWA_SEC Procedures and Functions

Procedure/Function	Parameters	Description
GET_CLIENT_HOST-NAME	None	Returns the web server's hostname
GET_CLIENT_IP	None	Returns the TCP/IP address of the client browser that executed the procedure
GET_USER_ID	None	Returns the username of the user executing the procedure
GET_PASSWORD	None	Returns the password used to log in
SET_AUTHORIZATION	scheme IN INTEGER	Forces the PL/SQL agent to call a custom authentication function called AUTHORIZE
SET_PROTECTION_REALM	realm IN VARCHAR2	Forces the user to provide a valid login name and password for the specified security realm

8

Developing Applications

In the last chapter, we learned about the individual packages of the PL/SQL toolkit. In this chapter, we'll use these packages to create two realistic web applications. The first application allows us to create and distribute anonymous surveys; the second allows users to communicate over the Web in a threaded discussion forum.

Designing a Web Application

Before looking at these two systems, however, let's take a quick look at four simple steps that can improve the design process. When you are confronted with any design task, it can greatly help to break the process down into manageable pieces, as follows:

1. Evaluate your development options; be sure PL/SQL and HTML are really the right tools for the job.*

2. Create a storyboard that will help you visualize the relationship between an application's various web pages.

3. Create a data model to help you create the screens.

4. Use PL/SQL packages to actually structure the code.

The next few sections describe these steps in more detail.

Evaluate Development Options

Choosing the right development language is always the critical first step in building any application. While you can use HTML and PL/SQL to create very powerful

---

* We'll assume that in this chapter!

systems, there are still some things you should think about before you start coding. For example:

- Does the proposed application require a lot of sophisticated data entry screens?

- Will users accept a new kind of interface?

- Do all users have modern browsers?

- Is the system brand-new, or is it replacing an existing system you could easily retrofit for the Web? For example, you could take an existing Oracle Forms application and access it using the web-enabled version of Developer.

The first of these questions is the most important. As a rule of thumb, it's probably better to use Java or client/server than HTML for mission-critical applications with sophisticated data entry screens requiring lots of user interactions, which would be very difficult to code from scratch. For example, you would not want to develop an accounts payable system in HTML. In my own experience, the most effective use of PL/SQL and HTML is for creating systems that generate information from a database, not those that put information into a database.

Also, once again, it's important to remember that you must always accommodate your design to the stateless nature of HTML. For example, a complex, hierarchical system where users progressively drill down to lower and lower levels, all the while picking up extra state information, might be difficult to implement in a web environment.

Create a Storyboard

Once you've decided to build an HTML system using PL/SQL, the next step is to create a diagram, called a *storyboard*, that helps you visualize the relationship between an application's various web pages. Figure 8-1 shows a simple storyboard for an organizational chart application.

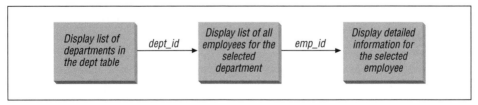

Figure 8-1. A simple storyboard

Each block on the diagram represents a page. The arrowed lines represent links between the pages. The labels on the link represent the information needed to move from one screen to the next. For example, to generate the second screen of the organization chart application, we must use the department ID code (dept_id) to fetch the correct employees.

There are several benefits to building a simple storyboard before you begin an application:

- Since a storyboard gives even a casual observer an overview of the entire system, you can get useful feedback from potential end users before you begin any actual coding.

- The elements on the storyboard translate almost directly into PL/SQL structures. For example, a quick look at the organization chart storyboard shows that we need at least three procedures. The labels on the links give us the formal parameters for each of these procedures.

- The storyboard, even if sketched out on the back of a napkin, is a useful piece of system documentation that can help future developers to quickly grasp the system's major functions.

Create a Data Model

Once you have completed the storyboard, you should build a simple data model to help you create the screens. Tables and relationships are your bread-and-butter resources; put them to work in your web systems. For example, suppose your company reorganizes and adopts some crazy new management plan. Inevitably, you will be called upon to develop hundreds of online surveys, with questions such as "Do you meet your core objectives?" or "How can you better align your personal life to the strategic goals of the company?"

We could take two approaches to this problem. In the first, we'll simply wait by the phone until someone in human resources (probably Bob) calls and asks us to create a particular survey (perhaps "Cross-Functional Teams and You"). Unfortunately, every call means that we have to build a new form, as well as analyze the results. This really cuts into our recreational web surfing.

A second, more interesting approach is to build a data-driven system that uses a data model to create any survey. Each time we have to create a new survey, we can simply enter the questions into the tables of our model, and out pops a complete form. Since the forms are standardized, we can also build a general system to store the user's responses and analyze the results.

Building a robust data model is a key part of this idea, and data models require data entry forms to populate their tables. We could build these tables with HTML, but it makes more sense to use a WebDB form or a client/server tool. If we, as IS developers, are the only people who will use a maintenance application, why spend the effort developing a complex system no one else will ever see?

Use PL/SQL Packages

The final step in building an application is to actually structure the code. As we've seen, the best tool for organizing PL/SQL is the package. Breaking your systems down along logical lines can simplify the design process and eliminate huge, monolithic programs. Package design is the most important PL/SQL skill to master, and simple web applications are a great place to practice your techniques. Here are some guidelines you should keep in mind when designing your systems:

- Separate the "business rule" parts of your code from the user interface code. This will help you reuse these business rules in non-HTML applications, such as Java, client/server, and even Pro*COBOL.

- Build a standard library of web functions that you can use over and over. Coding is hard work; anything you can do to reuse what you've already done (or better yet, what someone else has done) makes your life much easier.

- Follow best-practices coding standards. A good PL/SQL book will help get you started; see the Appendix for further information.

- Follow best-practices naming conventions for parameters and variables. As we've seen in earlier chapters, WebDB and OAS are very picky about variable names and types.

Okay, enough sermonizing. Let's look at some code.

Example 1: An Anonymous Survey

Our first application will let users fill out anonymous surveys using a web browser. Surveys and opinion polls are some of the most common web applications, and usually consist of a list of questions. Users respond by selecting an answer from a small list of options. Most systems also have an option that lets users see the tabulated results for each survey.

This section walks through a simple process you can use to create a generic survey system. Our first step is to design a storyboard to define each screen in the system. This sketch helps us in the next step: designing a generic data model that we can use to construct each page. Our last step is to actually code the system.

Storyboard

In a typical survey application, the first screen presents a list of all available surveys. There are usually two options for each survey: to answer it or to view its tabulated results. If the user decides to answer a survey, she's presented with a bunch of questions and a corresponding list of possible answers. She then answers the questions and presses "Submit" to save the responses in a database table. If the user chooses to view the results of a survey, she's presented with a table summarizing all the previous responses. Figure 8-2 is a simple storyboard that captures these functions.

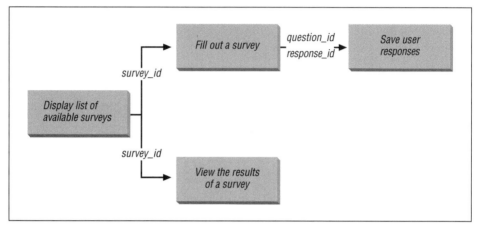

Figure 8-2. The storyboard for the anonymous survey

Data Model

We can use the storyboard to design a data model. The first storyboard screen tells us that we need some sort of table to hold the survey list. The screen used to respond to a survey suggests three more tables. The first table holds the text of each question, the second holds the possible answers for each question, and the third holds the actual user responses. The "view results" screen queries these tables.

Figure 8-3 shows a data model that uses these four tables. The SURVEY table contains information about the survey itself, such as its name, description, and the date range during which it is available. The rows in QUESTIONS represent the individual questions on a survey. ANSWERS defines the list of valid responses for each question. The final table, RESPONSES, holds the actual responses given by the respondents.

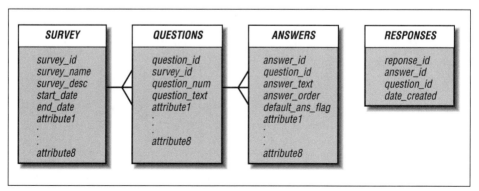

Figure 8-3. A data design for the anonymous survey

Implementation Notes

Since the survey application is a fairly simple system, we can implement it using a single package, which we'll call EMP_SURVEY. We'll store all the application objects, including code and tables, in a schema named SURVEY.

The EMP_SURVEY Package

Now that we've got the basic screen layout and data model, we're finally ready to develop the actual package. Table 8-1 shows the five procedures contained in EMP_SURVEY.

Table 8-1. The EMP_SURVEY Package

Procedure	Parameters	Description
display_survey_list	None	Generates an HTML list of available surveys, with descriptions.
answer_survey	i_survey_id IN VARCHAR2	Creates the HTML form that allows a user to respond to the survey.
process_survey	question IN response_array DEFAULT emp_survey.no_response response IN response_array DEFAULT emp_survey.no_response	Inserts the user's answers into the RESPONSES table.
view_results	i_survey_id IN VARCHAR2	Prints each question in the survey. Together, view_results and print_answers tabulate the results for the survey.
print_answers	i_question_id IN VARCHAR2	Prints the corresponding summary information for a question. Together, view_results and print_answers tabulate the results for the survey.

Like all packages, EMP_SURVEY requires a specification and a body.

Specification

We can translate the storyboard almost directly into a package specification. The four boxes on the diagram, each of which represents a screen in the system, indicate that we'll need at least four procedures. The lines connecting the boxes give us the formal parameter list for each procedure. Not everything is on the storyboard, though; we'll also need to declare an array to hold the user's survey answers. We'll discuss how to use this when we write the program to create the form.

The code for the EMP_SURVEY package is as follows:

```
/* Formatted by PL/Formatter v.1.1.13 */
CREATE OR REPLACE PACKAGE emp_survey
AS

    /*
    || Datatype used to hold the responses to the survey
    */
    TYPE response_array IS TABLE OF VARCHAR2(20)
        INDEX BY BINARY_INTEGER;
    no_response response_array;

    -- Display the list of available surveys
    PROCEDURE display_survey_list;

    -- Display the form so that the user can respond
    PROCEDURE answer_survey (i_survey_id IN VARCHAR2);

    -- Save the responses
    PROCEDURE process_survey (
        question IN response_array DEFAULT emp_survey.no_response,
        response IN response_array DEFAULT emp_survey.no_response
        );

    -- Display the results of a survey
    PROCEDURE view_results (i_survey_id IN VARCHAR2);

END;
```

Body

With the basic design complete, all that's left is to fill in the pieces. In the survey system, this consists largely of building screens based on the information in our data model. Recalling the specification, we have to write five procedures for the package body: display_survey_list, answer_survey, process_survey, view_results, and print_answers.

The display_survey_list procedure. The first procedure, display_survey_list, generates the first page of the storyboard. This page presents an HTML list of all available surveys along with their descriptions. Each survey requires two hyperlinks: one to link to the "response" page and one to link to the "view results" page.

The following procedure uses the SURVEY table to create the list. For each row in the table, the procedure creates a new HTML list item based on the survey_name and survey_desc columns. It also creates the two hyperlinks that include the survey_id as a parameter in the query string:

```
PROCEDURE display_survey_list
IS
    -- Create cursor of all surveys that are active
    -- Done by testing the start_date and end_date columns
```

```
   -- of the SURVEY table
   CURSOR survey_cur
   IS
       SELECT *
         FROM survey
        WHERE SYSDATE BETWEEN start_date AND end_date;
   survey_rec survey_cur%ROWTYPE;
   rec_count NUMBER DEFAULT 0;

BEGIN
   HTP.print ('<title>Available Surveys</title>');
   HTP.print ('<body bgcolor=white>');
   HTP.print ('<ol>');    -- Begin an ordered list
   OPEN survey_cur;
   LOOP
       FETCH survey_cur INTO survey_rec;
       EXIT WHEN survey_cur%notfound;
       HTP.print ('<li>');
       HTP.bold (survey_rec.survey_name);
       HTP.print ('<br>');
       HTP.print ('<i>' || survey_rec.survey_desc || '</i><br>');
       -- Put an anchor to take the survey
       HTP.anchor (
           'emp_survey.answer_survey?i_survey_id=' ||
           survey_rec.survey_id,
           'Take the survey'
       );
       -- Put an anchor to view the results
       HTP.anchor (
           'emp_survey.view_results?i_survey_id=' ||
           survey_rec.survey_id,
           'View the results'
       );
       HTP.print ('<p></li>');
   END LOOP;
   HTP.print ('</ol>');
   CLOSE survey_cur;
END display_survey_list;
```

Figure 8-4 shows the procedure's output.

The answer_survey procedure. The next procedure creates the HTML form that
allows a user to respond to the survey. answer_survey has one parameter, survey_
id, to indicate the survey the user selected on the preceding screen. answer_survey
uses the rows of the QUESTION table for the specified survey to build corresponding rows in a two-column table. The first column in the table holds the question's
text. The second column holds two form `<input>` elements. The first element, a
hidden field containing the question's ID, is needed to associate the user's answer
with a corresponding question. The second element, created by the OWA_UTIL.
LISTPRINT procedure, is a selectable list of the question's possible answers as they
appear in the ANSWERS table. When the user submits the form, both the hidden

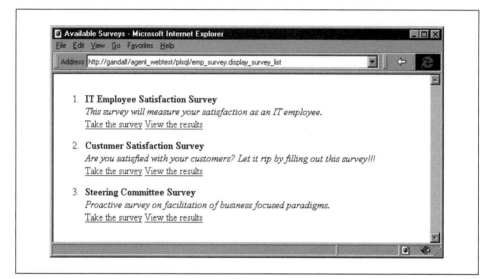

Figure 8-4. The main screen of the survey application

field and the response field are passed as parameter arrays to the process_survey procedure.

The code for this procedure is as follows:

```
PROCEDURE answer_survey (i_survey_id IN VARCHAR2)
IS
   CURSOR q_cur
   IS
      SELECT *
        FROM questions
       WHERE survey_id = i_survey_id
       ORDER BY question_num;

   q_rec q_cur%ROWTYPE;
   stmt VARCHAR2(500);

BEGIN
   HTP.title ('Survey');
   HTP.print ('<body bgcolor=white>');
   HTP.print ('<form action=emp_survey.process_survey>');
   HTP.print ('<table width=80%>');
   OPEN q_cur;
   LOOP
      FETCH q_cur INTO q_rec;
      EXIT WHEN q_cur%notfound;
      -- Start a new row in the HTML table
      HTP.print ('<tr>');
      -- Print the question in column 1
      HTP.print ('<th align=left valign=top>');
      HTP.print (q_rec.question_text);
```

```
        HTP.print ('</th>');
        -- Put the question_id and select list in column 2
        HTP.print ('<td>');
        -- Put the question_id in as a hidden field
        HTP.formhidden (
            cname => 'question',
            cvalue => q_rec.question_id
        );
        -- Use owa_util.listprint to build the LOV for the answer
        stmt :=
            'select answer_id, answer_text, default_ans_flag ';
        stmt := stmt || ' from survey.answers where';
        stmt := stmt || ' question_id = ' || q_rec.question_id;
        stmt := stmt || ' order by answer_order';
        OWA_UTIL.listprint (stmt, 'response', 4, FALSE);
        HTP.print ('</td>');
        HTP.print ('</tr>');
    END LOOP;
    HTP.print ('</table>');
    HTP.formsubmit;
    CLOSE q_cur;
END;
```

Figure 8-5 shows the output of this procedure for a sample survey.

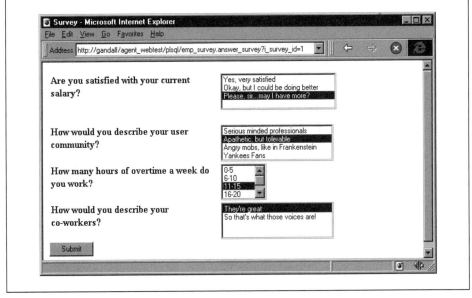

Figure 8-5. The form used to answer a survey

The process_survey procedure. The third procedure, process_survey, inserts the user's answers into the RESPONSES table. It accepts two response_array parameters (see the specification), question and response. For each question on the answer form, these parameters hold (respectively) the ID of the question as defined

in QUESTIONS and the ID of the user's corresponding answer as defined in
ANSWERS.

The procedure loops through each element, inserting a new row in the
RESPONSES table for each question. The procedure calls the display_survey_list
procedure to return the user to the main screen:

```
PROCEDURE process_survey (
    question IN response_array DEFAULT emp_survey.no_response,
    response IN response_array DEFAULT emp_survey.no_response
    )
IS

    count NUMBER DEFAULT 0;

BEGIN
    HTP.title ('Saving Responses');
    HTP.print ('<body bgcolor=white>');
    -- COUNT attribute available in PL/SQL 2.3
    FOR count IN 1 .. question.count
    LOOP
        INSERT INTO responses (response_id,question_id,answer_id)
            VALUES (
                response_seq.nextval,
                question (item_count),
                response (item_count)
            );
    END LOOP;
    HTP.print ('<h1>Values Saved</h1><hr>');
    display_survey_list;
END;
```

The view_results procedure. The last procedure in the application tabulates the
results for the survey specified by the survey_id parameter. The procedure is split
into two parts: a main procedure (view_results) to print each question and a secondary procedure (print_answers) to print a corresponding summary. The code for
the main procedure is as follows:

```
PROCEDURE view_results (i_survey_id IN VARCHAR2)
IS
    CURSOR q_cur
    IS
        SELECT *
          FROM questions
         WHERE survey_id = i_survey_id
         ORDER BY question_num;
    q_rec q_cur%ROWTYPE;
BEGIN
    HTP.title ('Survey Responses');
    HTP.print ('<body bgcolor=white>');
    HTP.print ('<ol>');
    OPEN q_cur;
```

```
    LOOP
        FETCH q_cur INTO q_rec;
        EXIT WHEN q_cur%notfound;
        HTP.print ('<li>');
        HTP.print ('<b>' || q_rec.question_text || '</b>');
        HTP.print ('<br>');
        -- Call another procedure to generate the response summary
        print_answers (q_rec.question_id);
        HTP.print ('</td>');
    END LOOP;
    HTP.print ('</ol>');
    CLOSE q_cur;
END;
```

The secondary procedure, print_answers, generates the summary information for a
question. The procedure opens a cursor based on the ANSWERS table to retrieve all
the answers for a particular question. It then queries the RESPONSES table to calculate the percentages for that response. The code for the procedure is as follows:

```
PROCEDURE print_answers (i_question_id IN VARCHAR2)
IS
    CURSOR ans_cur
    IS
        SELECT *
          FROM answers
         WHERE question_id = i_question_id
         ORDER BY answer_order;
    ans_rec ans_cur%ROWTYPE;
    total_responses NUMBER;
    num_responses NUMBER;
BEGIN
    -- Fetch the total number of responses
    SELECT COUNT (*)
      INTO total_responses
      FROM responses
     WHERE question_id = i_question_id;
    HTP.print ('<table width=50%>');
    OPEN ans_cur;
    LOOP
        FETCH ans_cur INTO ans_rec;
        EXIT WHEN ans_cur%notfound;
        HTP.print ('<tr>');
        -- Print question text
        HTP.print ('<td nowrap>' ||
                    ans_rec.answer_text ||
                    '</td>');
        -- Fetch and print number of responses
        SELECT COUNT (*)
          INTO num_responses
          FROM responses
         WHERE answer_id = ans_rec.answer_id;
        HTP.print ('<td align=right>' ||
                    ROUND (
                        num_responses / total_responses * 100,
                        2
```

```
                        ) ||
                        '%</td>');
        HTP.print ('</tr>');
    END LOOP;
    HTP.print ('</table>');
    CLOSE ans_cur;
END;
```

Figure 8-6 shows the combined results of these procedures.

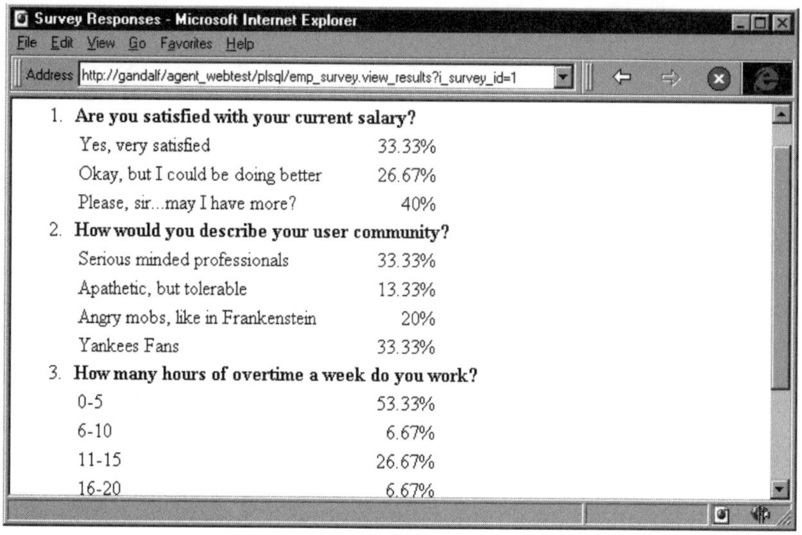

Figure 8-6. A sample summary

Security Privileges

Our last formal step is to make the package accessible to the user's web browser. Rather than creating a new PL/SQL agent for the SURVEY schema, we can make the package available to an existing agent's schema (in this case, WEBTEST). This makes the system more secure and reduces maintenance for the webmaster. Here are the steps to follow:

1. Log in to the SURVEY schema using SQL*Plus.

2. Grant EXECUTE privileges on the EMP_SURVEY package to the agent account (WEBTEST).

3. Connect to the agent account (again, WEBTEST).

4. Create a synonym called EMP_SURVEY for survey.emp_survey.

Figure 8-7 shows how these commands are used in SQL*Plus.

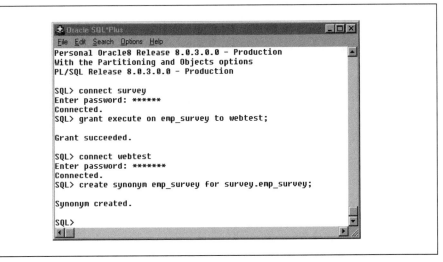

*Figure 8-7. Using SQL*Plus to grant privileges to the PL/SQL agent*

Summary

Developing the anonymous survey has taught us several things about web development. First, we have seen that a storyboard is a good place to start when faced with a new application. We can use the information on our diagram to define how the user will navigate, get a good idea of the database tables we'll need, and get a jump-start on defining the package specification. Second, this example has illustrated how to use parameter arrays to pass multiple field values, as well as how (and under what circumstances) you should use hidden fields. We'll expand these ideas further in the next sample application.

Example 2: A Discussion Forum

Our second, more complex example allows users to post messages in a browser-based threaded discussion forum. The granddaddy of all discussion lists, Usenet, allows the Internet community to share its views on literally thousands of topics, ranging from C programming to *The X-Files*. A more focused list, run by Reveal-Net at *http://www.revealnet.com*, is geared to PL/SQL developers.

The system presented here is based loosely on the forums run by the online version of *InfoWorld* computer magazine (*http://www.infoworld.com*). Each week, the editors at *InfoWorld* select a number of topical issues in the computer industry for its readers to discuss. These forums allow registered users to express their opinions on both the forum topic and the posts from other readers. Figure 8-8 shows the user interface for the discussion forum we'll develop in this section.

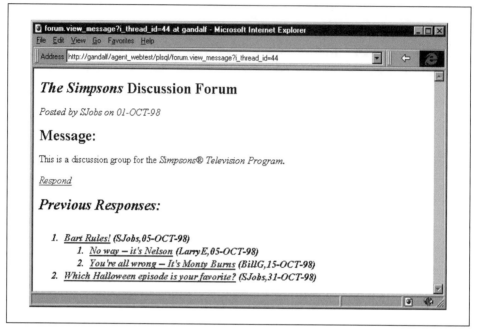

Figure 8-8. A typical discussion list

A vibrant internal discussion forum is a great way for users and developers to communicate simply and efficiently. For example, a forum about an IS application provides users with the ability to report bugs (e.g., "the total dollars on this report should be double-underlined") and suggest new, potentially interesting ideas ("It'd be cool if we could click on the client number and get an AR report"). Monitoring these discussions can help you design better systems and establish your department, or at least you, as responsive and customer friendly.

Storyboard

Our system follows a well-established format. Users begin at a login screen where they provide a username and password. To allow users to express both personality and anonymity in their postings, we'll create our own list of users and not use the OWA_SEC package described in Chapter 7, *The PL/SQL Toolkit*. (This also saves the DBA from user maintenance.) Of course, the downside is that you now have a new list of users, possibly increasing maintenance. However, building maintenance features into the system (such as allowing a user to create a new account) helps shift the burden some so that users are maintaining their own information.

Initially, a user must enroll in the system and provide some optional information, such as a real name, an email address, and a personal description. Once the user logs in, he is presented with a list of the various forums. He can choose to create a new forum topic or respond to a previous post. If he chooses to create a forum, he is brought to a screen where he can enter the forum subject and its topic. If he chooses to view a forum discussion, he is brought to a list of all the previous responses.

These posts are arranged hierarchically, meaning that responses to a particular post are indented beneath the original message. Each post shows the subject of the message, the author, and the date it was created. Clicking one of these posts presents its full text, as well as a hyperlink labeled "Respond." Clicking the link allows the user to enter a response to the message. Figure 8-9 shows the storyboard for the system.

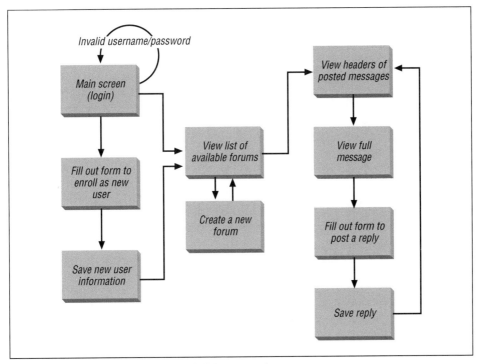

Figure 8-9. A storyboard for a threaded discussion list

Data Model

Figure 8-10 shows a straightforward data design for the discussion list. The first table we'll need is one to hold information about the forum members. The table, called MEMBERS, contains fields for the username, password, real name, and a personal description. All fields except the username are optional.

The second table, named MESSAGES, holds the posts submitted by the forum members. Its fields include a primary key based on a sequence value, the username of the member who submitted the message, a subject line, and the text of

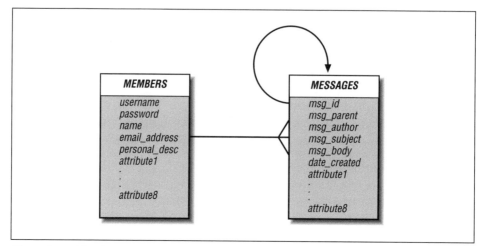

Figure 8-10. The data model for the discussion forum system

the message itself. To represent the hierarchical relationship between the messages, MESSAGES is defined recursively: an additional field must hold the primary key of the message's parent.

Notice that it isn't necessary to create a separate table to hold the forums. Instead, we can simply treat a forum as a message that is the root of a thread of other messages. By convention, we'll differentiate a forum from a normal post by setting its parent field to zero.

Implementation Notes

The threaded discussion list is complex enough that we should break it into simpler parts. The storyboard suggests at least two components: a package to register new members and a package to display the discussion list itself. Breaking the system into pieces lets us tackle the problem in discrete, logical steps.

In the next sections, we'll implement the system using three packages. The first package, GENERAL_FORM, will contain useful formatting procedures that are shared between the other packages. The second package, FORUM_USERS, will handle user management. The third package, FORUM, will handle all the code needed to allow users to post and view messages. Table 8-2 shows these packages with their procedures.

Table 8-2. The Discussion Forum Packages

Package	Procedures	Description
GENERAL_FORM	print_input_row print_textarea_row	Contains formatting procedures for the various forum procedures

Table 8-2. The Discussion Forum Packages (continued)

Package	Procedures	Description
FORUM_USERS	login_form login get_current_user create_user_form save_user_info	Handles user management for the forum
FORUM	print_thread_links current_forum_list view_message create_msg_form save_message	Handles users' posting and viewing of forum messages

Finally, we'll create all the application's objects (tables, packages, etc.) in a database schema named DISC_LIST.

The GENERAL_FORM Package

The GENERAL_FORM package contains two procedures that format form input elements into an HTML table. Both do the following basic things:

- Open a new table row.

- Print the passed label in the first column.

- Print an input element in the second column; the element's attributes are set using the various parameters.

Conceptually similar to the HTP package procedures, the GENERAL_FORM procedures use parameters to set the tag attributes. Creating a library of simple procedures like these can encapsulate line after line of clumsy HTML code in a single call, resulting in cleaner and shorter programs. Table 8-3 shows the procedures and functions of the GENERAL_FORM package.

Table 8-3. The GENERAL_FORM Procedures

Procedure	Parameters	Description
print_input_row	i_label IN VARCHAR2 i_input_name IN VARCHAR2 i_hidden_flag IN BOOLEAN DEFAULT TRUE i_size IN NUMBER DEFAULT 40 i_value IN VARCHAR2 DEFAULT NULL	Formats a text input box using a table
print_textarea_row	i_label IN VARCHAR2 i_input_name IN VARCHAR2 i_cols IN NUMBER DEFAULT 40 i_rows IN NUMBER DEFAULT 7	Formats a textarea input box using a table

Specification

Here's the specification for the GENERAL_FORM package:

```
/* Formatted by PL/Formatter v.1.1.13 */
CREATE OR REPLACE PACKAGE general_form
IS

    PROCEDURE print_input_row (
        i_label IN VARCHAR2,
        i_input_name IN VARCHAR2,
        i_hidden_flag IN BOOLEAN DEFAULT FALSE,
        i_size IN NUMBER DEFAULT 40,
        i_value IN VARCHAR2 DEFAULT NULL
        );

    PROCEDURE print_textarea_row (
        i_label IN VARCHAR2,
        i_input_name IN VARCHAR2,
        i_cols IN NUMBER DEFAULT 40,
        i_rows IN NUMBER DEFAULT 7
        );

END;
```

Body

The GENERAL_FORM procedures are simple enough that they don't require any annotation. Here's the code:

```
/* Formatted by PL/Formatter v.1.1.13 */
CREATE OR REPLACE PACKAGE BODY general_form
IS

    /*
    || Prints a single two-column table row;
    ||     Column 1 is description,
    ||     Column 2 has either an input element plain text
    */
    PROCEDURE print_input_row (
        i_label IN VARCHAR2,
        i_input_name IN VARCHAR2,
        i_hidden_flag IN BOOLEAN DEFAULT FALSE,
        i_size IN NUMBER DEFAULT 40,
        i_value IN VARCHAR2 DEFAULT NULL
        )
    IS
    BEGIN
        HTP.print ('<tr>');
        HTP.print ('<th align=right>' || i_label || ':</th>');
        HTP.print ('<td>');
        IF NOT i_hidden_flag
        THEN
            HTP.formtext (
```

```
                cname => i_input_name,
                csize => i_size,
                cvalue => i_value
            );
        ELSE
            HTP.formpassword (
                cname => i_input_name,
                cvalue => i_value
            );
        END IF;
        HTP.print ('</td>');
        HTP.print ('</tr>');
    END;

    /*
    || Create a two-column table
    ||    Column 1 is description
    ||    Column 2 is a <textarea> field
    */
    PROCEDURE print_textarea_row (
        i_label IN VARCHAR2,
        i_input_name IN VARCHAR2,
        i_cols IN NUMBER DEFAULT 40,
        i_rows IN NUMBER DEFAULT 7
        )
    IS
    BEGIN
        HTP.print ('<tr>');
        HTP.print ('<th align=right>' || i_label || ':</th>');
        HTP.print ('<td>');
        HTP.formtextarea (i_input_name, i_rows, i_cols);
        HTP.print ('</td></tr>');
    END;
END;
```

The FORUM_USERS Package

Our second package, FORUM_USERS, will implement the user management portions of our discussion list. It performs two basic functions: user authentication and user enrollment. The authentication code is responsible for displaying a login form, verifying the username and password, and setting a cookie to save the username throughout the user's session. The enrollment code is responsible for displaying a user information screen and saving that data in the MEMBERS table.

One thing to note about the enrollment system is that it only inserts new users; once created, a user cannot update his profile. Although it would be relatively straightforward to also update a row, doing so would require considerably more code. Since updating a row adds little that is interesting to the example, users of the application in its current state (after all, this is just an example) simply have to make sure they spell their names right on the first try!

Table 8-4 shows the procedures and functions of the FORUM_USERS package.

Table 8-4. The FORUM_USERS Procedures and Functions

Procedure/Function	Parameters	Description
login_form	i_username IN VARCHAR2 DEFAULT NULL i_message IN VARCHAR2 DEFAULT NULL	Creates a login screen for users
login	i_username IN VARCHAR2 i_password IN VARCHAR2	Verifies the user's login
get_current_user	None	Assigns the author of a message
create_user_form	None	Displays the data entry form to create a new user
save_user_info	i_username IN VARCHAR2 DEFAULT NULL i_name IN VARCHAR2 DEFAULT NULL i_password IN VARCHAR2 DEFAULT NULL i_email_address IN VARCHAR2 DEFAULT NULL i_desc IN VARCHAR2 DEFAULT NULL	Inserts new user data into the MEMBERS table

Specification

The leftmost portion of the storyboard lays out how users log in to the system. By referring back to the diagram, we can see that we need at least three procedures in the specification: a procedure to create the login form itself (login_form); one to enroll new users (create_user_form); and one to insert the new user's information into the MEMBERS table (save_user_info). Since HTTP is a stateless protocol, we'll also need a function to pass the user's login name to the package that implements the discussion list code. This function is named get_current_user.

Here's the specification for FORUM_USERS:

```
/* Formatted by PL/Formatter v.1.1.13 */
CREATE OR REPLACE PACKAGE forum_users
IS

    PROCEDURE login_form (
        i_username IN VARCHAR2 DEFAULT NULL,
        i_message IN VARCHAR2 DEFAULT 'Please Log-In'
        );

    PROCEDURE login (
        i_username IN VARCHAR2,
        i_password IN VARCHAR2
        );
```

```
        FUNCTION get_current_user
            RETURN VARCHAR2;

        PROCEDURE create_user_form;

        PROCEDURE save_user_info (
            i_username IN VARCHAR2 DEFAULT NULL,
            i_name IN VARCHAR2 DEFAULT NULL,
            i_password IN VARCHAR2 DEFAULT NULL,
            i_email_address IN VARCHAR2 DEFAULT NULL,
            i_desc IN VARCHAR2 DEFAULT NULL
            );
    END;
```

Body

In the following sections, we'll develop each procedure in the specification for USER_FORUM.

The login_form procedure. This procedure creates a login screen that has three elements: a username field, a password field,* and a hyperlink used to enroll as a new user. The procedure has two parameters: the first parameter, i_username, sets the default text of the username. The second parameter, i_message, is used to change the message displayed on the form; this gives us added flexibility so that the form can serve multiple purposes. Note how this procedure calls the GENERAL_FORM package to create and format the form input elements:

```
    PROCEDURE login_form (
        i_username IN VARCHAR2 DEFAULT NULL,
        i_message IN VARCHAR2 DEFAULT 'Please Log-In'
        )
    IS

    BEGIN
        HTP.print ('<body bgcolor=white>');
        HTP.print ('<h1>' || i_message || '</h1>');
        HTP.print ('<form action=forum_users.login>');
        HTP.print ('<table>');
        general_form.print_input_row (
            'Forum User Name',
            'i_username',
            FALSE,
            30,
            i_username
        );
        general_form.print_input_row (
            'Forum Password',
```

---

* While the HTML `password` attribute adds a measure of security to the password field, it's important to remember that the text has only been masked, not encrypted! When the user submits the form, hackers can use a program called a *packet sniffer* to intercept and read the password. Your database administrator or webmaster must secure your site with a tool such as SSL to prevent this possibility.

```
        'i_password',
        TRUE
    );
    HTP.print ('</table>');
    HTP.formsubmit (cvalue => 'Login');
    HTP.print ('</form>');
    HTP.print ('<p><p>');
    HTP.anchor (
        'forum_users.create_user_form',
        'Enroll as a new user'
    );
END;
```

Figure 8-11 shows the output of the login_form procedure.

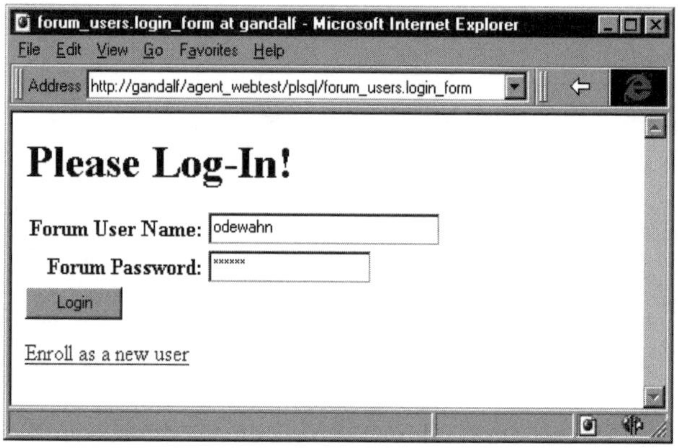

Figure 8-11. The forum login screen

The login procedure. This procedure, called when the user submits the information from the login form, is the gateway to the FORUM package, which we'll describe later. The procedure begins by calling the verify_user function to determine if the person has entered a valid username and password. If the user has done this, login executes the set_user procedure, which saves the user's login name in a cookie named forum_user, then calls the procedure to display the forum topic list.

Since cookies are relatively easy to hack, this approach is very insecure. For a system in which security (in the "I wanna keep out the bad guys" meaning of the word) is a serious issue, you would also need to use a protocol like SSL or HTTP and set the cookies to expire so they aren't saved on the user's machine.

If the user has entered an invalid username or password, the procedure calls
login_form to display an error message along with the original login form:

```
/*
|| Check to see if username and password are valid
*/
FUNCTION verify_user (
    i_username IN VARCHAR2,
    i_password IN VARCHAR2
    )
    RETURN BOOLEAN
IS

    match_count NUMBER := 0;

BEGIN
    SELECT COUNT (*)
      INTO match_count
      FROM members
     WHERE username = i_username
       AND password = i_password;
    IF match_count = 1
    THEN
        RETURN TRUE;
    ELSE
        RETURN FALSE;
    END IF;
END;

/*
|| Save username into a cookie
*/
PROCEDURE set_user (i_username IN VARCHAR2)
IS
BEGIN
    OWA_UTIL.mime_header ('text/html', FALSE);
    OWA_COOKIE.send ('forum_user', i_username);
    OWA_UTIL.http_header_close;
END;

/*
|| Main procedure -- perform logic test and take
|| appropriate action
*/
PROCEDURE login (i_username IN VARCHAR2, i_password IN VARCHAR2)
IS
BEGIN
    IF verify_user (i_username, i_password)
    THEN
        set_user (i_username);
        forum.current_forum_list;
    ELSE
        login_form (i_username, 'Username/Password not found');
    END IF;
END;
```

The get_current_user function. This function, the third block of code in the
FORUM_USERS package, fetches and returns the original username stored in the
forum_user cookie. The function is used by the FORUM package to assign the
author of a message. While this function could also go in the actual FORUM package, there's a nice symmetry to keeping all functions that act on the same data
structure (in this case, a cookie) together in the same package. Here's the code:

```
FUNCTION get_current_user
    RETURN VARCHAR2
IS
    cookie OWA_COOKIE.cookie;
    ret_val VARCHAR2(50) DEFAULT NULL;
BEGIN
    cookie := OWA_COOKIE.get ('forum_user');
    IF cookie.num_vals != 0
    THEN
        ret_val := cookie.vals (1);
    END IF;
    RETURN ret_val;
END;
```

The create_user_form procedure. This procedure displays the data entry form to
create a new user. This screen, which the storyboard labels as "Fill out form to
enroll as new user," is displayed when the user clicks "Enroll as a new user" on
the login form. Here's the code:

```
PROCEDURE create_user_form
IS
BEGIN
    HTP.print ('<body bgcolor=white>');
    HTP.print ('<h1>Welcome, New User!</h1><hr>');
    HTP.print ('<form action=forum_users.save_user_info>');
    -- Existing users cannot change their name or username
    HTP.print ('<table>');
    general_form.print_input_row (
        'Forum User Name',
        'i_username'
    );
    general_form.print_input_row ('Real Name', 'i_name');
    general_form.print_input_row (
        'Forum Password',
        'i_password',
        TRUE
    );
    general_form.print_input_row (
        'Email Address',
        'i_email_address'
    );
    general_form.print_textarea_row ('Description', 'i_desc');
    HTP.print ('</table>');
    HTP.formsubmit (cvalue => 'Create New User Profile');
    HTP.print ('</form>');
END;
```

Figure 8-12 shows the output generated by the procedure.

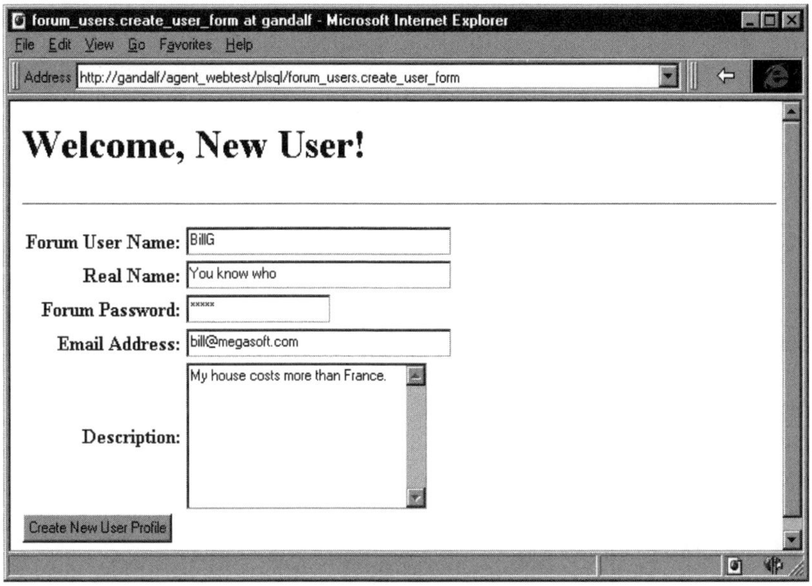

Figure 8-12. The "add new user" screen

The save_user_info procedure. This procedure, the last procedure in the FORUM_ USERS package, attempts to insert the data entered on the "Create User" form into the MEMBERS table after the user presses the "Create New User Profile" button. If the insert is successful, the procedure calls set_user to save the new username and calls the procedure to display the forum list. If the insert fails, either because the user already exists or because there is some other error, the exception section prints an appropriate error message.

Here's the code:

```
PROCEDURE save_user_info (
    i_username IN VARCHAR2 DEFAULT NULL,
    i_name IN VARCHAR2 DEFAULT NULL,
    i_password IN VARCHAR2 DEFAULT NULL,
    i_email_address IN VARCHAR2 DEFAULT NULL,
    i_desc IN VARCHAR2 DEFAULT NULL
    )
IS
BEGIN
    -- Create the new user
    INSERT INTO members (
        username,
        password,
```

```
        name,
        email_address,
        personal_desc
        )
          VALUES (
              i_username,
              i_password,
              i_name,
              i_email_address,
              i_desc
          );
    COMMIT;
    set_user (i_username);
    forum.current_forum_list;
  EXCEPTION
    WHEN DUP_VAL_ON_INDEX
    THEN
        HTP.print ('<h1>User already exists!</h1>');
    WHEN OTHERS
    THEN
        HTP.print ('<h1>An unidentified error occurred!</h1>');
  END;
```

The FORUM Package

Now that we've built our supporting packages, we can turn our attention to the real meat of the application. The FORUM package displays and manipulates the records in the MESSAGES table. Table 8-5 shows the procedures in the FORUM package.

Table 8-5. The FORUM Procedures

Procedure	Parameters	Description
print_thread_links	i_thread_list IN VARCHAR2 i_expand_thread IN VARCHAR2 DEFAULT 'N'	Private procedure used for for- matting other procedures
current_forum_list	None	Generates the list of available forums

view_message	i_thread_id IN VARCHAR2
	    DEFAULT NULL
	i_hierarchy_flag IN VARCHAR2
	    DEFAULT NULL
		Prints the full text of a message,
		a link for posting a response,
		and the threaded list of previous
		responses

create_msg_form	i_parent_msg IN VARCHAR2 DEFAULT NULL	Creates an HTML form used to respond to a message

save_message	i_parent_msg IN VARCHAR2
	    DEFAULT NULL
	i_subject IN VARCHAR2
	    DEFAULT NULL
	i_msg_body IN VARCHAR2
	    DEFAULT NULL
		Saves a message into the
		MESSAGES table

Specification

We'll need four procedures: one to display a list of forum topics, one to view the full text of a message, one to create a message, and one to save the new message into the MESSAGES table. Here's the specification for FORUM that includes procedures for each of these tasks:

```
/* Formatted by PL/Formatter v.1.1.13 */
CREATE OR REPLACE PACKAGE forum
IS

    PROCEDURE current_forum_list;

    PROCEDURE view_message (
        i_thread_id IN VARCHAR2 DEFAULT NULL,
        i_hierarchy_flag IN VARCHAR2 DEFAULT NULL
        );

    PROCEDURE create_msg_form (
        i_parent_msg IN VARCHAR2 DEFAULT NULL
        );

    PROCEDURE save_message (
        i_parent_msg IN VARCHAR2 DEFAULT NULL,
        i_subject IN VARCHAR2 DEFAULT NULL,
        i_msg_body IN VARCHAR2 DEFAULT NULL
        );

END;
```

Body

In addition to implementing the procedures listed in the specification, the body of the FORUM package contains a private procedure called print_thread_links. Even though it can't be called directly from the Web, this procedure is used in all of FORUM's public procedures. Consequently, we'll begin by examining this private procedure, even though it's not declared in the specification.

The print_thread_links procedure. This procedure calls itself recursively to produce the indented list of hyperlinked subject headers illustrated in Figure 8-8. Clicking on one of these links displays the full body of the original message.

The procedure accepts two parameters. The first, i_thread_id, is the primary key (as defined in MESSAGES) for the root of the thread. The second parameter, i_expand_flag, is used to make the procedure expand the child elements under the root thread. If the flag is "Y," then the procedure will call itself again, this time using the ID of the child message as the new root thread. Here's the code:

```
PROCEDURE print_thread_links (
    i_thread_id IN VARCHAR2,
```

```
    i_expand_thread IN VARCHAR2 DEFAULT 'N'
    )
IS

    CURSOR t_cur
    IS
        SELECT *
          FROM messages
         WHERE msg_parent = i_thread_id
         ORDER BY date_created;

    t_rec t_cur%ROWTYPE;
    link VARCHAR2(500);

BEGIN
    HTP.print ('<h4>');
    HTP.print ('<ol>');    -- Start a new ordered list
    OPEN t_cur;
    LOOP
        FETCH t_cur INTO t_rec;
        EXIT WHEN t_cur%notfound;
        HTP.print ('<li>');
        link := 'forum.view_message?i_thread_id=' || t_rec.msg_id;
        HTP.anchor (link, t_rec.msg_subject);
        HTP.italic ('(' ||
                        t_rec.msg_author ||
                        ',' ||
                        t_rec.date_created ||
                        ')');
        HTP.print ('</li>');
        -- Recursively print the children if necessary
        IF i_expand_thread = 'Y'
        THEN
            print_thread_links (t_rec.msg_id, 'Y');
        END IF;
    END LOOP;
    HTP.print ('</ol>');   -- End the ordered list
    HTP.print ('</h4>');
    CLOSE t_cur;
END;
```

The current_forum_list procedure. This procedure generates the list of available forums that serves as the main entry point of the forum system. From here, the user selects the forum topic that he or she would like to discuss.

If you'll recall from the "Data Model" section, we defined a forum (as opposed to normal posts) as rows in the MESSAGES table where the parent column equals 0. current_forum_list works by passing the print_thread_links a value of 0 for the root thread and a value of 'N' for the expand flag, as shown in this example:

```
PROCEDURE current_forum_list
IS
    link VARCHAR2(200);
```

```
BEGIN
    HTP.print ('<body bgcolor=white>');
    HTP.print ('<h1>Forums</h1><br>');
    link := 'forum.create_msg_form?i_parent_msg=0';
    HTP.anchor (link, 'Create a new forum');
    HTP.print ('<hr>');
    -- Print the threads, but do not recurse
    print_thread_links (0, 'N');
END;
```

Figure 8-13 shows the output of the procedure.

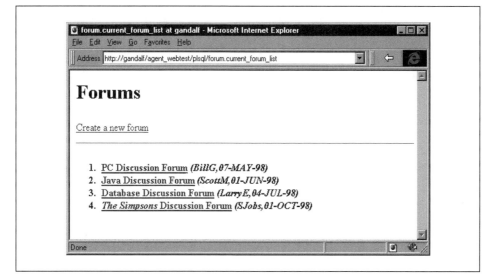

Figure 8-13. The available forum list

The view_message procedure. This procedure prints the full text of a message, a link that allows the user to post a response, and the threaded list of previous responses:

```
PROCEDURE view_message (
    i_thread_id IN VARCHAR2 DEFAULT NULL,
    i_hierarchy_flag IN VARCHAR2 DEFAULT NULL
    )
IS

    m_rec messages%ROWTYPE;
    msg_found BOOLEAN;
    link VARCHAR2(500);
BEGIN
    SELECT *
      INTO m_rec
      FROM messages
     WHERE msg_id = i_thread_id
     ORDER BY date_created;
```

```
HTP.print ('<body bgcolor=white>');
HTP.print ('<h2>' || m_rec.msg_subject || '</h2>');
HTP.print ('<i>Posted by ' || m_rec.msg_author);
HTP.print (' on ' || m_rec.date_created || '</i><p>');
HTP.print ('<h2>Message:</h2><p>' || m_rec.msg_body || '<p>');
link := 'forum.create_msg_form?i_parent_msg=' || i_thread_id;
HTP.anchor (link, 'Respond');
HTP.print ('<h2>Previous Responses:</h2><p>');
print_thread_links (i_thread_id, 'Y');
HTP.print ('<p>');
IF m_rec.msg_parent != 0
THEN
    link :=
        'forum.view_message?i_thread_id=' || m_rec.msg_parent;
    HTP.anchor (link, 'Previous Message');
END IF;
EXCEPTION
WHEN NO_DATA_FOUND
THEN
    HTP.print ('<h1>Message Not Found!</h1>');
END;
```

The create_msg_form procedure. This procedure creates an HTML form used to respond to a message. Before displaying the form, the procedure first confirms that the user is logged in. If not, the procedure calls FORUM_USERS.login_form to force the user to log on. Here's the code:

```
PROCEDURE create_msg_form (
    i_parent_msg IN VARCHAR2 DEFAULT NULL
    )
IS
BEGIN
    -- Only allow users that are logged in to post
    IF forum_users.get_current_user IS NULL
    THEN
        forum_users.login_form (
            NULL,
            'You must login to post a message'
        );
    ELSE
        -- Print message form
        HTP.print ('<body bgcolor=white>');
        -- Print a header; a msg_id of zero indicates a forum topic
        IF i_parent_msg = 0
        THEN
            HTP.print ('<h1>Create Forum Topic</h1><hr>');
        ELSE
            HTP.print ('<h1>Post response</h1><hr>');
        END IF;
        HTP.print ('<form action=forum.save_message method=POST>');
        HTP.print ('<table>');
        HTP.formhidden (
            cname => 'i_parent_msg',
```

```
                  cvalue => i_parent_msg
          );
          general_form.print_input_row ('Subject', 'i_subject');
          general_form.print_textarea_row (
              'Body',
              'i_msg_body',
              80,
              10
          );
          HTP.print ('</table>');
          HTP.formsubmit;
          HTP.print ('</form>');
      END IF;
   END;
```

Figure 8-14 shows the output of the procedure.

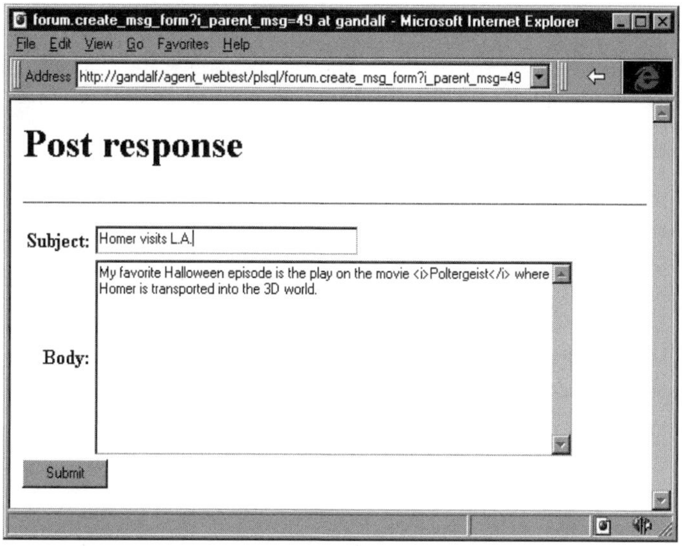

Figure 8-14. Posting a response to a message

The save_message procedure. This final procedure inserts the user's posts into the MESSAGES table. Like create_msg_form, the procedure first checks to make sure that the user is logged in.* Otherwise, people would be able to easily forge messages from other users, which can lead to big trouble. If the user checks out, the procedure inserts the record and redisplays the updated message list. If not, the

---

* Despite our best efforts, users are still free to jump into the application at any point simply by entering the URL into the browser's "Navigation" box. The cookie simply allows us to determine if the user has logged in.

exception section traps the error and prints a message. Here's the code for this procedure:

```
PROCEDURE save_message (
    i_parent_msg IN VARCHAR2 DEFAULT NULL,
    i_subject IN VARCHAR2 DEFAULT NULL,
    i_msg_body IN VARCHAR2 DEFAULT NULL
    )
IS

    author members.username%TYPE
        := forum_users.get_current_user;

BEGIN
    -- Only allow users that are logged in to post
    IF forum_users.get_current_user IS NULL
    THEN
        forum_users.login_form (
            NULL,
            'You must login to post a message'
        );
    ELSE
        -- Save message
        INSERT INTO messages (
            msg_id,
            msg_parent,
            msg_author,
            msg_subject,
            msg_body,
            date_created
            )
              VALUES (
                message_seq.nextval,
                i_parent_msg,
                author,
                i_subject,
                i_msg_body,
                SYSDATE
              );
        COMMIT;
        -- Now return to the original message to display the new post
        IF i_parent_msg = 0
        THEN
            current_forum_list;
        ELSE
            view_message (i_parent_msg);
        END IF;
    END IF;
EXCEPTION
    WHEN OTHERS
    THEN
        HTP.print ('<body bgcolor=white>');
        HTP.print ('<b>An error has occurred<p>');
END;
```

Security Privileges

We'll follow the same steps we used in the survey example to make the discussion list available on the Web. Since we have two packages, though, we'll have to use two sets of grants:

1. Log in to disc_list using SQL*Plus.

2. Grant the EXECUTE privilege on FORUM to the agent account (WEBTEST).

3. Grant the EXECUTE privilege on FORUM_USERS to the agent account (WEBTEST).

4. Connect to the agent account (WEBTEST).

5. Create a synonym named FORUM for disc_list.forum.

6. Create a synonym named FORUM_USERS for disc_list.forum_users.

Figure 8-15 shows how these commands are used in SQL*Plus.

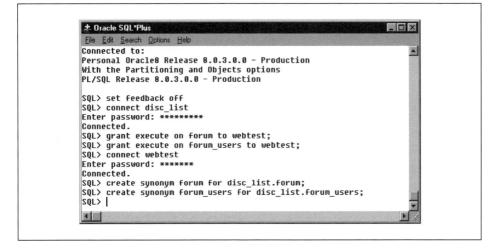

*Figure 8-15. Using SQL*Plus to grant privileges to the PL/SQL agent*

What Next?

The FORUM package is the most complex example we'll look at in this book. It illustrates how to break complex systems into multiple packages, how to create reasonably complex navigation schemes, and how to use cookies to save state information. If you have understood this example, you're well on the way to being able to write almost any PL/SQL-and-HTML-based system.

9

XML

Extensible Markup Language (XML) is an emerging standard closely related to Standardized General Markup Language (SGML), the granddaddy of all markup languages, which was designed by the U.S. government to create complex documents. Realizing that SGML was simply too complicated for his purposes, Tim Berners-Lee (the inventor of the Web) used SGML to create HTML, and the rest is history.

Now that the Web has matured, however, developers are starting to miss some of SGML's capabilities. XML is an attempt to find a middle ground between the complexities of SGML and the ease of use of HTML. Like HTML, XML employs a tag-based syntax to mark up ASCII text. Unlike HTML, which controls the appearance of a document, XML describes the meaning and structure of a document by defining a syntax and grammar for creating new tags. XML is extensible because it lets you define your own tag vocabulary (as long as it follows the rules of the XML specification) for creating meaningful documents.

Although it's currently being touted as "HTML done right," XML is actually a lot more. It has a number of potential uses as a tool for integrating disparate systems and building electronic commerce systems. The XML specification provides an open framework for exchanging complex, structured documents (such as purchase orders, invoices, insurance claims, etc.) among different computer systems. In one fell swoop, XML eliminates network dependencies such as TCP/IP or IPX, protocol dependencies such as SQL*Net or ODBC, hardware dependencies such as Intel or Alpha, operating system dependencies such as Windows NT or Unix, and even database dependencies such as Oracle or SQL Server. In fact, the implications of XML are so profound that it even threatens the Fort Knox of the database world—delimited flat files!

While you might expect XML to be enormously complicated, it's really just a formal implementation of a wonderfully simple idea: that the structure and meaning of a document's contents should be indicated inside, not outside, the text of the document itself. An example can help make this idea clear. Suppose you receive the following comma-delimited file:

```
876514234,05/21/1999, Megaplex Industries
PN-5324,Super Duper Widget,5,19.99
PN-6354,Not So Super Duper Widget,2,9.99
119.93
```

While it's clear that this file contains some sort of structured information, we have no way to tell exactly what it might be; about all we know for certain is that the first line might contain a date. This is the problem with delimited files. Until you have the file's columnar layout, its secret decoder ring, you can't do anything meaningful with it.

Now suppose you receive the same information in XML format:

```
<?xml version="1.0"?>
<!DOCTYPE INVOICE SYSTEM "invoice.dtd">
<INVOICE>
    <INVOICE_NUMBER>876514234</INVOICE_NUMBER>
    <DATE>05/21/1999</DATE>
    <CUSTOMER>Megaplex Industries</CUSTOMER>
    <INVOICE_ITEMS>
        <ITEM>
            <ITEM_NAME ITEM_NUM="PN-5342">Super Duper Widget</ITEM_NAME>
            <QUANTITY>5</QUANTITY>
            <PRICE>19.99</PRICE>
        </ITEM>
        <ITEM>
            <ITEM_NAME ITEM_NUM="PN-6354">Not So Super Duper Widget</ITEM_NAME>
            <QUANTITY>2</QUANTITY>
            <PRICE>9.99</PRICE>
        </ITEM>
    </INVOICE_ITEMS>
    <TOTAL>119.93</TOTAL>
</INVOICE>
```

The XML version leaves no doubt about the file's purpose or structure: it's an invoice consisting of two items. Knowing this, we can deduce the structure of the original file. The first line contains basic information, such as the invoice number, the invoice date, the invoice total, and the customer to whom it is being sent. The next two lines are invoice items, and consist of a part number, a name, an order quantity, and a unit cost. The last line is the invoice total.

The difference between the first file and the second is that the XML file contains a decoder ring within its own text, making the meaning of each element in the document explicitly clear. While XML certainly doesn't eliminate the need for comma-delimited files (for example, they will always be useful for loading data in bulk),

the previous example shows how it could be used in an electronic commerce setting to exchange invoice data. XML, combined with encryption and digital signature technologies,* offers a reasonably straightforward way for businesses to
exchange information simply and securely.

 Of course, to take advantage of XML's full potential, everyone must
adopt a standard set of domain-specific tags and nomenclature.
Although this is probably a greater challenge than XML's technical
aspects (since it requires people to agree on something!), several
industries' experiences with SGML give some hope, at least, that this
can happen. Companies in the semiconductor industry (Intel, Hita-
chi, Texas Instruments, etc.) have adopted an SGML standard for
exchanging chip data.

This chapter will help you get your feet wet with XML by showing you how to
generate XML documents using WebDB or OAS. We'll start with a brief discussion
of the motivations behind XML, then move on to the major skills you'll need to
generate XML from the Oracle database: creating syntactically correct XML documents and formally defining rules that they must follow. From there, we'll cover
how a program called an XML parser is used to check the structure of the document and, if it's valid, break it into a hierarchical structure called a document tree.
After that, we'll write a PL/SQL program to generate the invoice we looked at earlier. Finally, we'll examine the future directions of XML and how it relates to
Oracle8*i*'s Internet File System.

Motivations for XML

You probably noticed that the invoice example looks remarkably similar to a standard HTML document, except that there are a lot of new tags. These similarities
are intentional. The XML specification was created in response to the evolution
(some would say devolution) of HTML.

HTML started as a simple way to define the structure of a document. The <head>
and <body> tags separate descriptive information from the main text. The header
tags (<h1>, <h2>, etc.) break the text into logical sections, much like the A and B
headings in an outline. The emphasis tag <em> denotes particularly important
information.

---

* A *digital signature* computes an encrypted checksum (also called a hash function) for a document that
guarantees the document's integrity and authenticity. *Integrity* means that no one has tampered with
the file, and *authenticity* means the file is actually from the person who says he or she sent it. Phil Zim-
merman's Pretty Good Privacy (PGP) is a widely available and popular encryption system that can produce a digital signature.

As the Web has evolved, however, the original intent of these tags has been lost. They are now used to control a document's appearance, rather than its structure. Browser vendors have exacerbated this trend by adding new tags explicitly for formatting. Some of these tags have been good (`<table>`), some not so good (`<blink>`), but the net effect is that HTML no longer has much to say about the purpose of the information it presents.

While this trend is not particularly important for many applications, such as creating attractive user interfaces for our PL/SQL systems, there are several reasons why it has been a change for the worse:

- HTML is no longer simple.

- HTML designers place more emphasis on a document's appearance than on its content.

- HTML documents are very difficult for computers to understand.

The last of these problems is probably one of the most important motivations for XML. As the Web becomes increasingly automated, it has become more and more important that software "robots" understand and interpret a variety of documents. If we're ever going to make a search engine smart enough so that the query "Where can I buy a leather attaché case?" doesn't turn up links to an S&M site, we must create online catalogs a computer can easily parse and understand. HTML is simply not designed to provide this type of information. XML is.

XML Syntax

XML achieves its flexibility by allowing you to extend a base markup language (the XML specification itself) with tags of your own design. You create tags to structure the text within a document so that its underlying meaning is clearly presented. For example, to denote an item on an invoice, you could use an `<ITEM>` tag.

While XML and HTML documents look a lot alike, there are several important syntactical differences. HTML is fairly flexible. You can omit end tags from many of an HTML document's most important structures, such as list items, and most browsers will happily display the document as best they can. XML documents, however, must meet a more rigid set of requirements:

- A document must begin with a line that identifies it as XML. It must also include the XML specification with which it complies. Since XML is a brand-new standard, this line is currently `<?xml version="1.0"?>`.[*]

---

[*] The line can also include additional metadata that I've omitted for purposes of simplicity.

- Tags are case sensitive. For example, <INVOICE_NUMBER> and <invoice_ number> are not the same. In general, the convention is to always use upper-case.

- All attribute values must appear in quotes, as in <CUSTOMER CUST_ ID="12345">.

- A start tag must always have a corresponding end tag. The combination of a start tag (plus any attributes), an end tag, and any intervening text is called an *element.*

- Elements cannot overlap. For example, the following set of markups is illegal: <INVOICE_ITEM><PART_NUM>PN-1234</INVOICE_ITEM></PART_NUM>.

- "Empty" tags that don't mark up any text, like HTML's <p> or <br>) must have corresponding end tags. For example, if you want to use a <PAID_IN_FULL> tag to indicate that an invoice has been paid, you must end with a </PAID_ IN_FULL> tag, even though there is no text in between. XML also has an alter-native notation for empty tags that lets you simply append a "/" to the end of the start tag (for example, <PAID_IN_FULL/>).

A document that follows all these rules is called *well-formed*, which means that it is syntactically correct. Even more so than with HTML, XML requires a precise syn-tax to make sure the documents follow a predictable structure. Fortunately, there are several commercially available tools that help you create well-formed XML documents. Figure 9-1 shows Vervet Logic's XML Pro (*http://www.vervet.com*).

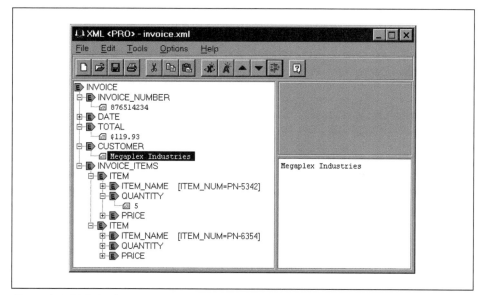

Figure 9-1. XML Pro by Vervet Logic

In the next section we'll look at how you can define strict rules the tags in your documents must follow.

The Document Type Definition (DTD)

If we're going to use XML to exchange documents electronically, we must be able to judge whether a document meets a certain set of necessary requirements. For example, an electronic invoice must, at minimum, include an invoice number, a date, and at least one item. Our systems should be smart enough to reject an invoice if it doesn't contain the required information. Additionally, we should be able to create these requirements ourselves.

You can associate a document type definition (DTD) with an XML document to enforce these sorts of rules. You can either create a DTD or use one that already exists. A major goal of XML is to encourage various groups (industry, community, academic, etc.) to form standards bodies to define collective DTDs. Eventually, these DTDs will form the basis for a variety of electronic data exchange systems.

A DTD is a lot like a database schema.* Just as you would define the columns in a database table, you can use a DTD to define the name and datatype of every element that can appear in an XML document. Just as you define a column constraint, you can require that particular elements appear within the document. Just as you would normalize a set of database tables into one-to-many or one-to-one relationships, you can create the same relationships by defining how the elements can be hierarchically nested.

Let's revisit the invoice example from the beginning of this chapter. If we were to simply model a basic invoice using an entity relationship diagram (ERD), we might wind up with something like Figure 9-2.

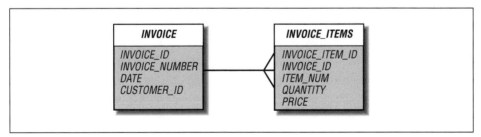

Figure 9-2. An ERD for a simple invoice

---

* Oracle Corporation is an active participant in the World Wide Web Consortium's (W3C) "XML Schema" working group. The W3C oversees the development of almost all the major Internet standards.

We can use this diagram as a guide to constructing a corresponding DTD. For clarity, though, we'll start with the finished DTD and work backwards:

```
<!ELEMENT INVOICE (INVOICE_NUMBER, DATE, CUSTOMER+,INVOICE_ITEMS,TOTAL?)>
    <!ELEMENT INVOICE_NUMBER (#PCDATA)>
    <!ELEMENT DATE (#PCDATA)>
    <!ELEMENT CUSTOMER (#PCDATA)>
    <!ELEMENT INVOICE_ITEMS (ITEM+)>
        <!ELEMENT ITEM (ITEM_NAME, QUANTITY, PRICE)>
            <!ELEMENT ITEM_NAME (#PCDATA)>
            <!ATTLIST ITEM_NAME
                ITEM_NUM CDATA #REQUIRED>
        <!ELEMENT QUANTITY (#PCDATA)>
        <!ELEMENT PRICE (#PCDATA)>
    <!ELEMENT TOTAL (#PCDATA)>
```

As you can see from the example, the majority of the DTD consists of instructions to define the elements that can appear within an invoice. The first line defines the root element, INVOICE, the highest element in the nesting tree, as well as the names of all the elements that INVOICE can contain. A single character that indicates how often the element can appear follows each element declaration. Table 9-1 summarizes the function of each character.

Table 9-1. Characters Used to Define Element Occurrences

Character	Translation	Rough Database Equivalent
Blank	Element must appear exactly once.	Non-NULL column constraint
?	Element can appear 0 or 1 times.	Constraint/one-to-one relationship
*	Element can appear 0 or more times.	Constraint/one-to-many relationship
+	Element can appear 1 or more times.	Constraint/one-to-many relationship

As we can see from the preceding code example, the INVOICE must include an INVOICE_NUMBER, an invoice DATE, at least one CUSTOMER (the + character leaves open our double-billing options), and an INVOICE_ITEMS section. Finally, it can include an optional invoice TOTAL (why should you have to do all the work?).

Declarations for each of these elements follow the root declaration. The first four items are the simplest declaration, and consist of a name and a datatype. XML datatypes are much more limited than the standard NUMBER, VARCHAR2, and RAW types used to define table columns. The datatype used here (PCDATA) tells the XML parser that the element consists of formatted text.

The next declaration, INVOICE_ITEMS, is an example of a nested element (notice how similar it is to the declaration for the root element.) The INVOICE_ITEMS section must contain at least one ITEM, which is itself a nested structure consisting of an ITEM_NAME, a QUANTITY, and a PRICE. As a final wrinkle, the ATTLIST command is used to further refine the <ITEM_NAME> tag by defining a tag attribute called ITEM_NUM.

That's it—we've defined everything we need for our simple example: the name of each element, the number of times each element can appear, and the allowable nesting arrangements they can follow. All that remains now is to make sure our XML documents are valid, which means that they are both well-formed and comply with the associated DTD. This is the job of the XML parser.

The XML Parser

The XML parser is responsible for reading an XML document and making sure it complies with the necessary rules. There are two kinds of parsers: non-validating and validating. The non-validating parser is the simpler of the two, and simply checks to see if a document is well-formed. The more complex validating parser will not only check for *well-formedness*, but also for *validity* (i.e., that the document actually follows all the rules laid out in an associated DTD).

If the document passes these tests, then the parser breaks it into a structure called a *document tree*. As the name implies, a document tree is simply a hierarchical data structure created from the nested elements in the document. The left-hand side of Figure 9-1 illustrates a typical document tree.

Once the document is parsed and loaded, you can use a wide variety of languages (such as Java, JavaScript, etc.) to write programs that use the Document Object Model (DOM) API to traverse and manipulate the information in the tree. For example, you could write a JavaScript program to build a hierarchical view of an XML invoice by programmatically expanding and collapsing the tree's branches. This sort of client-side manipulation is very fast because it acts on information stored in memory, rather than having to requery the server each time a user requests a new view of the same information.

In the next two sections, we'll see how you can generate XML documents from information stored in the Oracle database. In the first, we'll develop a package to build an XML invoice. In the second, we'll look at a set of experimental packages that you can use to build a variety of XML applications.

Example: Generating an XML Invoice from Oracle

Like HTML, XML is stored in plain ASCII documents. Consequently, we can use the PL/SQL toolkit to generate almost any XML document. In this section we'll write a package called XML_INVOICE_PKG to generate the XML invoice we've been discussing.

Specification

We'll start, as always, with the package specification. For this particular application, we'll need just one procedure: print_invoice. The procedure will accept the invoice number for a particular invoice and generate the corresponding XML invoice. Here's the code:

```
/* Formatted by PL/Formatter v.1.1.13 */
CREATE OR REPLACE PACKAGE xml_invoice_pkg
IS

    PROCEDURE print_invoice (
        i_invoice_number IN VARCHAR2 DEFAULT NULL
    );

END;
```

Body

The next step is to define the package body, as follows:

```
/* Formatted by PL/Formatter v.1.1.13 */
CREATE OR REPLACE PACKAGE BODY xml_invoice_pkg
IS

    -- Include code annotated below

END;
```

In addition to the print_invoice procedure defined in the specification, we'll need a private function, get_attribute, and two private procedures, print_xml_tags and print_items. The first two items are needed to format the output to the XML specification, since the PL/SQL toolkit doesn't have functions or procedures specifically for XML. The other local procedure fetches the invoice items from the database and prints them to the web browser. Table 9-2 lists the procedures and functions required in the package body.

Table 9-2. XML_INVOICE_PKG Procedures and Functions

Procedure/ Function	Parameters	Description
get_attribute	attr_name IN VARCHAR2 attr_val IN VARCHAR2	Private function that returns a well-formed attribute tag: attr_name = "attr_val".
print_xml_tag	tag_name IN VARCHAR2 tag_value IN VARCHAR2 tag_attr IN VARCHAR2 DEFAULT NULL	Private procedure that prints a well-formed XML tag: <tag_name tag_attr>tag_ value</tag_name).

Table 9-2. XML_INVOICE_PKG Procedures and Functions (continued)

Procedure/ Function	Parameters	Description
print_items	i_invoice_id IN NUMBER o_invoice_total OUT NUMBER	Private procedure to print the individual items on the invoice. The OUT parameter returns the total dollar value for all items.
print_invoice	i_invoice_number IN VARCHAR2 DEFAULT NULL	Public procedure, called from the Web, that generates the XML invoice.

The get_attribute function accepts an attribute and a value. It formats this information to the XML specification (`attr_name = "attr_val"`) and returns a string. Here's the function:

```
/*
|| Function to return an attribute tag
*/
FUNCTION get_attribute (
    attr_name IN VARCHAR2,
    attr_val IN VARCHAR2
    )
    RETURN VARCHAR2
IS
BEGIN
    RETURN attr_name || '=' || '"' || attr_val || '"';
END;
```

The print_xml_tag procedure has a similar purpose. It accepts a tag name, a tag value, and an optional string for tag attributes. The procedure then formats these parameters into a well-formed XML element. The HTP.PRINT procedure sends this element back to the browser. Here's the procedure:

```
/*
|| Simple wrapper procedure to print a tag
*/
PROCEDURE print_xml_tag (
    tag_name IN VARCHAR2,
    tag_value IN VARCHAR2,
    tag_attr IN VARCHAR2 DEFAULT NULL
    )
IS

    xml_str VARCHAR2(5000);

BEGIN
    IF tag_attr IS NULL
    THEN
        xml_str := '<' || tag_name || '>';
    ELSE
        xml_str := '<' || tag_name || ' ' || tag_attr || ' >';
    END IF;
```

```
    xml_str := xml_str || tag_value;
    xml_str := xml_str || '</' || tag_name || '>';
    HTP.print (xml_str);
END;
```

The last local procedure, print_items, uses the previous function and procedure to
generate the <INVOICE_ITEMS> section of the XML invoice. Like the other HTML
procedures we've seen, it simply opens a cursor, loops, and prints each row by
calling print_xml_tag. In addition, the procedure uses an OUT parameter to keep a
running total of the dollar amount of each item. The value is passed back to the
caller when the procedure completes. Here's the code:

```
/*
|| Print the items for the selected invoice. Return
|| the total of the invoice item using an OUT parameter.
*/
PROCEDURE print_items (
    i_invoice_id IN NUMBER,
    o_invoice_total OUT NUMBER
    )
IS

    CURSOR item_cur
    IS
        SELECT p.part_num, p.part_name, i.quantity, i.unit_cost
          FROM xml_invoice_items i, xml_parts p
         WHERE i.part_id = p.part_id
           AND i.invoice_id = i_invoice_id;

    item_rec item_cur%ROWTYPE;

    part_num_attr VARCHAR2(500);

BEGIN
    o_invoice_total := 0;
    OPEN item_cur;
    HTP.print ('<INVOICE_ITEMS>');
    LOOP
        FETCH item_cur INTO item_rec;
        EXIT WHEN item_cur%notfound;
        -- Accumulate costs
        o_invoice_total :=
            o_invoice_total +
            item_rec.quantity * item_rec.unit_cost;
        -- Generate XML tags
        HTP.print ('<ITEM>');
        part_num_attr :=
            get_attribute ('ITEM_NUM', item_rec.part_num);
        print_xml_tag (
            'ITEM_NAME',
            item_rec.part_name,
            part_num_attr
        );
```

```
            print_xml_tag ('QUANTITY', item_rec.quantity);
            print_xml_tag ('PRICE', item_rec.unit_cost);
            HTP.print ('</ITEM>');
        END LOOP;
        CLOSE item_cur;
        HTP.print ('</INVOICE_ITEMS>');
    END;
```

The main public procedure, print_invoice, uses the local procedure to actually create the invoice. Here is the implementation:

```
    /*
    || Main procedure to print the invoice.
    */
    PROCEDURE print_invoice (
        i_invoice_number IN VARCHAR2 DEFAULT NULL
        )
    IS

        CURSOR inv_cur
        IS
            SELECT i.invoice_id, i.invoice_date, c.customer_name
              FROM xml_invoice i, xml_customers c
             WHERE i.customer_id = c.customer_id
               AND i.invoice_number = i_invoice_number;

        inv_rec inv_cur%ROWTYPE;

        inv_total NUMBER DEFAULT 0;

    BEGIN
        -- Set MIME type to XML
        OWA_UTIL.mime_header('text/xml', TRUE);
        inv_total := 0;
        OPEN inv_cur;
        HTP.print ('<?xml version="1.0"?>');
        -- Note: the DTD is defined in a file stored on server
        -- The URL has been omitted for space
        HTP.print ('<!DOCTYPE INVOICE SYSTEM "invoice.dtd">');
        HTP.print ('<INVOICE>');
        FETCH inv_cur INTO inv_rec;
        IF NOT inv_cur%notfound
        THEN
            print_xml_tag ('INVOICE_NUMBER', i_invoice_number);
            print_xml_tag ('DATE', inv_rec.invoice_date);
            print_xml_tag ('CUSTOMER', inv_rec.customer_name);
            print_items (inv_rec.invoice_id, inv_total);
            print_xml_tag ('TOTAL', inv_total);
        END IF;
        CLOSE inv_cur;
        HTP.print ('</INVOICE>');
    END;
```

Figure 9-3 shows the XML output of the procedure.

You must use an XML-compliant browser such as Microsoft Internet Explorer version 5 to view XML documents.

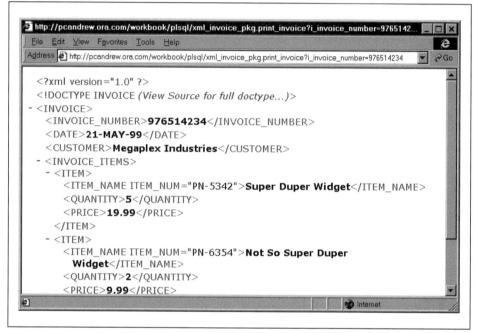

Figure 9-3. Output of XML_INVOICE_PKG.print_invoice

The XML_INVOICE_PKG is a very simple example of how to link XML and Oracle. In the next section, we'll look at a set of packages that really illustrate XML's potential.

PLSXML Utilities and Demos

Steve Muench, Oracle Corporation's "XML evangelist," has developed a very interesting set of PL/SQL packages called the PLSXML utilities and demos. While they are still experimental, they can give you a clear idea of the power of generating XML inside the database. Additionally, there are several examples of how to use JavaScript and XML to create rich interfaces. The PLSXML packages are:

DBXML

Uses dynamic SQL to automatically create XML documents from a SQL query. Based on the same technology as WebDB, DBXML reduces the package we developed earlier to a single procedure call.

DBDOM

> A PL/SQL implementation of the Document Object Model (DOM, the model used to create document trees) API that allows you to create, parse, and search XML documents.

DBXSL

> Generates formatting instructions called *XSL stylesheets* that control how the browser renders an XML document.

You can download the PLSXML and its full documentation (it's excellent) from:

> *http://www.oracle.com/xml/plsxml/index.html*

In the next section, we'll look at a product that takes full advantage of XML.

XML and iFS

Oracle8*i*'s Internet File System (*i*FS) has a built-in XML parser you can use to store XML documents directly in the database. As more and more vendors (including Microsoft, a big proponent of the XML standard) "XML-enable" their products, the *i*FS parser will become more and more useful. Widespread adoption of the XML format, as opposed to proprietary formats, will help alleviate the common, frustrating, and usually contentious problem of importing data from end user productivity tools into relational databases.

For instance, take spreadsheets. There is no denying the fact that these wonderful tools can help even the most unsophisticated (at least in terms of computer experience) user perform meaningful and important tasks. An analyst might use a spreadsheet to solve a finance problem, a manager might use one to schedule the phases of a project, and an accountant might use one to do almost anything. Some companies even use spreadsheets to create client invoices. Because they are easy to use and widely available, spreadsheets have become primary business tools, perhaps second only to word processors. While spreadsheets have many benefits, however, they have also created difficult information management problems.

For example, companies have spent millions of dollars on relational databases only to see them circumvented by spreadsheets. End users complain, sometimes quite correctly, that systems developed by IS are too complex or time consuming. Consequently, users simply create their own offline versions out of a ragtag collection of spreadsheets. As a result, the critical business information these database systems are designed to collect is strewn randomly throughout hundreds of spreadsheets on dozens of machines. This data is decentralized, unanalyzed, and insecure.

To remedy this problem, many companies try to force users to adopt standards. However, as anyone who has worked in IS knows, there are few issues that stir up more controversy than trying to replace a tool users like, such as a spreadsheet, with one that they don't like, such as a database. Any attempt to do so usually winds up in an "us versus them" battle. End users see IS taking away the tools they need to do their job, and IS sees end users wasting valuable company resources (time, money, sanity, etc.) by refusing to even consider the benefits of different approaches. In most cases, IS is on the losing end of these political battles.

*i*FS can help eliminate this problem. Once productivity tool vendors adopt XML (many of them are doing this as rapidly as possible), you can use *i*FS to simply import the relevant portions of the documents directly into the database. Users can use their favorite tools, or at least new versions of these favorites, and you can treat their data as standard relational data. As Humphrey Bogart said at the end of *Casablanca*, "This could be the start of a beautiful friendship."

Appendix: Resources for the Oracle Web Developer

In this appendix, I've pulled together a variety of resources—both online and offline—that you'll find helpful as you develop Oracle web applications.

Books

There are many books on the market describing Oracle and the Web. I list here those titles I find the most helpful and accurate:

Arnold, Ken, and James Gosling. *The Java Programming Language* (Addison-Wesley, 1997). Coauthored by the creator of Java, this valuable introduction explains much of the rationale behind the language.

Brown, Bradley D., Richard J. Niemiec, and Joseph C. Trezzo. *Oracle Application Server Web Toolkit Reference* (Oracle Press, 1998). This large book contains a lot of helpful information about OAS and Oracle's other web products.

Dynamic Information Systems, LLC. *Oracle Web Application Server Handbook* (Oracle Press, 1997). This book is not current with the latest Oracle software, but it contains useful discussions of building web systems with PL/SQL and other tools.

Eckel, Bruce. *Thinking in Java* (Prentice Hall Computer Books, 1998). A popular and comprehensive introduction to Java that doesn't pull any punches when it comes to criticizing aspects of the language that could be improved.

Feuerstein, Steven, and Bill Pribyl. *Oracle PL/SQL Programming, Second Edition* (O'Reilly & Associates, 1997). Hands down, the definitive guide to PL/SQL: if you need information about PL/SQL, it's in this book. The second edition has been updated for Oracle8.

Feuerstein, Steven. *Oracle PL/SQL Programming: New Features for Oracle8i*, (O'Reilly & Associates, 1999). This small book supplements *Oracle PL/SQL Programming* by providing an up-to-date discussion of the Oracle8*i* enhancements to PL/SQL.

Feuerstein, Steven, Charles Dye, and John Beresniewicz. *Oracle Built-in Packages* (O'Reilly & Associates, 1998). The follow-up volume to *Oracle PL/SQL Programming*. Presents detailed information about the vast array of packages built into the Oracle database.

Flanagan, David. *Java in a Nutshell, Second Edition*, (O'Reilly & Associates, 1997). Provides a compact reference to the classes, methods, and variables in the Java API, practical real-world example programs, and a comprehensive overview of Java.

Greenwald, Rick. *Oracle WebDB Bible* (IDG Books Worldwide, 1999). A very current and complete discussion of Oracle's WebDB product.

Musciano, Chuck, and Bill Kennedy. *HTML: The Definitive Guide, Third Edition* (O'Reilly & Associates, 1999). The most thorough description of all aspects of the HTML language, including models for writing your own web pages.

Rosenfeld, Louis, and Peter Morville. *Information Architecture for the World Wide Web* (O'Reilly & Associates, 1998). Describes architectural principles for web sites: how to design web sites that are easier to use, manage, and expand.

Simpson, John E. *Just XML* (Prentice Hall Computer Books, 1998). A breezy tone and simple style belies the wealth of information contained in this useful book. Bonus: you'll learn as much about B movie trivia as you will about Extensible Markup Language.

Spainhour, Stephen, and Valerie Quercia. *Webmaster in a Nutshell, Second Edition* (O'Reilly & Associates, 1999). A quick reference to a wide variety of information needed by web developers and administrators, including HTML, CGI, JavaScript, Perl, HTTP, and server configuration.

Stein, Lincoln D. *How to Set Up and Maintain a World Wide Web Site* (Addison Wesley, 1995). An excellent, clear, and complete book on installing and administering web servers and authoring in HTML, with a web page style guide and web security recommendations.

Theriault, Marlene, and William Heney. *Oracle Security* (O'Reilly & Associates, 1998). The definitive source of information on security and its implementation in the Oracle environment.

Other Publications

Select

> This publication, produced as a membership benefit by the International Oracle Users Group–Americas (IOUG–A), contains a variety of articles and columns on web issues, as well as web-related tips, techniques, and practices.

Oracle Magazine

> This magazine, published by Oracle Corporation, is primarily a marketing tool, but also carries articles (often by Oracle technical staff) on current web issues.

In addition, many Oracle user groups and special interest groups publish newsletters that contain useful information for Oracle web developers.

Organizations

International Oracle Users Group–Americas (IOUG–A)

> 401 North Michigan Avenue
> Chicago, IL 60611
> Voice: 1-312-245-1579
> Fax: 1-312-527-6785
> Email: *iouga@ioug.org*

Asia-Pacific Oracle Users Group

> PO Box 3046
> The Pines, Doncaster East
> VIC 3109, Australia
> Voice: +61 3 9842 3246
> Fax: +61 3 9842 3050
> Email: *100242.1746@compuserve.com*

European Oracle Users Group (EOUG)

> Brigittenauer Lände 50-54
> A-1203 Vienna, Austria
> Voice: +43 1 33777 870
> Fax: +43 1 33777 873
> Email: *eoug@at.oracle.com*

Web Sites

http://www.oracle.com

> The web site of Oracle Corporation. Contains a wide variety of pages of interest to Oracle web developers, as well as links to other web development resources, including Oracle Support.

http://www.ioug.org

> Operated by the IOUG-A. Contains technical articles from *Select* magazine, papers from IOUG-Alive conferences, a technical discussion forum, and other areas of interest to Oracle web developers.

http://www.eoug.org

> The web site of the EOUG. Contains information of general interest to Oracle web developers, information about EOUG conferences and educational events, and information about European, Middle Eastern, and African user groups.

http://apoug.oracle.com.sg

> The web site of the Asia Pacific Oracle Users Group. Contains information of interest to Oracle users in the Asia and Pacific Rim regions, as well as useful links to other Oracle resources.

http://www.oug.com

> Operated by a consortium of Oracle user groups and special interest groups. Contains a number of useful Oracle-related links.

http://www.revealnet.com

> An online resource with useful articles and discussion forums for DB2 and Oracle developers.

Discussion Groups

comp.databases.oracle.server

> This discussion group features a wide variety of information relating to Oracle server technology. It should be of interest to both new and experienced Oracle web developers

http://www.ioug.org

> This web site includes a discussion area where items of interest to Oracle web developers are posted and discussed.

http://www.revealnet.com

> Operated by a commercial vendor, RevealNet, but contains many free and useful resources. See especially the PL/SQL Pipeline, a discussion forum for PL/SQL developers. Includes archives full of papers and software, monthly tips and puzzles, and other useful links.

Index

About the Author

Andrew Odewahn is an Oracle application developer and consultant who lives in Davis Square in Somerville, Massachusetts. He has a degree in computer science from the University of Alabama, where he was a fellow in the Computer-Based Honors Program. He has presented at the East Coast Oracle Developers (ECO) Conference and other Oracle events. He and his wife both love the outdoors and, as this book goes to press in the summer of 1999, are hiking the Appalachian Trail from Georgia to Maine.

Colophon

Our look is the result of reader comments, our own experimentation, and feedback from distribution channels. Distinctive covers complement our distinctive approach to technical topics, breathing personality and life into potentially dry subjects.

The animal on the cover of *Oracle Web Applications: PL/SQL Developer's Introduction* is a boll weevil. The boll weevil is one of several snout beetles with a small beak or snout, which it uses to puncture the flower buds of the cotton crop as well as the fruits, which are known as bolls.

The boll weevil is regarded as a notorious pest—possibly the most destructive insect in North America—for its devastation of cotton crops in the southern United States since its migration from Mexico in the late 1800s. Although 90 percent of adult boll weevils die over the winter, the egg cycle from larva to adult takes only three weeks, so in one year between four and seven generations can be born. It's estimated that boll weevils destroy 10 percent of the cotton crop per year, which amounts to over $200 million in damage and affects at least 13 states in the U.S. Controlling the population of this small beetle is very difficult, as the chemicals that can eradicate them often cause too much environmental pollution to be safely used.

These beetles are not despised everywhere, however. The town of Enterprise, Alabama, is home to the Boll Weevil Monument—the world's only known monument to a pest. When boll weevils proved so destructive to their cotton crops in the early 1900s, farmers in this Alabama town (as well as across the Southeast) had no other recourse but to grow crops other than cotton, including hay, potatoes, and corn. Peanuts, however, were the most profitable crop, and brought so much wealth to the area that the town decided to erect a monument honoring the boll weevil, without whom the town never would have experienced such prosperity.

Madeleine Newell was the production editor and copyeditor for *Oracle Web Applications: PL/SQL Developer's Introduction*. Clairemarie Fisher O'Leary proofread the book; Ellie Cutler and Nicole Arigo provided quality control. Mike Sierra provided FrameMaker technical support. The index was written by Pamela Murray.

Edie Freedman designed the cover of this book, using an illustration created by Lorrie LeJeune. The cover layout was produced by Kathleen Wilson with Quark-XPress 3.32 using the ITC Garamond font. Whenever possible, our books use RepKover™, a durable and flexible lay-flat binding. If the page count exceeds RepKover's limit, perfect binding is used.

The inside layout was designed by Alicia Cech, based on a series design by Nancy Priest, and was implemented in FrameMaker 5.5 by Mike Sierra. The text and heading fonts are ITC Garamond Light and Garamond Book. The illustrations that appear in the book were produced by Rhon Porter and Robert Romano using Macromedia FreeHand 8 and Adobe Photoshop 5. This colophon was written by Nicole Arigo.